PRAISE FOR
OLD HOUSE AND RED NECKTIES

"A timely work that addresses the ways the construction of race goes beyond the Black–White dichotomies, particularly in the United States. It expands the BLM imperative to encounter the different ways race signifies in other parts of the diaspora and in that sense is as salutary a nuance for the African American as it is for the White American discourse. In both discourses, we often face the problem of flattening, or worlding, that treats all Black contexts as one or the US situation as *the one*. This perspective from someone who has navigated both the Jamaican/Caribbean and US contexts is very helpful. . . . Lyrical and poetic at times, and always riveting in its descriptions of Jamaica's natural beauty and its complex social environment."

—**CURDELLA FORBES**, PhD, Author, Professor of Caribbean Literature, Howard University

"This book took me down so many roads! Sometimes in dialogue with her, sometimes admiring her journey, and sometimes just arguing with her! Surely this is the sign of a good read? A modern-day Jamaican DeTocqueville, Grace critiques political and civil society and helps us see them in revealing new ways. On a dissenting note, I disagree with her characterization of both Barack Obama and Hillary Clinton. Her values are better than theirs."

—**MATTHEW CREELMAN**, Journalist, Guatemala

"Dr. Virtue's story is poignant, heartbreaking, complicated, infuriating, and fascinating. She uses a deceptively casual approach to make searing observations about the pervasive nature of systemic oppression, the risks of confronting it, and what is lost to society when huge swathes of people are trapped within destructive systems. This book is enlightening, poetically engaging, and deeply relevant to today's America, and for our world."

—**KIRANDEEP SINGH SIRAH**, Storyteller, TEDx Speaker, Johnson City, Tennessee

"*Old House and Red Neckties* is a riveting story of courage and compassion that is evocative of my grandmother and our experiences in her 'old house' in the Cayman Islands in the '60s and '70s. Searing and sober in its examination of the insidiousness and hurtfulness of bias and racism at all levels of society, it is an inspiring testament to one woman's determination to tear down those barriers for herself and others. By situating contemporary challenges in a personal and historical context, Grace demonstrates how much has changed and how much remains the same. This story is a treasure. It deserves to be told and to be read by everyone!"

—**CATHERINE TYSON-SEWELL**, Author, Host, CTS Wind Down Radio Show, Georgetown, Grand Cayman

"The women of Old House were incredible! This highly engaging story of struggles and triumphs is a classic example of how the 'pull yourself up by your bootstraps' edict is such a cruel joke for people of color, poor people, or other marginalized communities without advocates in their corner. Grace raises the important issue of the role of dangerously simplistic narratives in sustaining cultures and systems of oppression. Could not be a better time for this conversation!"

—**RAVEN PADGETT**, Journalist and Communications Professional, Washington, DC

"*Old House and Red Neckties* is a fascinating and thought-provoking commentary on culture, race, and power. Through powerful storytelling, it reminds us of the parallels found in the immigrant experience in the United States, regardless of which country we first called home."

—**A. GRACE TESNAU**, Creative Principal, The Write Design, LLC, Silver Spring, Maryland

"Courage, authenticity, and steadfastness are some of the unmistakable lessons from this inspiring story of one woman's journey to defy the odds while remaining true to herself and the virtues she learned from her father. Kingdom blessings on this beautiful piece of work."

—**L. ROO MCKENZIE**, EdD, Author, Educator, and Ordained Minister, Lanham, Maryland

Old House and Red Neckties
A Memoir of Race, Resilience, and Selfhood

by Grace Virtue

© Copyright 2024 Grace Virtue

ISBN 979-8-88824-385-5

All rights reserved. No part of this publication may be reproduced, stored in a retrieval system, or transmitted in any form or by any means—electronic, mechanical, photocopy, recording, or any other—except for brief quotations in printed reviews, without the prior written permission of the author.

Published by

3705 Shore Drive
Virginia Beach, VA 23455
800-435-4811
www.koehlerbooks.com

OLD HOUSE AND RED NECKTIES

A MEMOIR OF RACE, RESILIENCE, AND SELFHOOD

Old House and Red Neckties

A Memoir of Race,
Resilience, and Selfhood

Grace Virtue

VIRGINIA BEACH
CAPE CHARLES

All the events and characters are real, but some names have been changed at the author's discretion.

To the memory of my grandmothers, Georgianna Langley, and Loretta Wilson-Reid; my father, W. S. Virtue; my mother, Icy May (Mary) Virtue, and her twin, my aunt Lyn (Martha) Hennie; my companion, Mayer Ray Resnick; and my dear friends Major Katherine Cousins and Chief Petty Officer Conor Minto. To everyone whose presence and friendship have helped me feel safe in the world.

If you do not find the time to document your own history, it is likely to be forgotten or, worse still, misrepresented.

—Hon. Ralston "Rex" Nettleford, OM

TABLE OF CONTENTS

Prologue 1

Chapter One: Old House 5

Chapter Two: Schooling 41

Chapter Three: Kingston 69

Chapter Four: New York! New York! 95

Chapter Five: Great Expectations 119

Chapter Six: Hope and Change? 140

Chapter Seven: The American Dream? 163

Chapter Eight: Red Neckties 171

Chapter Nine: Grace 209

Epilogue 234

PROLOGUE

The United States loomed large in my life as one of the most important places on earth, as it does for millions of people around the world. Politically, it is the earth's epicenter, a status that was solidified after the Cold War and the dissolution of the Union of Soviet Socialist Republics (USSR). It is a great country but not without enormous contradictions.

Chief among these contradictions, particularly as I have experienced the country over the almost three decades I have lived here, is a penchant for bipolarity—seeing and structuring life and human experience as a set of binary choices—and an accompanying preference to process humanity through a narrow list of preferred attributes. While official rhetoric champions multiculturalism, for example, there is a core and periphery model when it comes to issues of race, ethnicity, gender, religion, and nationality. Even the diversity, equity, and inclusion (DEI) framework, championed by so-called liberals as an antidote to an endless array of biases, is locked into this approach.

The US, because of its great successes, is a magnet for immigrants from places like Jamaica, Haiti, and Kenya, former European colonies still wrestling with colonialism's impact on their economy and psyche. People come for jobs, education, and better living standards than they can afford in native lands often mired in poverty or internal political strife. However, those who come soon realize that implicit in their status—as Black people, women, foreigners, Muslims, people with accents and different cultural behaviors and expressions than the

American majority—are entrenched beliefs about their inadequacies as human beings.

The systemic and cultural constraints significantly erode the advantage of space and opportunities that immigrants seek. The difficulty of overcoming these barriers accounts for why most accept the value of migration as mostly lost to the first generation and a sacrifice for their offspring. Professionals from developing countries must often be content to survive as janitors, taxi drivers, maids, waiters, and waitresses because the system does not allow them to catch up in time to recover their careers. However, many immigrants will invest heavily in their children to secure the better lives they had hoped for.

For those who flee extreme poverty or conflict, life does get better. Neighborhoods are generally safe despite the prevalence of guns and catastrophic mass shootings, the outcome of politicized gun laws; and some social safety nets are available to catch those who qualify. Overall, though, being an immigrant in the US is a profoundly challenging experience. Being a Black immigrant is doubly so. Black immigrants from developing countries face the added burden of being perceived as inferior because of where they come from, effectively captured in the vulgarity of a president who denigrated these countries as "s**tholes" and expressed his preference for people from Norway. His raw articulation might have been shocking, but immigrants know that the underlying assumption among many Americans is that those who come from the "Third World" are correspondingly third rate. To a good extent this is the framework that shapes how immigrants are treated in the US. The reality is, while most Americans might not be racists, the US is a racialized society with White people at the top of a stratified system and Black people at the bottom, with their inherent worth subsumed by their race and negative views around it, and the implicit suggestion of subhumanism.

This idea of subhumanism is central to how the US has treated Blacks throughout history. Enshrined in the Constitution was the stipulation that, for tax purposes, the "Negro" should be treated as three-fifths of a human being. The Fourteenth Amendment sought to correct that by granting equal rights to all citizens, but inequalities remained the norm, officially sanctioned by the 1896 Supreme Court's ruling on *Plessy v. Ferguson*, which posited a doctrine of "separate but equal." The ruling legalized segregation and ensured that Black people remained on the fringes of society, with limited access to opportunities and with substandard facilities.

This remained the law for more than half a century until it was overturned by the 1954 court ruling on *Brown v. Board of Education*, argued by Howard University School of Law graduate Thurgood Marshall. It would take the long struggles of the civil rights movement for the country to begin to integrate, and efforts continue today, often under misnomers implicit in the DEI efforts.

As a Black woman and an immigrant from the Global South, I live at the intersection of these multiple tensions, more so because I belong to what my Mexican friend refers to as "the intelligent poor"—educated people without status or money but who possess a heightened ability to see into the underbelly of the system and the extent to which it needs to be challenged and changed. I do challenge it, sometimes. It is existentially exhausting whether one pushes back or simply tries to ignore these persistent trials and live with things as they are.

The election of Barack Obama in 2008 seemed like a giant step forward in the diminution of race-based bigotry, and his conduct and character in many ways made life more hopeful—though he too was unable to break entirely free of damaging old models, particularly how the US uses its power in relations to countries it regards as enemies.

Then came the backlash. Then came Donald Trump. Then came years of ugliness and accelerated attacks on people who were not White, male, rich, or Christian. What did it all mean?

Two years into Trump's presidency, I had expended a lot of energy in hoping that something would make him go away. Instead, he seemed to consolidate his power, nominating his second Supreme Court justice, for example, and infecting the court with some of his worst instincts. The hearings into sexual allegations against the nominee, now Supreme

Court justice Brett Kavanaugh, were especially disheartening. Led by Senate leader Mitch McConnell, the process smacked of deception and depravity. They revealed the underbelly of power ruthlessly applied—how anything can be staged or manipulated, and supportive narratives constructed to mislead rather than illuminate. The whole circus reinforced an increasingly niggling belief that the system is untrustworthy—that there is a tremendous focus on how things appear rather than how they are.

The need to process my emotions, including powerlessness, disappointment, and enlightenment, inspired me to write *Old House and Red Neckties*. It explores issues of oppression and the struggle against it as I experienced growing up in Jamaica and living in the United States.

More than anything else, *Old House and Red Neckties* is about resilience and determination in the endless struggle for dignity and liberation, grounded in an unwavering belief that I was born free, equal, and entitled to live with dignity and pursue my dreams. It is about making choices, what informs them, and, ultimately, why they are not difficult even when they result in suffering, as they have at times. It is about the determination to live my truths and a fool's mission, perhaps, to measure up to the power of my name: Grace Virtue.

My small, quiet victories, which hopefully eliminated some barriers for those who have walked in my footsteps, reinforce my belief that the struggle against oppression rests with the willingness of those who desire change to fight for themselves and others. We do this with the full recognition that we will suffer damages to our careers, finances, and livelihoods; some of us will even lose our lives. Positive changes, big or small, are only possible through effort and sacrifice. *Old House and Red Neckties* is my story of challenging, overcoming, and surviving.

CHAPTER ONE

OLD HOUSE

I was born in Jamaica 127 years after the end of plantation slavery. For nearly 500 years, my island was a European colony: Spanish for 161 years and British for 307.

The first Jamaicans, the Taíno, were annihilated just forty years after the Spaniards arrived, casualties of the colonizers' diseases and brutality. The Spaniards replaced the free labor they extracted from them with Africans brought from the Canary Islands, laying the foundation for mass human trafficking, which the British accelerated after they chased out the Spaniards in 1655.

For three centuries after, Africans in enforced servitude provided labor on sugarcane plantations, the fruit of which fueled the British economy. The freedom they doggedly sought came in 1838. Then began the never-ending journey to reclaim their stolen humanity and their dignity.

This is the shortcut to a story of oppression, intergenerational poverty, trauma, and the ongoing quest for liberation that continues to shape island life. It is also the context in which I was born—poor, Black, and female—and it explains why I am primarily Nigerian, though I have never set foot in Nigeria, and part Ghanaian, Senegalese, Sierra Leonian, and British. Other parts of my DNA include a sliver of Italian and Ashkenazi Jew and a small portion deemed too complicated to be assigned anywhere. This scattered composite is par for the course among descendants of people kept in bondage by enslavers who took advantage even as they dehumanized.

I was born at a symbolically hopeful time, on the first day of the new year, a few years after Jamaica gained independence from Great Britain; but circumstances were less than auspicious. My birthplace was an old, pale-yellow one-room house with two windows and two doors. A wooden structure attached to it served as the kitchen. The windows flanked the front door in the middle of the house. The second door was directly opposite.

There was symmetry and balance in the tiny, nondescript structure, with rotting shingles that were often ineffective against heavy tropical rain. I have lived with this need for symmetry, and I believe it began and was reinforced by that little house where my family lived for the first ten years of my life.

Mama kept the place spotless and taught me one of my earliest life lessons: that even in conditions of great paucity, it is possible to affirm one's dignity by controlling what is within one's power to control. Her insistence on a clean, orderly house and clean physical environment overall was one of the reasons I have never felt poor or disempowered. Somehow, those two things seemed incompatible. The two beds were neatly made in the daytime, the floor polished to a high sheen with Rexo, and the outside swept with branches of wild rosemary tied together.[1]

In short, we did not live within the narrative of poverty. I understood the difference between not having enough for one's material needs and haplessly existing without the agency, capability, or desire to live as a dignified and productive human being.

The allure of the outdoors was another reason I knew, without being told, that I lived in a beautiful place, and that too seemed incompatible with poverty. From the riot of diverse, untrained vegetation around me to the sparkly glimpses of the Caribbean Sea to the endless high-spirited chatter of a million birds, the landscape fed my soul in vastly more powerful ways than the forces that said we did not have enough and were therefore not good enough.

I can still smell the tangy fragrance of orange blossoms tinged with

---

1   Rexo was a popular brand of polish for concrete floors at the time.

honey from the trees outside the back door, where they grew in the shadow of a tall coconut tree, surrounded by clusters of wild lilies. I can still see darting hummingbirds, hear bees buzzing, the *rat-a-tat-tat* of a woodpecker on the coconut tree, and the hoarse, rattling call of an "Old Man Talker," a large, otherworldly, chestnut-bellied cuckoo endemic to Jamaica, buried deep in the shrubbery, which blessedly concealed the pit latrine on the southeastern border of the property.[2] Hunger was hard but sitting on the toilet seat over the carefully cut-out hole, fearing I would fall into the dark, stinking abyss below, and watching the sleepy geckoes—croaking lizards, we called them—staring warily back at me from the roof just above the doorway was torture. I am a great lover of all living things, but I could have done without those lizards.

Mama never opened the back door; we needed the space. She kept a small table against it with a few prized possessions: pieces of glassware and china that were her wedding gifts and a few souvenir plates and cups marking Jamaica's independence on August 6, 1962.

My parents had a proper wedding sometime after I was born. I was about four years old, but I remember the day and the preparations for it, most notably because I was stung by a bee when I put my bare foot over a hole where it had been resting. The hole had been dug for a post that would form part of a temporary lanai with a roof of coconut boughs that my father had been building in his mother's front yard, where the reception would be held.

My parents already had two children, a girl and a boy, before I came along, so fussy, frail, and refusing to thrive that people were soon insinuating that unfriendly spirits, or duppies, were playing with me. Everything changed when my mother began calling me Desie, after my

---

2 The Old Man Talker of my childhood, identified by Birds of the Caribbean (https://www.birdscaribbean.org/) as Old Man Bird, is described as a stunning bird endemic to Jamaica. It stands at 48 cm (19 in) and is "distinguished by its thick, dark gray decurved bill, creamy white throat fading into pale gray on the breast, and contrasting chestnut belly and underparts. Its broad, long, dark gray tail is tipped with large white spots, while its legs are gray."

long-dead maternal great-grandmother. I have fuzzy memories of some childhood illnesses—skin rashes, mostly, and the discomfort that came with them—but obviously no accounting for them or why I suddenly got better once they changed my name.

I eventually learned that my paternal grandmother and my mother loathed each other, but my father named me Grace on his mother's insistence. Mama grudgingly agreed but always resented it. My illnesses provided her the opportunity to concoct a duppy story and nickname me after her grandmother. As a result, I was entirely Desie until I reached school age, when my teachers, and by extension my classmates, called me by my registered name: Grace. The duppies never resurfaced, and I simply grew into my names—the North Star that life handed me at birth.

The little village where I was born was called Old House. It was a small place trapped in a time warp after emancipation brought no new order, no bridge to transport the formerly enslaved to a life of not merely freedom but dignity, hope, and a real chance of progress.

The smattering of people who lived in Old House was nearly all related, mainly with a few common last names, such as Reid, Wilson, Shaw, Hutchinson, Allen. Many were my great-aunts, uncles, and close and distant cousins. For the most part, we were equally poor, equally Black, equally deprived of opportunities—equally, it seemed, children of the same God, whose plans for us were much the same: lives of normalized struggle, feeling our way in the dark through no fault of our own.

There were no privileged classes, though some people were marginally better off than others, and there was always that slight sense of entitlement from the few folks with lighter skin, whose DNA contained a little more of the planter classes than of their enslaved ancestors. But they were still poor. I recognized this colorism, as we call it now, but it never interfered with how I felt about the person looking back at me in the mirror.

Old House had one semicommercial building, a one-room shop my great-uncle Alvin owned where everyone else bought flour, sugar, cooking oil, or half a stick of butter. There was no electricity, no refrigerator, no cold storage—not even a water cooler. I do not know where or how he kept the butter. Maybe the hard, salty sticks did not need to be refrigerated. But how could that be in a tropical country where it is always hot?

There were and still are no street names or road signs. There was no tidy convenience of a 12 Virtue Boulevard or 15 Wilson Terrace or arrows pointing in the right direction, nor signposts of any kind. Instead, we had majestic cedar trees with trunks big enough to carve out doors, headboards, and caskets; luxuriant pimentos with silvery bark and little berries called green gold because of their color and value as the main ingredient in popular island spices and liqueurs; clumps of sleepy bamboo; random patches of marigolds or clusters of hibiscus blooming amid untamed shrubbery; tombs freshly whitewashed or old and mossy green; or a boulder jutting out of an embankment.

Those were our landmarks. They guided visitors to our home, whether they were Papa's coworker, the public health nurse, or the police. Directions to our house, therefore, could have sounded like "Pass the shoemaker shop in Top Hill and come down the hill until you get to the deep corner. You will see a marl hole on the left and some yellow flowers on the right side. Come round a little more until you see rosemary bushes on the left side behind some fence posts. A little bit after that, you will see the bamboo trees on the right side. The little yellow house is behind them."

Directions were anchored in some basic facts but required intuition and discernment, like knowing how much "a little more" is or differentiating a deep corner from a shallow one. It also required patience and persistence for those times when the person giving the directions forgot there was more than one deep corner and that the marl hole was no longer in use and covered with overgrowth. It was a highly interpretive culture, not an either-or one by any stretch. It organically honored the multidimensional nature of the human spirit and shaped my perspectives in fundamental ways.

About three miles north of Old House lay Cross Keys, a little village of two asphalt roads that intersected like a cross, with a few grocery stores and bars on the edges. The post office was in the right corner, and a small concrete arch with a few shrubs, "the park," was to the left. My father helped build it as part of a national Labour Day project in the 1970s when Prime Minister Michael Manley encouraged recognition for workers and volunteerism to improve communities. There was a branch of the National People's Co-operative Bank, health center, gas station, and an open-air market from Thursdays to Saturdays where small farmers and artisans sold their goods. Villagers patronized them and converged at the full-service post office to collect mail from "foreign" and catch the village gossip.

Overlooking it all was a stately, multistory, colonial-era police station. At the back of the blue-and-white Georgian building, a judge held petty session court on the first Monday of each month, presiding over land disputes, dog bites, farm thefts, and countless community squabbles. Unlike Old House, Cross Keys was on the map. It was connected to the outside world and held a vision of what burgeoning rural development might look like. It was where politicians stopped when they came looking for votes and where people from Old House and other communities went to catch buses or taxis into Mandeville, Kingston, or even Alligator Pond, a thriving fishing village on the southwest coast.

About the same distance south of Old House was Canoe Valley, a mass of untouched forestry opposite the Caribbean Sea where redwood, logwood, and palm trees touched the sky and Guinea grass grew in mounds over old Taíno graves. Along with other villagers, Papa grazed a few dozen goats there on Crown land where the government exercised no oversight—fortunately, in some ways, for the struggling families desperate to earn a living. Weak governance mostly allowed us unsupervised used of the lands, but it also meant lack of oversight and infrastructure that would have protected the farmers and their herds.

My older brother, Ian, and I were often responsible for our goats if my father had daywork in directions away from Canoe Valley. We tended them before or after school and frequently suffered the trauma of finding some killed by wild dogs or others missing. Missing livestock usually meant people were stealing from the herd, a prized ram or a ewe and her kids at a time, rendering all our investment and effort at even subsistent living a constant source of frustration. After a while, it was more of a hobby for Papa, providing a semblance of consistency and meaning rather than monetary benefits.

As little as we had, we persistently lost more than we gained. My family epitomized the futility of fighting persistent structural poverty in the absence of legislative or actual support like the ability to keep our animals on Crown land closer to home or providing rangers to patrol the areas where small farmers like us kept them. These ideas would have been too far ahead of where the country was and still is in some ways. Praedial larceny (farm theft) remains the scourge of small farmers in Jamaica and a driver of violent crimes. More effort is being made to address it, but it is still not enough.

Yet I remember Canoe Valley as far more than a place where we kept and lost so much of our livestock. It was eerily compelling, with infinite skies and an endless vista of brooding forest. I remember the lone palm tree near where we kept our goats, and a few others silhouetted against the western skies. I remember how loudly the silence screamed at us, telling us perhaps of something out there in the great beyond, in the underbrush, over the treetops, and all around—something other than my brother and me, the goats, the grass, the trees, or the roar of the sea on the wind. It reeked of the spirits of ancestors who likely followed the coast to freedom from slavery or searched for a new life after emancipation, and the Taíno people who roamed the land freely before the Europeans came.

I could not shake the feeling of otherworldliness, but I was not afraid. I just wanted to head back as soon as I could, toward the light. Toward home. I was just seven or eight at the time, and my brother was two years older—too young to be so far into the wilderness all by ourselves. But it was not abnormal for that life and time. My parents would not have let us go if they thought it was unsafe.

Beyond the attempts at animal husbandry, Old House people survived on what they planted—corn, pumpkins, potatoes, gungo peas, bananas, yams, potatoes, and tomatoes—and the occasional slaughter of livestock—chickens, goats, and pigs—and fish caught from dugout canoes on the Caribbean Sea, which lay a few miles south of Canoe Valley through challenging terrain marked by untamed woodland and huge, craggy rocks. They sold or exchanged surplus with each other or to a few vendors who ventured further afield, like to Mandeville, the capital of Manchester Parish, about twenty miles away, or to Coronation Market in Kingston, about seventy miles or so east and hard to get to. Even travel to Mandeville was a struggle since no public transportation existed.

Migration to Great Britain, England mostly, and later the United States became a way out for some residents around my parents' age during the 1950s and '60s. Those who returned brought back new habits and enough money to improve material conditions for themselves and their families. Old wood-and-mud houses slowly gave way to ones made with cinder blocks and good roofing. Kerosene and gas stoves replaced brushwood and charcoal as the primary fuel for cooking. Among the ultimate signs of progress, flush toilets replaced pit latrines.

My parents did not leave. Family lore says Papa had an opportunity to migrate in the late 1960s to early 1970s. By then, he had five children. He was uninterested in leaving us behind, and quite frankly, I could not envision him living in cold weather or being in the grinder, as life in the US often demands of new immigrants. Still, he had many skills that might have translated into better material conditions for us in the early days, had he taken that route. I cannot imagine, though, how much we would have lost without the wisdom and direction he brought to our lives.

Even at the worst times, he loomed large as a morally authoritative figure, my first and most consistent example of what it means to be fully human—to live with compassion, honor, dignity, and decency even in the face of great suffering. He gave me a name to live up to, and he provided me an example. I needed his presence and influence more than I did clothes and shoes. I remain enormously grateful for his wisdom and sense of responsibility.

Mama was not interested in migration either. It never came up in contemplations of how to better our lives financially. If we could have emigrated together, I suspect she would have been fine; but a fragmented family, with parents and children separated from each other, was out of the question.

Still, she was curious about the world and eventually took steps to see a little of it. In her forties, after she had given birth to eleven children and the older half had grown to adulthood, she took my youngest brother, Marlon, then about seven years old, and traveled to the United Kingdom to spend a whole summer with her older sister, Minzie, one of eight children on my maternal grandmother's side who left Jamaica as part of the Windrush generation.[3] In 2012, Mama spent the last summer of her life with my sisters in Fort Lauderdale, returning home in late August. I regret that I never got a chance to see her in America and bring her to Maryland, where I live, even though it was her express wish to do so. By October, she was gone.

Gender divisions manifested in intriguing ways in Old House. Some of the men were engaged and high functioning, but the women held the social structure together. Lower-functioning men tended mostly to hold themselves in high esteem, believing all power resided with them.

---

3 The Windrush generation left the Caribbean between 1948 and 1973 to help rebuild Britain after World War II. The term derives from the name of a large ship, HMT *Empire Windrush*, that took the first group of more than 1,000 people from Jamaica to London in 1948.

Those were the ones who tried to dictate what women wore, how they combed their hair, who they chose to be their friends, and whether they could use birth control or not. But the women's workload often quadrupled theirs. They had the babies and took them to the clinics for their vaccines. They cleaned, cooked, fetched water over long distances sometimes, and worked grung too—the one main task automatically associated with men's work. The women of Old House did not hold up half the sky; they held up two-thirds of it.[4]

Much as I loved my father, and an outlier though he was, I never wanted to be a man like him. Not once during my growing-up years did it occur to me that having a penis instead of a vagina or wearing pants instead of dresses and skirts, which was a deeply entrenched cultural distinction then, would have meant a more elevated status for me or that it was a necessary precursor to a more useful life. It would have been hard to arrive at such a conclusion when the everyday heroes in my eyes were the women I saw sinuously navigating what life threw at them. I looked up to them. I wanted to be them. They had little materially because opportunities were scarce and not because of their gender. The men were not any better off and were often less versatile, resilient, or self-assured.

It took the experiences of adulthood and the power of memory to help me understand how pervasive and intractable systems of oppression are—that much of what I took for granted as central to my humanity, like being a woman, would become obstacles or conditions to be exploited by others the farther from Old House I moved. It would not matter how much I like myself or how perfectly made I am; society had a designated space for people like me: Black, female, materially deprived, and culturally grounded in the ethos of my enslaved ancestors and the values of a small rural community. That space was below people with white or light skin, below men, and well below rich people, no matter how their wealth came to be.

Living inside these social constructs became more challenging as I got

---

4 "Grung" is a Jamaican word for ground/small farm or garden.

older, particularly because the system expects accommodation from the people it wants to keep in positions of subservience. It expects us to use any discernible talents or abilities to sustain it instead of challenging it; to facilitate our continuing oppression; to be accommodating of "superior" people; to never make the mistake of considering ourselves equally human. This condition is maintained and advanced by concepts like the word "poor," for example, which, just like "n****r," is meant to demean and dehumanize. It otherizes people lacking the trappings of materialism, views us through a subhuman lens, and associates us with character flaws like laziness, slothfulness, dishonesty, and inferior social and intellectual ability. As far as the system is concerned, these qualities then become the root causes of a person's situation rather than the systemic exploitation rooted in institutions like plantation slavery and their corresponding biases, and continuing in many aspects of neocolonialism and modern capitalism. In many ways, "n****r" and "poor" are interchangeable in their connotations except that one is race specific and the other is not.

Ultimately, the intersecting narrative about slavery and poverty somehow concluded that our Blackness qualified or caused us to be enslaved, and for that reason, Blackness should be loathed, and the oppressor's role justified. This perspective, taught relentlessly in the social systems, is at the heart of anti-Black oppression and Black self-hatred, and it feeds the underdevelopment of societies like Jamaica and the racial tensions in the United States. Decades as an outsider and insider of both systems have taught me the similarities.

About a mile up the road from where we lived, a family owned a small, black-and-white TV that operated on a Delco. I did not know then that Delco was a brand of electronics rather than the equipment itself, a gas-operated generator on which the family also ran a refrigerator and a few light bulbs. This put them in an elite position among the rural people who could afford no such luxury.

I remember the loud, continuous sputter of the machine in the evenings and on special occasions when they turned it on. Seared in my memory still was going to the house once with my father specifically to watch the television. It was September 7, 1969, the day of the funeral service for Norman Washington Manley, a mixed-race Jamaican who led the island to independence from Great Britain.

Papa was a Manley devotee, embracing his vision of a just society and equal opportunity for everyone. Known for his reticent personality and formidable intellect, Manley, a British-trained barrister, focused on carving out a path to progress and bringing every Jamaican with him.

"The mass of the population are the real people," he declared at the founding of his People's National Party (PNP) in 1938, exactly a century after emancipation. "Those who will not unite with them on all fundamental matters, are the real aliens in the land. . . . [The] people must consciously believe in themselves and their own destiny and must do so with pride and confidence."[5]

Papa believed in those words, and I grew up doing the same because it made perfect sense to me. Watching the funeral on the neighbors' television was the one choice he had short of a trip to Kingston, which he could not afford. The owners were his ideological opponents, which mattered immensely even in rural Jamaica, but ceding a little pride was a small price to pay. Nothing could stop Papa from paying tribute, however simple, to a man he regarded as a hero.

I remember sitting uncomfortably on a forest-green sofa in the tiny living room with its floral linoleum floor. It seemed then like the height of luxury to have multiple rooms, including one devoted solely to chairs for people to sit in and watch television—more so to own this rare, spectacular piece of equipment. I took it all in, but I could not shake the feeling that Papa and I were betraying some cause by being in their home, watching shadowy black-and-white images on a box with two silver poles sticking out from behind.

---

5 In the prologue to "Cultural Action and Social Change: The Case of Jamaica – An Essay in Caribbean Cultural Identity" by Rex Nettleford (1979).

I had never seen a TV before. I did not understand how it worked—how the people inside were reduced to such small sizes and how they got out and returned to being normal-sized people. I spent much of the broadcast trying to figure out this peculiar form of magic that had brought Kingston inside our neighbor's tiny living room and allowed Papa to see and participate in the national goodbye to his hero.

My memory of the event is as ghostly now as the images on the screen then, but it still spits out one image clearly: a woman named Joyce Lalor, head covered with a black mantilla tied under her chin, performing a solo in full operatic drama.

This was a mere seven years after Jamaica gained independence from 314 years of British rule. I was just emerging from my toddler years and only partially absorbing, in some vague ways, the liberating future my parents hoped for me—and far less cognizant of how much the strange box and what it represented would shape the world I was growing into.

Owning a TV would take vastly more resources and infrastructure than we had; we could not afford a Delco, and public electricity was not in the realm of possibility. We barely knew what it was. But another device came into the mix—one with the same capacity to bring us news from the outside world, just without the pictures: radio. Much less expensive than television, they came in different sizes and were battery operated and easy to move around.

Amir, my teenage cousin, lived with our grandmother about 200 yards diagonally from our little house. He was the neighborhood hipster and techie, and he wanted a radio. He had no father figure, and his mother, Papa's younger sister, Susan, had immigrated to the US, leaving him with Mammy. Papa was a loving uncle to him.

Mammy did not want a radio, calling it the idiot box built in the devil's workshop. If Amir ever brought one into her house, she said, she would throw it where grass never grew!

Susan sent it anyway: a red, medium-sized acrylic radio with a little gold-colored handle like a handbag. It was left to Papa to mediate the rows between Mammy and Amir in the days after the radio came. When she threw him out of her house, we made room for him in our tiny one-room for a night or two. Papa would have it no other way. Amir clung fiercely to the radio.

We gathered around him daily, stooped in loose circles, and listened to the strange-sounding voices inside the box. We listened to music and the news, and when the West Indies played cricket against Australia, New Zealand, Pakistan, or England, we followed the series on the radio. Soon, Mammy began to listen to the local news and religious services from the United States. She became acquainted with Oral Roberts, and with the money her children sent her, she bought postal orders and supported his Seed Faith campaign. By then she had gotten her own large, black and silver radio. She kept it in the compartment of her headboard near her Bible and hymn book until she died in 1977.

Radio soon became a staple, as exalted and commonplace as mobile phones would become generations later. Men carried them around and listened to cricket or festival songs while they worked during the days or at night as they played dominoes by torchlight. Women listened to daytime soap operas, some set in faraway places with people speaking in strange accents and others in communities like Old House, with characters who sounded like us, living lives like ours. Soon, we would have our own radio, a smaller black and silver version of my grandmother's that a man named George brought back from Florida at Papa's request.

George was a farmworker, traveling for about six months each year to pick apples or oranges or cut sugarcane in the southern United States and returning home when the crop was over. He made a career out of it, provided for his family, and served as a reliable connection to the US for people like my father in the early 1970s. Ahead of his departure, Papa sometimes gave him a list, usually including a wristwatch, a fountain pen, or a radio—objects that, as time passed, he would update by the same medium. Amir's mother also sent home goods that way, such as clothes and food for him and Mammy, and sometimes for Papa and the rest of us.

The radio brought us local news daily at 6 and 7 a.m. on RJR (Radio Jamaica Rediffusion), BBC World News at 8 a.m., and local news again at 10 a.m. and midday.[6] Reggae music played in between local soaps, *Dulcimina* and *Life in Hopeful Village*. There was a special thrill in processing our own lives through a mediated space.

Local news kept us up to date about things in Town and what the government was doing that bore no relationship to our lives.[7] Meanwhile, BBC held me spellbound with stories of conflict around the world: sectarian violence between Catholic "nationalists" and Protestant "loyalists" in Northern Ireland; Nelson and Winnie Mandela's resistance to apartheid in South Africa; the Popular Movement for the Liberation of Angola, or MPLA, fighting for independence from Portuguese colonial rule; the civil rights movement in the United States; and the soul-crushing battle between the Israelis and the Palestinians. That conflict was seared into my consciousness, likely with the war of 1973 and the United Nations General Assembly in 1974, which reaffirmed "the inalienable rights of the Palestinian people to self-determination, national independence, sovereignty, and to return."[8] Mama paid close attention. She believed that every such conflict was likely the beginning of Armageddon, the great war that would signal the end of time. Her interpretations were always religious or biblical instead of political as Papa's tended to be.

I do not pretend to remember a single detail, only that those were the major issues of the day from our one overseas news source, which I listened to in the mornings while I brushed my teeth outside and spat foamy white toothpaste on the dusty earth under the pimento trees. These experiences have had a lifelong impact on me.

---

6 Owned by the British Rediffusion Group, RJR (Radio Jamaica Rediffusion) emerged from colonial wartime shortwave transmissions in the 1930s and became Jamaica's first radio station in 1949. It remains the island's leading news station.

7 In Jamaica, Town is commonly used as a synonym for Kingston, the country's capital.

8 See "The Question of Palestine and the General Assembly" at https://www.un.org/unispal/data-collection/general-assembly/.

Radio would become central to my understanding that there was a giant world out there, far different, and more complicated than Old House. News told the story of that world constantly in trouble and darkly fascinating compared to our humdrum existence. I listened fiercely. I have carried with me that fascination with news and narratives of conflict, and later an equal or more profound interest in how to arrive at solutions, especially when some of them seem so obvious. It connects to my firm belief that it is the purpose of every life to leave things better wherever we can—and that we must act in the interest of justice, peace, and progress.

I have more happy memories of my childhood in Old House than sad ones. My sense of well-being stemmed from my lack of awareness of what "poverty" was or what wealth should look like. The absence of such comparison in my early life meant there was no room to feel better or worse about what I had or did not have. Life was just life.

I also had something of incalculable value: two strong, functional parents with solid values and fine human qualities, regardless of their weaknesses. They loved me, and I loved them as a matter of course. Holding on to Mama's frock tail while she balanced a four-gallon tin of water on her head or Papa grasping my little hand in his big one, on my first trip to Mandeville, provided a feeling of security that nothing in my adult life has transcended or ever will.

A vast circle of siblings, two grandmothers, a great-grandmother, aunts, uncles, and cousins both nearby and far away in the United Kingdom, Canada, and the United States extended a tightly woven net of unconditional love around me. That and the leisurely pace of life and the peace of the natural world made home—an idea more than a physical place—as comfortable as a soft, fuzzy old blanket. I belonged.

A left turn at the end of the narrow, dusty pathway from our house, flanked by a naseberry tree on the left and a coconut tree on the right, led to Mammy's lovely little bungalow, painted pale yellow on the outside and aquamarine under the veranda. As with my parents' house, there was no electricity or running water. We lit the house with kerosene lamps at night and harvested rainwater in old construction drums. The sanitary convenience was about seventy-five yards from the house. We used portable enamel or plastic pails or chamber pots—chimmies—kept under the beds and emptied each morning. That ritual disposal of nighttime waste was the first chore for little country girls like me. Boys were above that. Not a single family would consider emptying or washing chimmies an appropriate chore for boys.

Things changed for Mammy over time. By the mid-1970s, the children had added two bedrooms and a kitchen to the large single room she previously lived in. The original house became a living room where she kept a three-piece aquamarine settee and a coffee table bearing a vase with stiff plastic flowers. The bright-red terrazzo tiles and new louvered windows were a novelty in a community where many houses still had wattle-and-daub concrete floors. Later, Uncle Maurice built a new pit latrine closer to the house. Besides the lack of running water, it was a perfectly modern sanitary space, similar to what is now called a compost toilet.

Set among coffee, soursop, tangerine, and pimento trees, the little bungalow was a haven for my grandmother. Keeping her few cherished pieces of furniture polished and shining and all the leaves at bay from the walkway kept her sufficiently occupied as old age advanced and she no longer worked for a living.

She reinforced the cleaning habit I had already learned from my mother. I swept and cleaned constantly and brought those habits into adulthood. So much lay beyond our capacity to effect change, so we overdid what we could control, even fighting with nature. We could not always accept that with some things, the fight would basically be futile—like staying ahead of falling leaves.

——— ✀ ———

Mammy, more so than Papa and Mama, was my earliest and greatest reason to reject the poor person's construct.

She was the first woman I knew who used a double-barreled surname, even though she was never married nor formally educated. Without the influence of the internet or even television, and against the norms of the times, she insisted on the importance of identifying with and honoring her mother's family and heritage. She attached her mother's name to her father's and insisted that both were equally her name. Throughout my life, therefore, I knew my grandmother, a single woman, as Loretta Wilson-Reid. My father called her Mammy, and so did I.

She was born in 1907. I have never forgotten because when she told me, she said she was five when the Titanic sank in 1912. The year of her birth marked the seventy-fourth anniversary of emancipation from plantation slavery. This means that her grandparents were likely enslaved people intermingling with some plantation owners or their relatives.

I remember her mother, my great-grandmother Advira Reid, Mumma or Granny Vira to us, from whom I inherited some of that 13 percent European DNA. She was old, stooped, and toothless, with blue eyes and skin so fair that the tropical sun could not tame it. She wore her long hair parted down the center and contained in two plaits hanging down her chest. I remember her brown walking stick and her clothes—the layers of white petticoats under a pale-pink overdress. I remember everything physical about her except her voice. I cannot conjure up a single memory of how she sounded or anything she ever said, although I saw and interacted with her often up to about age eight or nine.

Mammy's deep-bronze coloring reflected the commingling of a dominant Black gene with those of her mother, whatever her ancestry, and she looked sunbaked where Granny Vira did not. Tall and elegant, with gold-flecked eyes, Mammy had an arresting quality—a fluid grace and haughty, dignified bearing that conveyed nothing about deprivation, disempowerment, lack of agency, or, God forbid, "lower class."

She had her first child, a girl she named Priscilla, at age sixteen, a not-unusual trajectory among the descendants of slaves, who had limited pathways to education or health care like contraceptive solutions.

Priscilla was a mulatto. I do not know the circumstances of her birth, only that her father was connected to a landholding family of Scottish men in the community who treated women like an extension of their property—theirs for the taking. The man who sired Priscilla was rumored to have had twenty-one children.

Mammy, thankfully, recovered from that early first pregnancy. Her second child, my father, came eleven years later. She would have two more children in her thirties and one in her forties. All of them became high-functioning adults, moving to London, Miami, and New York, with two remaining in Jamaica—my father, who eventually became a works overseer with the Public Works Department, and my youngest uncle, an accountant for Bernard Lodge, a nineteenth-century former slaveholding sugar estate in St. Catherine parish, bordering Kingston.

Mammy was not just a feminist. She was a woman with a well-thought-out philosophy on both human and animal rights. It is mainly to her and my father that I owe my early understanding and appreciation of the sentiency of all life and that animals, like people, deserve to be treated with care and dignity. She always had cats, and they held pride of place in her house and were even allowed privileges, like sleeping on the sofa, that humans were denied.

To this day, I remember the Sunday evening when her beloved cat Polly was killed by a car across the road from her house. In rage and sorrow, she excoriated the driver for being a reckless show-off and driving too fast. We stood behind her as she scooped up Polly's broken body with old newspaper and marched stoically home to bury her at the back of the coffee piece. She never forgave the man, and neither did Amir and I.

Mammy believed in education and raised her children to value it too. Papa did the same for us, scrimping and saving to buy us whatever we needed and never allowing a missed day at school. Illness was the only exception, and he needed to be convinced.

Unlike Mammy and Mama, Papa was agnostic and did not feed me on the Bible. Where the Bible was the go-to for Mama, he read the newspapers and whatever else he could get his hands on. Although he had his radio, Papa bought the paper every day, often brought by the postman—under some special arrangement, looking back. Then he became a rural correspondent for both the *Daily Gleaner* and RJR, sending them press releases and cables about deaths, bad roads, storm damage, the absence of proper toilets in the community, and political news, whatever it was.

In retrospect, I realized that Papa did not just take me along to keep him company when he attended his group meetings or like he did to watch Manley's funeral on the neighbor's TV. Rather, these were deliberate efforts to expose me to life outside Old House. He took advantage of every small opportunity to communicate to me a sense of a bigger world and path to a better life.

He did not exert much control over what I read and did. Mammy assumed that role while I was between ages six and twelve, and I spent most of my time with her. She recommended library books with the same themes as the stories she made me read from the Bible: justice, humility, grace, virtue, and the importance of moral conduct. *The Basket of Flowers*, *Dick Whittington and His Cat*, and "The Little Match Girl," all old European folktales, were some of her favorites.

By age six, I was reading the Bible to her every night. I read from Psalms, beautiful, evocative verses about God's righteousness and commitment to protecting His people or the wrath that would befall those who persecuted them or disobeyed Him. From the book of Job, I read powerful lessons about the redemptive power of faith and the suffering God's chosen people must endure in His name. And over and over, she made me read the story in Genesis about Joseph, the son of Jacob, sold into slavery in Egypt by his jealous brothers for twenty pieces of silver.

She praised Joseph's goodness, lamented his brothers' duplicity, and reveled in the supreme belief that what had been intended as a grave injustice to Jacob's young son inured to his favor because he was a man of integrity. Joseph did not just survive; he thrived, elevated to a position of great power, and in the end saved his family from famine because he was a righteous man.

The story about David, a young Israelite who confronted the Philistine giant Goliath, was another favorite. The simple narrative was that of a brave boy who took on a bully—older, bigger, and better armed. When King Saul offered his heavy armor for the confrontation, David refused, opting for the basic tools he knew how to use: a slingshot and five pebbles from a brook. David's first shot struck Goliath's forehead, knocking him off his feet. When the giant fell, David cut off his head with his sword and took it to the king.

I took from those stories what I believed my grandmother intended: the certainty that integrity matters and, in the battle between justice and injustice, the size and circumstances of those in the fight do not always predetermine the outcome. Therefore, I should never be afraid to stand on the side of righteousness. She wanted me to believe, too, that in all things, the law of God prevails, if not the law of man.

In my life, in the epic struggles against multiple forms of oppression, I have often questioned that premise, sometimes despairing that there is a supreme being who is both righteous and caring. Each time, my soul-searching ended in the same place. Regardless of what name we call Him or whether we accept that there is a deity, there is a force out there with a distinct preference for justice and the power to make it happen, even if the pace is most often long and slow.

This belief is truncated in a now familiar quote by the great civil rights leader Rev. Dr. Martin Luther King Jr., paraphrasing portions of a sermon delivered in 1853 by the abolitionist minister Theodore Parker. America's first Black president is said to have loved the quote so much that he had it woven into a rug in the White House: "The arc of the moral universe is long, but it bends toward justice."

As I grew older, my reading expanded beyond the Bible and what I could find on Mammy's nightstand. I joined the community library, a one-room structure measuring approximately twelve by twelve and attached to the Presbyterian church, about two and a half miles from our house and a mile from my infant school. The school was a thatched hut, about twelve by sixteen, made with sturdy damsel posts and roofed with dried palm fronds. It was unenclosed, so there was no need for windows or doors. Tropical breezes flowed unencumbered throughout. The floor looked like brown clay, smooth and slippery from the persistent trampling of little feet over time. When it rained, Miss Lou, the founder, and my teacher most of the time, guided us all up a flight of concrete steps and into her three-bedroom house about fifty feet away. This was where I learned my times tables, alphabet, days of the week, months of the year, nursery rhymes, clock times, and to read my Nola books—our primers.

Miss Lou served us lunch for five cents a day if we could afford it. When we could not, we would get it on credit. Even then, I felt an acute absence of dignity whenever I had to tell them that Papa would pay later. I wanted to pay those five cents when they called my name. It is safe to say my desire for self-sustenance developed at a young age. It endures.

The library and the books I found there would be crucial to that effort, though I did not know it then. I would crawl around the polished red floor, struggling to find something in the children's section that I had not already read. It became more challenging as the years went by, but I discovered most of my childhood books there, primarily European folk and fairy tales.

I do not recall identifying with the golden-haired maidens I found in these stories or wanting to be them. I thought they belonged to some faraway world in which I could never venture, but I did connect with elements of their character, the morals of the stories, and their lives. In those earliest years, I learned to separate people's appearances from their inner lives—their characters. It remains a profound source of frustration to me that so many otherwise intelligent and educated adults are still unable to make that distinction. It is equally maddening and deflating each time I am the object of their misjudgments.

By age ten, I had graduated to American mysteries like the Bobbsey Twins and, soon after, the Nancy Drew and Hardy Boys series. If nothing else, they kept me gainfully occupied in my leisure time, encouraged my love of reading, built my vocabulary, strengthened my written English skills, and took me to fascinating places and cultures far from Old House. I often lost track of time and place, drifting in my beautiful web of dreams that seemed too far removed from my reality to be anything else. Nonetheless, these stories anchored many of my aspirations away from the least desirable aspects of our reality, like food insecurity or living in a house that was both inadequate and not our own. I am not over my fear that whoever owns my dwelling owns my life too. It is always a disempowering contemplation.

Around the same time, Claire, an older cousin, started working as a maid to a wealthy family in Kingston and brought me more books. It was from her that I received Johanna Spyri's *Heidi*. I promptly fell in love with the Swiss Alps and the notions of nature as healing and humanity as one with the universe. It was among the first books that presented the natural world to me in a way that lingered in my imagination as something to reach for in a valuable and wholesome way. I grew into it. I went to the library and found the sequels, *Heidi Grows Up* and *Heidi's Children*. Again, I did not want to be Heidi, but I loved her world and would have loved to play and herd goats with her and Peter.

For a while, I harbored an intense yearning for the Swiss Alps. Life there seemed as simple as in Old House, but processed through the written word and the prism of distance and newness, it seemed infinitely more alluring, more romantic. There was the magic of changing seasons and golden daffodils popping out of the earth on cue, so unlike the dusty valley where I woke to the warmth of a tropical sun year-round, only occasionally interrupted when the rains came with big, galloping drops on the roof. It was never long before the sun shone and the hibiscus, marigold, and myriad ferns and lilies slowly raised their heads again, hydrated and happy. What could be alluring about that?

Reading was my best escape from everyday life, and the cultural difference I found from one setting to another was infinitely exciting. It was a solitary activity too and therefore empowering. I did not need a partner as I did for a game of jacks or hopscotch or to play school in the bamboo roots. Even more than that, reading appealed to the side of me that was deeply introverted and enjoyed being alone with my discomfitures and my dreams.

When I found a copy of *The Fire Next Time* by a man named James Baldwin inside Mammy's nightstand, I settled down with my first introduction to radical Black intellectual tradition. By then, Mammy had suffered her first stroke and paid less attention to me and what I read. She did not notice when I took the book from the drawer or sat outside on the walkway, my brown-haired doll beside me, lost in Baldwin's fluidity and fury at injustices facing Black people in the United States. I finished and went looking for more Baldwin at the library. I found *Go Tell It on the Mountain* and finished that too.

I cannot say how much of it resonated then. I did not yet have a broader context for what it meant to live as a Black person in the US, but these books placed Baldwin in my consciousness as an advocate against racial oppression and began to inform how I saw myself in Jamaica—and in the world.

Next door to Mammy and me, my cousin Beatrice was raising her seven children—five boys and two girls. She was Mammy's niece and the same age as Aunt Priscilla, or Priss, Mammy's oldest child, who had lived in New York since before I was born. That meant Beatrice was a little older than my father and by blood only a second cousin to me, but in deference to her age and status, and as a mark of deep affection, Beatrice Harrison-Allen was Sister (Sa) Bea throughout my life.

Whenever and wherever I saw her, Sa Bea was a comforting presence, with her silky black skin, piercing dark eyes always dancing with merriment, and reams of laughter and worry lines forming half circles from just below her cheekbones and leveling with her lower lip. Warm and fulsome, she had little apparent allegiance to vanity. She nearly always wore a checkered red bandanna covering all but the ends of her black-and-white plaits and loosely tied in a bow at the nape of her neck. Over brightly colored dresses, she wore sturdy denim or calico bibs with deep pockets where she kept her thread bag—a homemade drawstring purse with money to purchase goods in and around Old House, which she then sold as a vendor in Coronation Market in Kingston.

While Aunt Priss went off to Kingston and later to New York in early adulthood, Sa Bea remained in Old House. When her husband—Thomas, one of my two godfathers—died, leaving her a widow at forty, she set out on her own. She billowed over the entire village with her joyful strength and determination to make a life for herself and her children. In her radiance, authenticity, and resilience, she epitomized the strength and character of the kind of women who make a difference. She was my Mother Earth.

The rhythm of Old House revolved substantively around Sa Bea's quest to survive during my early years. Rising early on Mondays, she canvassed the immediate and nearby communities, sometimes on the back of a little gray donkey and other times on foot, to find cash crops and other goods to sell. The search continued until noon on Wednesdays, when fresh tomatoes, naseberries, pumpkins, cabbages, watermelons, sweetsops, and soursops would be packed in wooden boxes lined with old newspapers bought from my father. Around 3 p.m., a small truck with wooden sides arrived to take her and a few other women to the market, where she spent the rest of the week hawking her goods before returning home between 9 p.m. and midnight Saturday.

Early Sunday morning, much of the village would come to collect whatever she had brought back for them, either in exchange for goods they had given her or as gifts sent by relatives in the city. It was also a good time for my cousins and me to raid the wooden boxes, competing with flies and bumblebees for leftover naseberries, sweetsops, or mangoes.

The exchanges over, Sa Bea would get ready for church, switching out her bib and bandanna for a floral dress, or white on communion Sundays, and a curly black wig under a broad-brimmed nylon hat with a dainty bow tied at the back. Gone were the black socks and comfortable loafers. In their place were brown nylon stockings and black or white wedge-heeled patent shoes.

Sa Bea was not only a woman trying to provide for her family. She was a crucially reliable connection between the small farmers of our community and the housewives of Kingston and St. Andrew who purchased her fruits and vegetables for their kitchens, week after week over two decades. On her return trips, she brought letters, goods, and messages from people in Kingston to their relatives in Old House and surrounding communities.

Through it all, I never saw a hint of helplessness, passivity, or lack of agency to manage and control her life. I never saw Sa Bea cry. Never saw anger, fatigue, vulnerability, or self-pity. I never saw a man in her life, either, or knew her to be involved with anyone from the time her husband died around 1969 until her passing almost forty years later. I only saw what was normal for her: taking charge of her life, doing her best with what she had, and helping a lot of people in the process.

Yet there was an odd but not uncommon dynamic in the family. Sa Bea was the darkest member on my grandmother's side. My awareness of the weight of skin color crystallized around the stories I heard about how she was treated as a child compared to Priss, the half-White or high-Brown family member. Despite Sa Bea's outsized impact on the family and the whole community, people seemed to take her for granted; meanwhile, Priss was regarded reverently. Family lore says she always had the first and best choice of whatever needed to be shared between her and Bea during their childhood—not by their choosing but because the adults around them made that distinction.

I still recall a family member telling a story that, even then, he found funny, about how one of our great-uncles had caught young Bea eating a naseberry intended for Priscilla. Furious, he choked her, forcing her to spit out the half-eaten fruit, which was no longer useful to her cousin. If Priss could not have it, neither should Bea. Both girls were his nieces, each by a different sister.

Priss was the family princess as a child and the queen in adulthood. With her flawless olive skin and mass of long, brown hair, she appeared closer to the former plantation owners than she did to the descendants of the formerly enslaved. She was therefore above the relatively menial roles that Sa Bea had to play in search of a living.

While Aunt Priss enjoyed a relatively comfortable life in the US, Sa Bea remained in Old House, their experiences offering a useful example of the differing trajectories shaped, in part, by race or skin color. Life was not easy for Sa Bea, but selfishly, I am happy that, like my father, she did not leave. Alongside my grandmother and my mother, she gave form and direction to my life. She was a boss.

Mama was twenty-four when she had me, her third child. She would have nine more children, including one stillbirth brought on by the stress of losing her mother as she approached her due date. I missed out on a fifth sister.

Like Mammy and Sa Bea, Ma had little formal education. I never saw her read anything besides the Bible or an occasional letter from her brother or sister in England. I only ever saw her write in response to those letters. She deferred to my father's splendid and much-heralded cursive in business or even personal letters to us once distance made them necessary.

Mama had a love affair with Psalms, and a limited few at that: 23, 27, 46, and 91. She read them aloud so frequently during my childhood that I also regarded them as my favorites because they were always in my head. At her funeral in 2012, I included all four, along with the hymns she sang when she was happy, agitated, beseeching the Lord for help in her anguish, or imploring his wrath upon her tormentors.

She was my heart outside my body, yet as a child, I quietly found fault with some things about her—like her thick, hard-to-tame hair, which she wore naturally. She did not look as important as my teachers or the public health nurse, with their hair straightened, curled with hot combs, and set on small plastic rollers overnight, resulting in professional-looking curls in the daytime. That was the epitome of sophistication of the day. I wanted Mama to be more like them, and why not? She was important, and I wanted her to look it. I was not at all immune to colonial acculturation, including notions of what "importance" is supposed to look like.

By my midteens, I began to appreciate how comprehensively and exquisitely lovely Mama was all around, with the same luminous dark skin as Sa Bea and her quick, hearty laughs. How brave she was to simply be herself and protect us with the vastness of her passions and fury, as she saw fit. I also realized, just about then, that I was becoming a lot like her!

Amid the travails of my life, and particularly after her death, I have often regretted having no images of her as a child, a teenager, a young woman at age eighteen or nineteen, or in her bridal dress on her wedding day. When my youngest sister described to me a dream she had of Mama in her early twenties, wearing a white sundress and happily walking through a field of yellow flowers, I let my imagination conjure how lovely she must have been at the culmination of youth and its radiance, with the energy and passion that was uniquely hers in early adulthood.

Family lore says my grandmother had not wanted my mother, a dark-skinned woman, for her eldest son, a Black man whose DNA became less so as the layers of ancestry were peeled back. He was not fair skinned like Aunt Priss, but they shared a maternal grandmother of obvious European origins. His father, John Milton Virtue, was the great-grandson of Daniel Virtue, a Scottish man who settled on the island in the late eighteenth century and eventually purchased

Roxborough Estate, now a national heritage site in central Manchester.

Historical records show that Daniel bought the property with sixty-four enslaved people and later added twenty to his "stock." In one of those little quirks of fate, the property was sold to T. A. S. Manley and became the birthplace of Premier Norman Manley, the great Jamaican leader Papa so admired. Papa tried to tell us as children about his ancestral connections to the old estate. We did not understand or care. To the extent that I was curious about the non-African part of his DNA, I had always thought it was Asian—South Indian perhaps. It has not proven to be true.

Compared to people with more obvious African ancestry, the lighter skin that resulted from forced sexual relationships between enslaved people and their captors or from cross-fertilization among other ethnic groups arriving after emancipation held significant value for some Jamaicans, cognizant of the privileges it brought them. Lighter skin remains valuable in a context that is still deeply colonial more than sixty years postindependence, but this eminence erodes a little every day because of better public policies, like those of the Manley era and new opportunities of a changing world that have allowed Black people to move into the so-called middle and upper classes.

As people emigrated, for example, and sent money back to build houses, start businesses, and educate the next generation; and as icons of contemporary society—academics, writers, athletes, musicians, and even TikTok stars—look increasingly more like the masses and less like old plantation owners, their wives, or their house slaves, race or skin color has become a much cheaper currency than it was during the late fifties when my father was a young man looking for a life partner in a small rural community. An increasingly conscious younger generation across the spectrum, integrated through school and social media, is dictating the future of racial relationships, and white or brown skin matters less to them.

Like most mothers looking out for their sons, and the first one at that, my grandmother had a suitably light-skinned woman picked out for Papa. He thwarted her and married my mother. Mammy never accepted her, and they kept each other at bay throughout their lives. As the grandchild most often exposed to both, I was often caught between them, constantly sensing the barely veiled hostility. It was uncomfortable knowing that they disliked each other, and worse because there was a wholly unacceptable explanation for it. In retrospect, and with neither of them still here to explain themselves, I wonder if the tension also drew from the fact that they were such different people. Maybe some, but not all. Colorism was in the culture, even in families like ours.

I now think of Mammy as a phenomenal woman with inherent flaws—one more example of why I am unpersuaded by the illogic of false choices I often encounter in my adult life. I understand that the woman who taught me so much about ethics, integrity, and human dignity, who made me read the Bible every night and in whose home I first read Baldwin, saw my mother as wanting, at some level, because her skin was too dark. I blame it on the scars of colonialism, which were deeper and closer for her.

Contrary to Mammy's biases, I grew to see my mother as beautiful, spirited, and sure-footed, with a tough outer shell and a heightened intuition. I recognized her undeniable psychic powers, and I knew they often overcame her, expressing themselves as emotional volatility, unpredictability, or paranoia. It could be draining at times, but they helped with the objective she cared about most: keeping her family safe and lifting us out of our precarious economic circumstances. In these important quests, my mother led my father more than he did her.

Her leadership mattered enormously to our progress as a family. Mama earned money less consistently and at more menial tasks than Papa did, such as washing or ironing people's clothes, picking up charcoal, or picking gungo peas or pimento for small farmers; but she made the big decisions about our lives and imposed them when Papa procrastinated or disagreed. This was how we moved from the little house where I was born.

The house at Old House sat on a strip of land between two parochial roads. It was owned by one of our cousins, my grandmother's nephew, who had also gone to England with the Windrushers. Next door to us, just beyond a little gully and a thick little grove of pimento, naseberries, and orange trees, lived Ubel, our cousin's half brother, with his wife and five children. He was unrelated to us and had inherited a solid house from his mother. Ubel resented that we lived in his brother's house and thought he could put us out if he wanted to. He asserted his authority as often as he wished—usually after too many ganja spliffs and when Mama was alone with us.

I can still see him stalking the house, his machete sharpened silver on both sides and tucked under his arm. I remember trembling in fear every time he walked by, repeatedly circling the house in silence before exploding in volcanic rage and screaming obscenities at us for no reason at all.

"Dutty bombo claat unooh!"

"A goin kill de whole a unooh!"

I feared that he would kill my mother or my father, both, or all of us.

As soon as my father found work at ALPART, the new bauxite plant in neighboring St. Elizabeth Parish, Mama began plotting our way out of that little house.

Papa now had a steady income, unwittingly giving Ubel one more reason to rage at us from the road beyond the bamboo. With Papa gone twelve hours a day, the explosions had become continuous rather than episodic and decidedly more persistent and vicious. Mama knew that we were barely staying ahead of a fiendishly angry man who was taking out all the frustrations of his life on us and leveraging his one source of power: We lived in his brother's house on their family land.

I heard the conversations as I lay in bed at night, Mama urging Papa from his very first paycheck to start putting away money to buy a piece of land and telling him where to look. Soon enough, they purchased a quarter acre about a mile north of Old House.

The location was not accidental. Moving north put us slightly closer to Cross Keys and its few amenities, including the primary school my father coveted for his children. It was a sign that we were moving up. Moving south would have meant heading further into the valley, with little of interest except the vast blue sea, splendid though it is. Papa, a skilled tradesman, began building as soon as the sale was completed, but before the structure was half-finished, he lost his job with the mining company.

In the anguished chatter that followed, I learned that Papa was fired for stopping too many times to repair an old pair of sandals he had made himself. He intended to replace them with good shoes as soon as he could but never reached that point; and the cycle of desperation, powerlessness, and vulnerability started all over again.

Mama cried despairingly as often as she prayed and sang. It wore me down like an anchor. The new house was incomplete, and Ubel's machete flashed as he glared at us, hurling obscenities through the bamboos. Mama knew time was not on our side.

He was going to kill us.

In the middle of one of his blistering rants late one afternoon around 1974, Mama decided enough was enough. He had been at it all day, orbiting the house in his usual way, moving from the street at the back near the coconut tree to the bamboo grove in front, his machete stuck under his arm. He singled me out, pointing the machete at me. I clung to Ma's frock tails. As usual, she hissed back occasionally, but something snapped that afternoon.

"Why you don't jus' come kiss mi ass?" she yelled, throwing her frock over her head for good measure.

Young as I was, I understood that voluntary loss of dignity born out of rage and frustration. It was intended as the ultimate insult to the person on the receiving end, and it was all she had in the fight against Ubel's unyielding madness. An hour or so later, when he had exhausted himself and temporarily disappeared from the front of the house, Mama shoved the six of us inside, including the youngest, about seven months old.

"Unooh lock the door," she threw over her shoulder as she ran up the path toward the bamboo and disappeared around the corner. "Mi soo come back."

Someone secured the door with the latch—a sliver of wood about three inches long, held in place on the jamb with a single nail and turned horizontally across the partially rotting door. At the time, I thought we were safe behind that "locked" door. Now I can only marvel at the childish innocence that protected me from even more anxiety. Ubel could have killed us if he wanted to. A one-handed push, or one medium puff from the Big Bad Wolf, could have taken the whole door down.

Mama came charging at dusk, and in the same state of heightened agitation with which she had left, she began frantically snatching our clothes from the hangers in the makeshift closet. She tossed whatever she could fit into the one brown imitation-leather grip we owned and the rest into two or three extra pillowcases.

I do not know why we had extra linens when we had so little of anything else. Mama likely made them herself in her rare moments of leisure. She was crafty in a way I am not and did not fully appreciate until recently, when I looked back at all the things she had made with her hands. She could sew but never could afford a sewing machine. She hand-stitched. She embroidered, too, whenever she could secure little pieces of fabric, rainbow-colored threads, and the larger needles she needed. It would have been simple enough to hand-stitch a pillowcase and complete it with bright-yellow sunflowers and green leaves. The images are still stuck in my mind's eye.

Mama's lightning run up the road had been to secure permission to occupy a small white house, about the same size as the one in Old House, owned by the woman who had sold us the land further north. The house was about 300 yards from the border of our new property and would be our home for just a few months before Mama moved us into our partially constructed three-bedroom house.

Months after Norman Manley's youngest son, Michael, won the national elections in 1972 on a social justice platform, Papa found a job with the Public Works Department. Michael's older brother, Dr. Douglas Manley, became our member of Parliament, and he looked out for us—not by giving us a handout but by setting up opportunities. He arranged for my father to take the civil service exams, which Papa passed easily. Mama immediately forced his hand, knowing that moving us into the unfinished house would compel him to finish it as quickly as possible. She was crafty in more ways than one.

The house had no windows, floors, or doors, just the cinder block walls and a corrugated zinc roof. Mama placed leftover sheets of zinc where the windows and doors were supposed to be and held them in place with stacks of cinder blocks and lumber. I do not know the trigger—what made her decide at that time that it was the end of the road for us in the little white house and that our incomplete house was where we needed to be. What I do know was that with her sixth-grade education, she was as astute a woman as I have ever met, and that extended to how well she knew her husband. On his own, Papa would have dithered, taken his time, enjoyed the process, debated whether to use cedar or mahogany for the finishes and whether the kitchen should be bigger than the dining room. Mama simply wanted us in our own home, on our own land, where no one could decide whether we went or stayed.

Papa had great intentions, of course. I had no say in the matter then, but from my perspective now, grounded in so many experiences in challenging spaces, I can respect Papa's idealism, but I am entirely with Mama and her need for speed when it comes to shaking off the yoke of oppression.

The first weekend after we moved in, Papa went to Mandeville, the nearest town with big hardware stores and supermarkets, bought new windows, doors, and ceiling material, and began working to complete our little bungalow. He modeled it on my grandmother's home, but with more amenities: a kitchen with cupboards and Formica finishing, the trend of the day; a tank built high above the ground to carry water to the kitchen; and a bathroom with American Standard fixtures. As the building progressed, Papa planted ortanique oranges and a hibiscus border parallel to the public road and branded our house "Hibiscus Place."

It became a haven for us and the countless friends and cousins who would form the core of my largely joyful teenage years. We still struggled with food insecurity sometimes, but we knew that as surely as the sun crept over the eastern hillside every day, there would be a break in the cycle of hunger, even if we did not know how.

Ubel, the first bully I encountered in my life, was no longer a threat to my existence or the people I loved, but his memory never left me. I have recognized his tactics in others, including in the workplace, where they might be more refined and the actions more subtle. He comes to mind whenever I must decide where to live, for example, and he appears whenever I see women in situations that heighten their vulnerability. He influenced my belief that housing is the greatest need among people without means around the world, the most effective protection against abuse of women, and the single most empowering agent for them.

In part, those memories propelled my contribution to the United State of Women Summit hosted by First Lady Michelle Obama half a century later, in 2016: a short blog post titled "For poor women, the answer is their own key," which was subsequently published on the White House conference site. In that post I argued that no anti-poverty eradication effort targeted at women is sufficient if it does not address affordable housing—places where they have agency and can protect themselves from abuse. I believe this to be inarguably true, particularly in the Global South.

This belief is also why, in May 2019, I wrote an open letter to billionaire philanthropist Melinda Gates, urging her to consider a housing program for women in Africa to complement her work on reproductive health. It was a response triggered first by my experience in Old House, what I had seen in Jamaica among other women living in poverty and later in Kibera, a sprawling slum in Nairobi, Kenya—and by what I perceived as insincerity and even high-handedness as Gates did the media rounds, promoting her book, *The Moment of Lift*. However unintended, it seemed to me that she was co-opting the struggles of underprivileged women, women like my mother, grandmother, Sa Bea, and Miss Lou, who made up the world of competent, forward-thinking, difference-making people I knew as a child, and who inspired me to confront even powerful people like Gates.

The women of my childhood needed no one's dictums on how to live. They merely lacked the resources to advance themselves in ways they could have otherwise. They were not poor in the ways that the word connotes, and I have come to believe it is loaded with psychological violence. Trapped beneath its weight is the bulk of society's talent, industry, creativity, and innovation, too often obscured by biases and misconceptions.

Increasing personal and professional exposure soon taught me that the material poverty of Old House was a microcosm of communities across Jamaica and the world where slavery, colonialism, and other systems of oppression created and sustained the exploitation of Black or non-White people. Politicians who benefit from these systems and have the power to initiate change do little to provide redress, leaving those who suffer most to battle the system as best they can. Within these constraints, the women of Old House were my first examples of strong, independent womanhood—long before Hillary Clinton, Oprah Winfrey, Michelle Obama, or #MeToo.

CHAPTER TWO

SCHOOLING

Life does not exempt any of us from its vagaries or leave any of us unchallenged and unencumbered. Even at twelve years old, I knew I was far worse off than some people, far better off than many, and quite alike a significant number who came into the world in circumstances much like mine. Hibiscus Place improved many things, but life continued apace. The obstacles came in different ways.

Mammy got sicker. She had been bedridden for a long time, and I became her hands and feet. I did my best before going to school; I emptied the chimmies, washed and brought them back inside, and placed whatever she needed on the bedside table within reach. At Aunt Priss's engineering, Sa Bea eventually stopped going to market as often to help take care of her. I went to school every day with a keen sense that my grandmother was slipping away. I prayed the day would never come. What would I do without her? How would I fill the inevitable hole in my heart? In my life?

I also had something called the Common Entrance Examination to prepare for. The school system used this national filter exam to determine what society did with children once they reached age twelve. We were either placed on a path to probable self-actualization and a meaningful life or on a much less certain, alternative track designed to keep those at the bottom, the descendants of the enslaved, in their places, forever battling the system like my father did and eking out a living until we die, all our passion and talent gone to waste.

Old British-inspired traditional high schools stood in contrast to new postindependence secondary schools, each functioning as distinct parts of a class-based dual-track education system that remains to this day, notwithstanding some superficial changes. Being awarded a Common Entrance pass where I lived meant a place at Manchester High, Bishop Gibson, or DeCarteret College, all about fifteen miles from home with neither school buses nor organized public transportation. Conversely, not being granted a pass meant going to Cross Keys, a newly built school less than two miles from home.

I took the exam near the end of sixth grade, not long after my twelfth birthday. I was joined by other children my age in the island's primary and preparatory schools, except those determined to be not worth "sending up." I had been at my new primary school for about two years, taking a six-mile roundtrip each day—seven when I added the journey to and from Mammy's house. Along with other children, I ran, walked, and played my way back and forth, building friendships, camaraderie, and cherished memories. We stayed healthy too. The distance did not feel like a burden. It was typical for children across the country, and for the most part, it was safe.

Our old school would have been closer by about two miles roundtrip, but my father wanted to give us a better education. Standards had declined at the old school since he attended, he said, resulting in lower performance by the children, evidenced by few to none advancing to anything meaningful. By comparison, the farther school was getting small but steady passes in the Common Entrance, which he attributed to better administration and accountability and more competent teachers. Much of this had to do with the woman principal, a supposedly strict disciplinarian I have renamed Selene.

She sounded formidable to me. I was terrified even before I started. Those fears turned out to be well founded, and I wondered if my father knew the extent of her cruelty. Miss Selene, as it turned out, was not a disciplinarian at all but a miserable crone who picked favorites among the children and violently abused those she did not like.

Unfortunately, she did not like me. She liked my older sister enough to have her fetch her lunch from her house, about a mile from the school, every day. I, however, committed the cardinal sin of befriending a student from Kingston who arrived at the same time I did—a bright, sassy, and defiant girl named Bridget. She did not wither under the principal's angry stare from behind owlish, double-lensed, horn-rimmed glasses or show any other sign of fear. Miss Selene's dislike of her soon extended to me. She branded me "Disgrace" and never once used my name in the two years I spent at the school. My loathing for her grew as I saw her push, punch, and batter one child after another for reasons I mostly did not know. The one time I did know why involved Bridget, our friend Mia, and me.

The sun was invigoratingly bright as usual one day when the bell rang for recess. I ran out with Bridget and Mia; we soon made our way between the school building and the concrete tank toward the back of the property. We clambered over a pile of stones onto a grassy field near the disintegrating remnants of an abandoned estate house. The building housed an independent infant school much like Miss Lou's, except that it was inside an old building.

In the southwest corner of the field was a neat little clearing under a tree that spread just over the playground's edge. We climbed onto the low limbs like carefree little monkeys, wrapped ourselves in the cocoon of interlocking branches, and chatted about whatever eleven- and twelve-year-old girls from rural Jamaica and Kingston would have talked about near the end of the 1970s. We lost track of time. We missed the bell.

Miss Selene was waiting for us in the doorway with a thick leather belt in her right hand. She ignored it and punched each of us hard as we walked past her. Mia's light skin turned crimson from helpless anger and embarrassment as she howled loudly. I followed close behind, still feeling the weight of the thump just below my right shoulder blade. Bridget remained stoic and dry eyed. Miss Selene wanted her to cry, though. She punched her hard, once, twice, three times, and again. She stopped only after Bridget collapsed to the floor, broken and weeping.

I knew her anguish was not just from the pain but perhaps more so from the injustice of it and the powerlessness to fight back. Bridget was spunky, but she also knew that the culture forbade her to hit back at an adult, particularly a teacher. As fully deserving of reprimand as Miss Selene was, it was Bridget who would have been expelled from school.

Within this space of mythologized cruelty, we prepared for the Common Entrance, with its many inadequacies and implicit and explicit contradictions. Space was limited in the traditional schools, for example. My sixth-grade teacher warned us that despite our rigorous preparation, the exam was a mere formality because there were only 10,000 spaces available nationally and more than 36,000 students competing for them. Most of those spaces would go to children in urban centers. Rural children faced numerous disadvantages.

For these reasons, poor families like mine placed enormous stock in the exams. A child's attire on examination day expressed this importance. Weeks before D-Day, we discussed who would get new uniforms or shoes. Almost everyone did, and those who wore no shoes to school normally had to get some for the occasion. My mother would have it no other way for me, so I too was appropriately decked out.

The examination center was another school farther away than my own. I left home much earlier than usual to walk there, dressed in my uniform—a rosy-pink, button-down cotton shirt and crisp, brown, pleated tunic starched and pressed by my mother with an iron heated on charcoal in a metal pot. Brand-new brown shoes and socks completed the attire.

My name was not in the newspaper when the results came a few months later as I prepared to graduate primary school. I remember being disappointed because the exam had been easy for me, but I was not devastated; even then I understood the odds. My teachers, though, were bewildered and openly expressed their frustration, partly because they had been counting me among their likely passes, for good reasons. In the competitive end-of-year internal exams after my first year, I had been second in the fifth grade. By the sixth grade, I was the top student in the class, ahead of the one boy who passed the external exam from the school that year.

For a wholly different reason, I went to my graduation ceremony—beautifully dressed in a lime-green, V-neck midi dress with little white spots, mandated for all the girls, and a triple-strand fake-emerald necklace, which I added—with my heart broken in thousands of tiny pieces. Mammy had died a few days before, slipping away one night while we both slept. Papa went to Delapenha's Funeral Home in Mandeville and asked them to collect her body and keep it there until his siblings could come for the funeral a week or two later. She was still there the Sunday I graduated, and I could not get my mind off her—off her empty bed at home, where she had lain for years, it seemed, her walking stick beside her even though she could not use it. Pain lodged somewhere between my throat and my chest and just behind my eyelids and stayed there for weeks. I went through graduation in a zombielike state that no one seemed to notice, and I even gave a speech on behalf of the graduating class.

Suffering this greater loss perhaps accounted for my minimal feelings of disappointment and quick acceptance of my "failure." But there was another genuinely positive response: relief. The traditional high schools were far away. My father's income could not support these additional expenses. I also walked past Cross Keys School every day on my way to and from my primary school and loved how serene the grounds were and the vibrance of the students I navigated through as they chatted animatedly in small or large groups.

But when I arrived at Cross Keys and met my homeroom teacher, she seemed perturbed by our interaction for reasons I did not fully understand. On my first day of school, I overheard her talking to another teacher about me.

"I had the little Virtue girl this morning," she said, sounding quite distressed. "She does not belong here. She does not belong in this school. She needs to be at Manchester High School."

A few days later, after taking the register, she called me outside the classroom. She had negotiated a place for me at Bishop Gibson High, a traditional high school owned by the Anglican diocese, no doubt with the help of her husband, a priest from Scotland. It was comparable to Manchester High and close by, but it was an all-girls school, and where I would have wanted to go. She wanted to get me out of Cross Keys—put me on a better path because she thought I was worthy—and had acted quickly to give me a fighting chance to get in before it was too late.

I was intrigued and contemplated the possibility on my walk home when school let out at 12:30 p.m. But even without asking my parents, I knew it would put an impossible strain on our family's budget. I also knew how young girls were preyed on by taxi drivers and other men with cars who exploited people struggling like themselves to survive in a country that was still not on our side. Pedophilia was normal. Older men openly molested young girls without fear of consequences. It was fodder for village gossip but nothing more. The police drank rum and beer with the molesters in the village bars. Back then, I thought some girls were bringing it on themselves. I applauded my twelve-year-old self for deciding not to be one of them. I would not compromise my dignity as a young woman in exchange for a ride to high school, no matter how much I wanted to be there.

I did not bother to say no to my teacher, one of the first figures of grace in my life, or even thank her more ardently for her kindness. Perhaps I did not have the facility or the desire to lay bare my family's deep financial insecurity and let her know why I was opting to remain close to home, where I could walk the two or so miles to and from school, past two old estates whose presence explained so much about the circumstances of our lives.

Great Valley estate ran most of the distance on the left, behind a handful of houses. The sprawling property included expansive but decrepit buildings overwhelmed by vegetation and several bulky concrete tanks where villagers sometimes fetched water. A slight distance from there and just past my maternal grandparents' home, the pattern repeated on the right side of the road, where the Cocoa Walk Estate accounted for much of the land. Manley built Cross Keys School on the northern portion, consciously or unconsciously establishing a template for what a nascent liberated people deserve and ought to strive for: accessible education and the better quality of life that it should lead to.

I made my choice, somewhat relieved that a Common Entrance award did not force me into it, and promised myself then that whatever I made of my life would begin right there in that school built by a society that needed but did not quite believe in them or us, still chained to the paradigm of the plantation and the idea that worth and dignity were things we had to fight for rather than something innate. I settled down at Cross Keys.

Like the deep-red, double-puffed hibiscus blooms in front of our house, life became richer, deeper, and infinitely more vibrant when I started at Cross Keys. It was the fall of 1977, about two years after we moved to Hibiscus Place and a year after Prime Minister Manley began his turbulent second term. Declaring his administration democratic socialist, he had become more strident in his anti-oppression rhetoric, nationally and internationally, and the backlash was growing from the US and the local capitalist class. News remained exciting but now induced much more anxiety. People were dying violently—often PNP people like my father, or so it seemed. Perhaps I noticed more when the victims reminded me of his, and our, vulnerability.

Cross Keys School was part of Manley's effort to decolonize the social structure, including making secondary education free and accessible to rural people like us and addressing the development needs of a small, newly independent country. This meant building new schools across the island, which he did. My older sister, Erica, and my brother Ian were part of the opening classes just two years before. I could see how they were blooming, reveling in learning opportunities we had not dreamed of, and I had secretly envied their head start.

Patience was not a virtue I possessed in abundance. I wanted to get on with it.

Erica was in the Literary and Debating Society. It was from her that I first heard "I Have a Dream," the most resonant work of civil rights leader Dr. Martin Luther King Jr. She recited it often, on the veranda and in the backyard, full throated and passionately capturing the frustrations and dreams of its iconic author. Ian, much quieter, was active on the Students' Council, an exciting new concept; Manley insisted on young people having a say in school governance and issues impacting their daily lives in the education sector and the country at large. Most of all, Ian was excited by his artwork. He did impressive charcoal sketches of human faces and paintings: of hibiscus blooms, of course, and coconut trees, the always aquamarine sea—the spirit guide for island people—and the lovely, ethereal little hummingbird, one of Jamaica's national symbols.

Along with English and social studies, I loved music, art, and the many extracurricular activities suddenly available to me, whether I participated in them or not—gymnastics, track and field, Glee Club, the Literary and Debating Society, and the Inter-School Christian Fellowship (ISCF). I could only pick two, so I chose the latter two, seamlessly integrating my faith and academic pursuits without even thinking about it. Like sails unfurling and propelling me into open seas, these activities were infinitely exciting and joyfully empowering.

Less than a month into the school year, I was drafted to represent the school at the Model United Nations Assembly at Church Teachers College, in Mandeville. September 1977 was mired in Cold War tensions between the United States and the USSR, and the themes we debated reflected those tensions. I pleaded for the abandonment of the arms race, a heartfelt cry for the powers that be to end their game in which vulnerable people far from the global center of power could become collateral damage. Manley's international stance and the US opposition to him and it meant that these very real fears and issues were being discussed both in the media and at the lunch table.

For as many years as the school participated in Model UN after that, I was a representative or leader of our debate team. I reveled in the opportunity to engage, albeit in a simulated way, in the global policy debates of the day. It was one of the high points of my secondary education and the genesis of a strong affinity for the United Nations. It persists even after further exposure to the global body, with its desperate need for reform laid bare, amid catastrophic conflicts in the twenty-first century: Russia's invasion of Ukraine and two years of war since; Hamas's horrific attack on Israel and their disproportionate response that looks like ethnic cleansing of the Palestinian people; Haiti's crippling gang violence and the absence of leadership to effect change. The world needs the UN—strong, functional, and relevant.

Overall, Cross Keys School was an idyllic place full of hope, promise, and the verve of young people grateful for an opportunity that most could not have foreseen. We were taking advantage of it all with great gusto. Besides the exposure to new academic opportunities, I loved walking along the newly asphalted driveway lined with cone-shaped evergreens fastidiously overseen by the principal and maintained by dedicated groundsmen, toward the school buildings painted sunshine yellow and olive green. The art teacher, Michael Escoffery, who would go on to earn some renown in New York, had painted an eye-catching mural on the wall across from the netball court, and just below that, the agricultural science teacher sowed beds of zinnias in every color of the rainbow.

This was the beginning of my wonder years, of learning and growing through work and experiences that were always fun for me, with a group of dedicated teachers to serve as useful guides. The school was achieving what education was supposed to; it challenged the mind with new opportunities to see the world differently, helped us see ourselves in it, and gave us something to aspire to.

Manley was right in his intention to decolonize the society, but even he, wise visionary intellectual and leader that he was, seemed to underestimate the magnitude of effort required to dismantle not just structural colonialism but the psychology underpinning it. Otherwise, he likely would have realized that his intent for the schools would be undermined by an obsessive elitist culture, which defines social value almost purely in exclusive terms.

The country did not like new schools like Cross Keys or even accept that there was a critical role for them. They trusted and preferred the old schools initially established by the British for the children of wealthy locals and expatriates. The student body of one such Kingston institution, Immaculate Conception High School, in 1941 comprised "wealthy Catholic residents in Jamaica, as well as those from Cuba, Haiti, Latin America, and Canada," according to the school's website. This generally meant non-Black students.

Even Bishop Gibson, the school that had offered to take me, was first established for White girls and only began taking Blacks when there was no longer an adequate supply of their preferred clientele, locally or from overseas. The demographics of these schools are now all predominantly Black, with the children of the wealthy and well connected still found at the top of the system. The cloak of exclusivity remains to some degree, and entering one of these institutions is perceived as a reward for a hard-fought academic battle—appropriately celebrated with much media attention for those whose matriculation and success are still perceived as anomalies.

The primarily rural profiles of the new schools and lack of barriers to access in the form of filtering exams also took them down a peg. The old schools were either boarding institutions or in locations that required long trips into urban centers, making accessibility difficult. People perceived this as part of what made these schools more important. Both types of schools were at the secondary level of the education system, but the term "high" had long been bastardized to mean superior. It therefore followed that schools designated "secondary," as the new schools were, were inferior. This is hardwired into the culture of education in my native country and holds a clue to the massive inequities, social dysfunctions, and most importantly low productivity and lack of economic growth.

The education ministry further disadvantaged the newer schools by underfunding and limiting the academic curriculum compared to the old, pre-independence schools. As much as I thought we were accomplishing, my contemporaries at high schools in Mandeville had access to much more. They had five years of history and geography as two separate subjects; we had three years of social studies and two years of history. They studied English language and literature; I generally had language only and eventually studied literature on my own, one of my best subjects. We had general sciences, while they had in-depth study of physics, chemistry, and biology. This effectively closed off careers in medicine, for example, since passing those subjects were prerequisites for that course of study.

They also had sixth forms (education from ages seventeen to nineteen) as an automatic progression if they did well academically. Meanwhile, our curriculum did not prepare us for the British-based General Certificate Exams at Ordinary or Advanced levels, without which there was virtually nowhere to go—unless I could somehow forge my own path.

The spring of my seventeenth year was grounded in two opposing realities. School was a lark. In many ways, life felt as light and easy as a little cloud scudding across a summer sky. The one challenge was that I was hungry—a lot; I was a tiny slip of a girl weighing a little over a hundred pounds and there was still not enough to feed me.

I was in the eleventh grade and was head girl, Students' Council president, Literary and Debating Society president, and Inter-School Christian Fellowship president. I was doing so well at everything else that no one cared that I could not catch a ball in physical education class. The teacher treated my attempts as entertainment, laughed cheerfully with me, and wrote about my efforts and attitude on my report cards rather than any actual mastery or accomplishment. My club affiliations provided new opportunities: weeklong sleepaway camps or daytime workshops and meetings in Mandeville with other secondary school students throughout the parish, sometimes farther away. I was engaging in, learning about, and understanding the many layers to life in my country.

The government had changed. Michael Manley lost the election in 1980 to his archrival, Edward Seaga, and his brother was no longer our member of Parliament. My father still had his civil service job, but in the true spirit of rotten, destructive politics, the higher-ups had started to transfer him, pushing him around to force him to quit. He refused to, but he often ended up miles away from home, as far as Kingston, obliging him to split his modest salary to pay for accommodation.

We still had our little house where the hibiscus never stopped blooming. Mama was as fanatically clean as ever. I loved coming home to the whole house polished so shiny that the floors looked like sheets of red ice. No one bothered us, but there was often not enough money for food. At school, the lunch ladies, Mrs. Joan Lawrence, and Mrs. Adlyn Hutchinson, made sure I ate, but where the next meal was coming from was never a certainty. Weekends were often bad. Sometimes I was so hungry that I cried.

Somewhere in the first quarter of 1982, my English teacher, Mrs. Barbara Walters, the expatriate wife of the principal, confronted me in the hallway just outside my classroom on the first floor of our new school building on the old Cocoa Walk Estate. She was formal and professional—cold, I used to think. Unlike the other teachers, she showed no emotion, and she never joked around. She was a great teacher, no doubt, but I found the unusual formality unnerving until I got used to her.

She made magic of even the dullest topic in English and found new and interesting ways to engage us. I also knew she believed in me.

She often used my best work as the template for what she expected from the class and directed my classmates to ask my opinion after they had done their best and were still off the mark. Perhaps even more empowering, she would appeal for my help when she did not quite understand what someone else was trying to explain or the use of local slang. I still remember the day she turned to me and asked: "Grace, what does 'irie' mean?" and nodded in dawning understanding when I explained that it was not a curse word or a bad thing at all. It was the rough equivalent of "good" with a special little vibe to it.

She also brought me her personal magazines—*Time*, *Newsweek*, and *Ebony*—and books that were outside the standard school curriculum, like *The Autobiography of Mrs. Jane Pittman*, and asked my opinion afterward. My interest in news and public affairs was cemented forever after the class did a unit on the Apollo 11 moonwalk. She assigned me to create a mock reproduction of a major newspaper's coverage, sending me and another student into Mandeville to the parish library to read real papers from the period and other publications and lending us a typewriter to produce our stories. It was a giant, exhilarating step toward a career in news.

That day in 1982, she showed me a flyer announcing a national essay competition under the theme "Growing up in Jamaica"; she suggested I enter. Without hesitation, I told her I wanted to. My world was expanding somewhat, and I thought I had enough to compare with life in Old House.

With the deadline fast approaching, I had to get started right away. She dispatched me to the library for the rest of the day to think it through, research as needed, and work on a draft.

It was enticing enough without the draw of the $500 first prize, more money than I had seen in my entire life. Here was the opportunity to process and articulate my understanding of the social construction of Jamaica through the lens of my seventeen-year-old self—a rural girl with a warm spirit and an ever-expanding view of the world, gained in large part from the books I read, the radio, and the wonderful adults in my life, including two decent, open-minded, and hardworking parents playing as best as they could the hand life dealt them; the aunts, uncles, and cousins who lived abroad and returned home routinely with stories about their lives; and teachers like Mrs. Walters, Mrs. Winnifred Syke, and Mrs. Girtis Reid, the latter two sometimes serving as guidance counselors. Mrs. Reid was also my second godfather's wife—Sa Bea's husband was the first—and sometimes invited me to her home to spend time with their children, Scherrie, and Rohan.

Almost certainly influenced by the socialist idealism of a few years prior and what seemed like common sense, I wanted to give voice to my experience of the class construct visible in society and in the education system. My life in rural Manchester was considerably different from my glimpses of "middle-class" life as I encountered it or of "upper-class" life as seen from a distance through the media or by limited associations.

I knew that the difference mainly had to do with money and the privileges connected to it, and that a good proportion of it was bound to skin color and whether one's ancestors were designated field slaves, house slaves, or plantation owners and their affiliates. Black people were in the middle and upper classes too, but non-Blacks were more likely to be, regardless of ethnicity, except for some poor Jamaican Indians in the old sugar belt. While some subsequently made it out of poverty, many remained near the plantations, tied to the deteriorating fortunes of those settlements, or otherwise combating poverty like many people of African descent.

For the most part, middle- or upper-class children lived in well-appointed homes in and around the parish capitals, with telephones, flush toilets, prep schools, and the best public or private high schools for those who chose to attend. They participated in organized after-school activities, played the piano, took swimming lessons, and traveled abroad, mainly to Miami and New York, on holidays. This was hardly the case for children like me, and as our childhood experiences diverged, so did our chances for meaningful career paths and success in adulthood.

I wrote the essay and turned it in to Mrs. Walters a week or so later. She made minor corrections and gave it to Miss Scott, the school's secretary, to type before putting it in an envelope and dispatching me to the post office with enough money to send it as express mail. After that, I promptly forgot about it and went on my merry way. Graduation was months away, and I was nearly grown up. I had important things to think about other than that pleasant aside.

"Yes, Grace. I understand that you write good essays."

The woman talking to me was heavily pregnant and dressed in white jeans and an empire-style blouse as colorful as the zinnias in the flower beds outside the office. Three women, including Miss Scott, sat with heads down behind typewriters on the neatly organized desks toward the front of the administrative office while this woman I had never seen before interrogated me about my work.

Miss Scott had met me halfway across the netball court as I walked toward my classroom on the first floor of the main building and directed me to the office instead because someone wanted to talk to me. She left me with the woman and buried her head in her work.

The bursar's office was to the immediate right, and the principal's was further down the narrow hallway on the same side. I was ending secondary school, having enjoyed a mutually respectful relationship with most of the teachers and administrators and only one quick strike from the principal's cane to speak of—when he had beaten my entire eighth-grade class for misbehaving after our teacher did not show up for class. We had chatted loudly, the room buzzing with unsupervised teenage energy as we waited, with some of my classmates getting up from their stools and walking around. The principal found the class in this state of dishevelment, lined us up, and caned all of us.

Mr. Walters was a diminutive man with an enormous presence. Though nothing like Miss Selene, he was an expatriate like his wife and not friendly like typical rural Jamaican folks. Plus, he had quite a bark. I maintained a cautious wariness in my relationship with him and did not enjoy going to the office for any reason. I had my eyes on the exit and my mind on joining my class and being with my friends and classmates for the day.

The woman introduced herself as Mrs. Gibbs, an education officer from the Ministry of Education in Kingston. Beyond the comment about my essay, she did not explain why she was there to see me or why she was interested in how well I wrote—and I had forgotten about the essay from months before. My inability to make the connection was also partly because I did not believe anything happened when people responded to things they saw in the newspaper; and if there was a response, it did not come with any speed or purposefulness. I had honored the process as best as I could, but I never seriously thought I would get a response to the essay. The cynic in me thought it was over when I covered the envelope with stamps and handed it to the postmistress. I had done it mostly for the exercise and for Mrs. Walters.

For every piece of work I showed her, Mrs. Gibbs asked me for more, displaying only cursory interest in what I pulled from my binder and the two short stories Mrs. Walters removed from the display board in my classroom and handed to her. When I told her I had more work at home, she immediately and unexpectedly offered to drive me there to find them.

About ten minutes later, at my direction, she pulled into our driveway at Hibiscus Place, now painted a soft coral under the veranda with a duck-egg-green exterior. There was the usual riot of red blooms at the gate, pink oleander at the northern fence, and the pots of red-and-pink anthuriums and white begonias I nurtured in a corner just below my parents' bedroom window.

Mama was at home as usual with my baby brothers, Richard and Marlon, aged three and six months, the last two of her eleven children. With a shouted explanation to her about why I had returned home from school in the middle of the day, driven by a strange woman in a white Peugeot, I ran into the middle bedroom I shared with my sisters. Kneeling on the floor, I pulled a carton box from under my bed and took out more samples of my work, including the original draft of the essay written in my untidy blue-ink scrawl, which Papa, with his unbelievable penmanship, could not live down. I returned to the veranda and held out the four sheets of legal-size pages, complete with a few corrections made in red by Mrs. Walters. Miss Scott had thoughtfully returned them to me after she finished typing.

"Oh! This is something I would be interested in," she said, snatching the paper from my hand.

With that, she was raring to go. She dropped me back at the netball court and sped off, back to Kingston, I assumed. I soon forgot about that whole episode too. I clearly had other things on my mind.

How naive life was then! I doubt if anyone so much as asked Mrs. Gibbs for identification before leaving me in her care. The school had no telephone, and there was likely no prior contact between the school and the Ministry of Education before she showed up and was granted full access to me—letting me get in her car and drive out the school gate. Challenging as things were, the time did not call for it. Shortly after that, maybe two weeks later, came the news that I had won the essay competition.

The principal announced it at devotions, and the whole school applauded. The punch line for him was that the second-prize recipient was a student from Immaculate Conception High, the "top" high school in Jamaica to this day, and the third-place recipient was a student from Knox College, another highly regarded traditional grammar school in Spalding, Clarendon, near the border with St. Ann and northern Manchester.

I was not one to get overly excited about anything, and I still am not, but I realized it was a big deal for a little country girl and for my school. There was no mistaking the pride in the principal's voice when he announced that I had taken first place in a national competition sponsored by Irving Burgie, a well-known African American songwriter of Barbadian descent living in New York. An inductee into the American Songwriters Hall of Fame, Burgie was the writer and composer behind some of the better-known songs by Jamaican balladeer extraordinaire Harry Belafonte, including the iconic "Jamaica Farewell." The competition had been part of Burgie's effort to encourage and inspire a new generation of Caribbean writers.

Soon, I was headed to Caenwood Center, a Ministry of Education facility in Kingston, for a formal presentation ceremony and, later, an awards luncheon at the Four Seasons Hotel. I made the "long" journey from South Manchester to Kingston with the principal and his wife, the vice principal, and my father as my chaperones.

I have little recollection of the event at Caenwood except walking nervously onto the platform when my name was called to receive the envelope with the prize money and a certificate of award and the trip back home, which would be quite revealing. But I have quite clear memories of the luncheon at the Four Seasons, where the elites of the Jamaican literati and the heroes of my childhood whose work I had read and frequently performed at school and parish competitions came out in full force: Louise Bennett, Mervyn Morris, Dennis Scott, Edward Baugh, Mikey Smith, among others, and a New York representative of Burgie. I sat at a table with an African American woman who had big, natural hair, shocking blue eyes—they had to be contact lenses, though I had no idea at the time—and a practiced smile. It was my first substantial social event outside of South Manchester, and she was my first experience with that American exercise, which was an arrangement of the lips but not a smile, though it could be mistaken for one.

I sat racked by anxiety over whether I was holding my knife—a piece of equipment I was unaccustomed to using—properly. What could I do besides hold the knife in my right hand and the fork in the left? Who was checking to see if I was holding it right or not?

I got through the event with no significant faux pax and afterward posed for pictures with the celebrities under a mango tree outside the hotel. They were all blissfully normal and eager to put the winners at ease. I enjoyed the experience and wondered how people could perceive them as anything other than normal. What we think we know of celebrities is likely only what is projected onto them rather than who they are, which is often the case when we only see people at a distance.

Coming home from the Caenwood Center ceremony, I recall the five of us set off for the journey in the principal's sprawling, blue Plymouth Valiant. From the passionate conversations between the adults, I began to understand that my essay submission had created a firestorm at the Ministry of Education and they had sought to invalidate my work.

"Why," the principal kept asking, "did the government build these schools if they did not believe in them?"

Mrs. Gibbs's role finally fell into place. Ministry of Education representatives on the panel of judges had found my essay quite impressive—too impressive for a child from one of "those" schools; so rather than award me first place, they decided to discard it. One of the judges, a history professor at the University of the West Indies named Patrick Bryan, objected, and demanded an explanation.

"There is no way that a child from one of those schools could write an essay like that," a representative said. "We should just trash it."

Bryan then refused to participate further and insisted that the Ministry of Education "owed it to this one child to find out whether she did write the essay or not." And so it was that the ministry launched an investigation into my work because I had performed above expectations based on where they had decided I should spend my secondary school years and what ultimately should be my lot in life.

A full five years after I "failed" my Common Entrance Exam, no one cared that perhaps I had not failed at all—that I might have been a victim of political interference that was and remains common in every facet of life. Moreover, the ministry itself had said that less than a third of the students who sat the examination would be awarded places in the traditional high schools based on available space; it was therefore quite possible that among the discarded 70 percent—the children of the poorest and most powerless—was talent or academic ability worthy of more than being relegated to life's scrap heap. Yet this went unacknowledged in their assessment of my work.

Discarding more than two-thirds of secondary school graduates means that most of Jamaica's children grow up in a society that does not believe in or make adequate provisions for them. Their status as the broad-based societal underclass is taken for granted, thereby perpetuating underproductivity, inequities, and the cycle of chronic poverty that replaced plantation slavery and remains substantively in place today.

With a grandmother who was literate and had been exposed to the world as a maid to Kingston's high society and with a father to whom she had passed on that precious gift, I fortunately overcame some barriers. I learned to read early, to understand and process information, and I practiced making sense of the world.

The principal's question would have increased resonance for me as I began to understand how much our life chances are determined by something outside the control of the majority—like the kind of public school we attend—and how those without autonomy suffer the blame for a system that does nothing for them or society at large and is, in fact, the result of worthless public policy, unethical leadership, corruption, and crony capitalism designed for the benefit of a minuscule few.

Winning the competition, a small enough victory in the scheme of things, was validating and played a big role in shaping the trajectory of my life after high school. Finally, it was not just my English teacher and a few friends telling me I write well, and my competitors were not just my classmates from Cross Keys who might not have read as much as I did then; the others came from the best schools in the country, and I had beaten them at something of consequence.

Incredibly, I owe this validation to one man who had more intelligence, common sense, and compassion than all the people at the Ministry of Education and dared to speak up. Had it not been for him, my efforts would have been thwarted again, erased without my knowing why. I could have been one more throwaway—the path I have followed closed off, life experiences unrealized, and contributions to society inhibited.

This was an early lesson about the work of unseen forces in our lives. Some are dark and malevolent and will act strictly with the intent of doing harm for no discernible reason other than that they can. Some, like the ministry representatives, are bungling incompetents who act with insufficient thought and ought not to be in positions of responsibility. And a minuscule few, like Patrick Bryan, with no skin in the game other than a commitment to ethics and fair play, ensure that people like me have a fighting chance. The quiet action of one person can make a difference in the life of another, a family, a school, a community, and even a nation. As much as there are oppressive people, there are also figures of grace like Patrick Bryan. They are sometimes too few and far between, but they exist.

This experience also offered more insight into the dysfunctions and paradoxes of postcolonial Jamaica. In some important ways, the needle has barely moved in the decades since independence. The poor majority, dispossessed since plantation slavery, believe passionately in education as their only pathway to self-development and out of poverty, and they generally make every sacrifice to ensure their offspring get the best available. The efforts, however, are often thwarted by government and other embedded structures.

For example, the government long permitted a pecking order wherein principals at the most selective schools could handpick who among the Common Entrance students they wanted in their institutions. They unremittingly chose the academically better prepared, and the most economically well off, many of whom, in a small society, would be easily identifiable by family names or home addresses. The top schools remained the exclusive preserve of the country's social and economic elites for decades. In a weak-kneed attempt to reverse the practice, the government now allows the children to choose their preferred schools. They pick the exact same ones. And the band plays on.

This subterfuge gives policymakers cover but does nothing to address the inadequacy of the system that drives persistent poverty, glaring and unsustainable inequities, economic stagnation, and social maladies such as extremely high levels of crime.

I used some of the prize money from the essay competition to buy my graduation outfit, a soft, powder-blue midi dress with a cape collar and fine accordion pleats worn under a gold graduation gown rented from the school. It was the first dress I ever paid for with my own money.

I used the rest to open my first bank account at the Workers Savings and Loan Bank, another Manley creation. In 1973, to operationalize his efforts at financial inclusion, which he saw as fundamental to decolonization, economic growth, and social transformation, he converted the Government Savings Bank into the Workers Savings and Loan Bank and used post offices like the one at Cross Keys as banking centers where people could open accounts and access money whenever they wanted to. Papa did his banking with the Workers Bank, and I followed him there. He and Mama let me deposit my check with no questions asked—no request to borrow any of it.

They sat near the front during my graduation ceremony, watching me take first prize in every subject and close out as class valedictorian. Papa sat in the corner of the bench near the aisle in his usual thoughtful posture, the right side of his face resting in his open palm. Mama sat beside him, smiling broadly, and trying to restrain my brother, still a toddler, who wanted to be with me on the platform.

Two prizes were incredibly meaningful to me. First was the one for vocation—the two-year required course of study during the final years of high school. The technical offerings were not a great fit for me. I saw myself as not physically nimble and was afraid of the sewing machine, so Clothing and Textile was out for me. I longed to cook like Mammy, so I thought Food and Nutrition might be a good option but soon became stressed by the need to buy weekly supplies and the teacher's constant reprimanding of students. Everything irritated her, from the sound of a pin drop to two girls exchanging a quick whisper. Her constant reprimands grated on my nerves. I quietly did my research on Child Care, the one remaining workable option.

I learned the department had a life-sized baby doll for practicing diaper changes. All I would have to buy in two years was a white smock and a copy of Dr. Benjamin Spock's *Baby and Childcare*, which was available in the library. The overall cost was almost equal to what I needed weekly in my Food and Nutrition class. I asked to be transferred, offering no explanation. The lack of money had again dictated my choice, but there was much to be gained by learning how to take care of children in their earliest years.

I topped the class at the end of the two years and placed third among all the eleventh graders in the spin-off two-week practical exercise, which I did at Bethabara Moravian Infant School, about a half mile north of my father's office in Newport. It was unexpected. I thought any number of students would have been better at the practicum than I was, but only two beat me.

The other prize, one they gave me for social studies, still sits on my desk today, more than forty years later: a copy of *Essays on Power and Change in Jamaica*, a book published in 1977, the year I took the Common Entrance. It was written by a cadre of the Caribbean's finest scholars at the University of the West Indies and overseas, including Donald Harris, father of Vice President Kamala Harris, and edited by two of the country's elite social scientists at the time, Aggrey Brown and Carl Stone. It remains among my most prized possessions, a go-to resource for insights into the Jamaican social and economic dilemma; it is also a memento of the country's finest intellectual effort, when the best-educated citizens were engaged in the process of leading change, and of the insight displayed by the teachers at Cross Keys who thought I needed it in my arsenal. It is also a great reference point for how much or little has changed in the country since then.

The thought that they put into that book and my other prizes, including the Oxford Dictionary, the most prized of the day, symbolizes a truth I have come to appreciate about Jamaica despite its many intractable issues: there are always individuals trying to make good decisions—a majority, I believe, and the nation's teachers being among them—and they are constantly battling systemic barriers and the biases that underpin them.

After Child Care, I flirted seriously with becoming a nurse. I did not see a place to take my interest in public affairs. I did not even have a name for it then. Nursing, meanwhile, seemed concrete and professional enough compared to being a nanny—essentially what the high school curriculum intended for me. I began to understand my homeroom teacher's urgency to reroute me somewhere else on that first day at Cross Keys; the school curriculum, whatever the intent, held no clear direction for me. Inasmuch as the Common Entrance determined the character of our secondary education, the British-based O and A levels determined our professional path afterward. Since I had no real path, I needed professional credentials before I could enter university, ultimately a tortured journey of six years for the grand purpose of acquiring an undergraduate degree!

With a combination of passes in the GCE (General Certificate of Education) levels, which I took privately, the new CXC (Caribbean Examinations Council) exams that would eventually replace them, and the secondary school exit exams, I qualified to enter Church Teachers College. Founded by the Church of England in Jamaica, the institution was in Mandeville. Several of my teachers had attended, and my older sister had been there a year already. It was the closest tertiary institution to me, and perhaps as far as I was ready to go.

I could leave Hibiscus Place for a safe environment while I continued to learn and grow. I could become a teacher. I could be self-sufficient. I could have a career, first choice or not. I could do something other than live a wasted life.

Thoughts of living closer to the bright lights both excited and terrified me. I was eager for growth and new experiences but not so much for leaving my parents and the simple, uncomplicated rural life I loved behind. The even distribution of poverty and lack of opportunities largely placed everyone on the same level. People knew each other for miles around. We took shelter on each other's verandahs from the smallest raindrops and heavy downpours. We even knew who the dogs on the roads belonged to. Spoken or unspoken, rural people depend on and look out for each other, rendering the need for pretentiousness useless. Honesty, brutal at times, was ingrained into the psyche of our lives. People were real. Life was real. I valued that realness.

Also, our folkways conspired with nature to conceal some legacies of our colonial past. Other than the sprawling, mostly unoccupied acreage where the old estates used to be, few overt symbols remained, with the old great houses at Canoe Valley, Great Valley, and Cocoa Walk hidden behind walls of wood and vines.

Mandeville was different. Bustling in the center and picturesque on the outskirts, the town was named for Viscount Mandeville, the son of William Montagu, the ninth Duke of Manchester and governor of Jamaica from 1808 to 1827. Its two most iconic structures, built during Manchester's tenure, are the Georgian-style courthouse in 1817 and the parish church, St. Mark, completed three years later. On the fringes, stately country homes with expansive lawns and luxuriant gardens owned by locals and expatriates attracted to the English-country vibes and cool mountain breezes evoke old-world charm and tranquility. It was only about fifteen miles away but quite distinct from where I grew up.

I went through registration and orientation with a mix of anticipation and trepidation. I was making friends already and liked the loud buzz of this new life, proud that I had made it so far, excited at the prospect of embarking on an intellectual path I had not conceived of even two years prior, but still fighting a deep desire to be back at Hibiscus Place with Mama. I stayed put only because the college forbade us from returning home the first weekend. I was out the gate as soon as possible the following Friday.

Sunday evening, I made my way back to campus. Somehow, it seemed to get better after that, as if I had given home and childhood a last, satisfying kiss and wrapped myself in the warmth and comfort of memories and goodwill I knew I had in abundance. I began to settle into my major, social studies and English—regarded as the most prestigious among the offerings—and into the new life college represented.

Right away, I used some of my prized books and deepened my interest in current affairs and the country's political landscape. I became the antagonist in the class of about thirty student-teachers, questioning the structure of the society as presented by some of my professors and the acceptance of colleagues who either agreed or never registered an opinion.

I rejected much of what I obtained, arguing fiercely against the class-caste system and the persistent marginalization of the Black majority. I rejected Edward Seaga's capitalism and dogmatic paternalism compared to Manley's democratic socialism, attempts at collaboration, and respect for the dignity of the individual. The professors welcomed the challenge for the most part, but many of my classmates did not. I was often the lone voice attempting a critical deconstruction of the basic structures of our society and suffered the same fate as anyone unaccepting of the normal way of things; they branded me a Marxist at age eighteen, before I even grasped what it meant. I do not think my classmates understood Marxism either, but it was a way to marginalize me—to identify me as outside the mainstream and attach a negative label to my "otherness." For them, based on what little they knew, Marxism was a useless or dangerous framework for examining society. With the little I knew, I did not think so then, and I do not think so now.

Literature classes offered a window into Georgian and Victorian England through the works of Jane Austen, George Eliot, Charlotte, and Emily Brontë, Thomas Hardy, and Charles Dickens, among others, and examined the power of writers as participants and bystanders in society. I carried *The Mill on the Floss*, Eliot's huge novel, with me to the toilet and the dining room, feeling exultant as I turned the last page. I had heard about the book before I entered college. Finishing it at all was an accomplishment.

The work of Langston Hughes, Paul Laurence Dunbar, Aimé Césaire, George Lamming, Samuel Selvon, Michael Anthony, Roger Mais, Earl Lovelace, James Ngugi, and Chinua Achebe gave me broader and deeper insights into the world of Black writers in the United States, the Caribbean, and Africa.

African literature was especially meaningful. I had gotten through secondary school without knowing much about the continent. I was therefore not oriented to associate Africa with scholarship or intellectual endeavors. Rather, I associated it with the little I learned about the Pygmies—short, stumpy, unrelatable forest creatures strange enough to be singled out for study. They became one of the templates I held for Africa or what it meant to be African. It was a strange, faraway place, a colossal jungle of exotic animals and people most worthy of being enslaved or abused. It was the Dark Continent, after all. Nothing about what I learned connected me to the continent or made me yearn to see the place where my ancestors came from.

It took years for me to begin untangling the simplistic paradigm through which Africa, the ancestral homeland of Black people, was presented—to understand instead how expansively rich and complex the continent is and the damage that is done to the Black psyche with the presentation of the continent as the place where disempowered subhuman Black people came from and where the populations were either Pygmies or Maasai, weird or warlike. College filled some of the gaps, opening my eyes and expanding my understanding of class differences in Jamaica beyond what I had written in my prizewinning essay at Cross Keys.

No one there was rich, or they likely would have been at school in Miami, but many students were properly middle class or even upper middle class and financially far better off than I was. There were also others just like me and some worse off. It was my first in-depth exposure to people from different socioeconomic backgrounds, including women who cared enough about their hair and had money to go to the salon every weekend. I was intrigued by the whole business of going to the beauty salon when their hair already looked like they had just come from there!

I also began to process some branches of the Christian church as rigid, oppressive, neocolonial social institutions grounded in bigotry and disconnected from the teachings of a simple Christ who modeled compassion and preached humility. There was a great deal of devotion to form, as well as insufficient acknowledgment of the student body as adults with agency and control over their lives outside the boundaries of reasonable institutional rules. Of course, the implicit preference for members of the Anglican faith often intersected with lighter-skinned students and economically better off. The bias seemed to be always present, and I thought there, of all places, it should not.

I was not fond of these aspects of the school, but Mammy's nudge toward challenging opposition in the name of a just God forever gave me the courage to respectfully ask questions as they appeared, with no undue deference to authority figures. I practiced the art of politely ignoring them too! I learned that like people, organizations have difficulty separating themselves from the past, and the Church of England is no exception. It would not expect the school to preach liberation theology, and it did not. The college then provided a particular kind of education—substantive and solidly traditional but neither consciousness raising, liberating, nor groundbreaking.

CHAPTER THREE

KINGSTON

What else was out there? How far could I go as a poor, young Black woman in Jamaica—in the world, perhaps—on passion, curiosity, and intellect alone? Navigating the social spaces and remaining my essential self without suffering further marginalization was an intricate dance, but I conquered college, again outperforming people much better prepared and with vastly more resources.

I took the prizes for the best student of English, the most promising teacher, and the most diligent student. I had edited the yearbook for two years and started a journalism club, coedited, and published an anthology of poems, and cohosted Mervyn Morris, once the island's poet laureate, at the college. I left with more books as presents and the highest regard for those professors who had no interest in the status of my chastity belt.

The day when I could feed myself was nigh. I landed my first job at Knox College, a highly regarded coed boarding school founded by the Presbyterian Church. Located in Spalding, a hilly mountain town in Clarendon Parish, about fifteen miles northeast of Mandeville, it provided a brief respite for me. I adored the children, who came from all over the country and a few from abroad. I liked Spalding too. It was bigger than Cross Keys, less congested than Mandeville, and known for its unusually chilly temperatures, complete with misty early mornings that could look and feel like eastern England or Scotland throughout the year. At a different time in my life, I could have settled in Spalding, but bigger hills beckoned.

I wanted a degree, not just a diploma. I wanted to make it inside the vaunted halls of the University of the West Indies (UWI), the only such institution in the country, educating a mere 3 percent of the population. It was the stamp of a pedigree education in the Caribbean, and I wished to discover whether I could find a place in the light of the rising sun. I moved to Kingston in the summer of my twenty-second year to pursue my dream.

I arrived in the Jamaican capital anxious about how I would afford my education but excited by notions of adventure and intellectual growth—of learning at the feet of legendary scholars I had read about in books or newspapers or whose books I had read or poems and dramatic pieces I had performed at the annual national speech and drama festival; or seeing in their natural habitat some of the literary icons who had turned up at the Four Seasons Hotel five years before for my award ceremony.

By the time I left Knox, I had taken several trips to Kingston. I was still apprehensive but a little less frightened by the traffic, the hustle and bustle, and being surrounded by hordes of unfamiliar people. Conventional wisdom suggests I should have had a game plan for such a big move, but what I had was fragile.

I had sent much of what I earned during the year back home to help my mother. No one asked for anything; I simply made a conscious decision to help my younger siblings as best as I could so they too could realize their potential, earn to whatever extent they could, and become something in a society too willing to see people like us as its dregs. My parents' hands were full, and they had no capacity to increase their earnings.

Yes, I did question, silently, why they had so many of us, but that was never a conversation for rural children like us to have with our parents, at least not in my family. In the fullness of time, the answers became evident: sex as entertainment in a place without much else to do; lack of reproductive health education; and misinformation about and resistance to limited birth control, arising from fundamentalist religious beliefs on my mother's part and patriarchal attitudes on my father's part, as he believed that birth control was the woman's responsibility. I overheard bits and pieces of adult conversations at times, and I could make sense of it. I realized that even Papa had some toes of clay.

The question was also irrelevant to me since we were already here. For the younger children, what mattered was how precious they were and how abundantly I loved them. I would not have negotiated any of them out of the picture even if I could have.

I had an invitation from my flatmate at Knox, a teacher from Kingston who had decided to return to the city after a year, to stay with her. Upon that alone, I applied to the university and began seeking a job in the city. My acceptance letter brought my impossible dream within my grasp. There would be a few tussles with fate, but I was not about to let go.

A heavy, distressed whisper when I called my friend from a pay phone on Washington Boulevard, a major artery in Kingston, was my first reminder that dreams are fragile things without guarantee of ever becoming anything more. I held my breath, waiting to hear what had changed.

Her mother, only in her fifties, had died suddenly the night before in her sleep. My friend was part of a large, close-knit family, and her mother had been at the center of it. The house was unexpectedly filled with relatives and friends from St. Ann and Kingston. I imagined the chaos, but her grief was palpable. She did not mention her invitation to me, and I did not have the heart to ask. I had no plan B.

A family I knew from Manchester rescued the dream. My younger sister had been working for them as a nanny to their toddler during the day and attending community college at night. I was grateful beyond words for the room they offered but eager to be on my way, a thought I could not entertain without a job to pay my bills and keep sending money home to Mama.

The period between July and August was the best time to find a teaching job, but deep into September, after schools started and I had completed orientation and started my first classes at UWI, I had found nothing. Unless I found a job soon, I would not be able to continue my education.

I despaired.

An opportunity appeared at the end of September, at St. Hugh's, a traditional high school for girls at Cross Roads in Kingston. Though just about five miles from where I lived, conditions made it seem longer by far. Jamaica's public transportation system was still an embryo, and a deformed one at that. There were no schedules, written or otherwise. There was simply a cluster of buses, insufficient to meet the needs, that would come racing up the boulevard during rush hour, one behind the other. Teachers, nurses, store clerks—the working poor and high school students—would pack together on them too tightly for air to penetrate. The comparison to the Middle Passage was frequent, with no intent to trivialize our ancestors' pain. The trips were uncomfortable and grossly dehumanizing, and the people on board were entirely the descendants of the enslaved.

I refused to get on the buses my first two mornings, seeing no possible way to fit, and arrived at work hours late. By day three, I understood I had no choice and forced my way onto the step. The conductor, dirty and unkempt even in the early morning, stood between me and others crowded on the steps and the asphalt as the bus sped through Kingston. I got used to it because I had no choice.

Plus, having a job made even the buses look better, blunting the despair of prior months and the sense of dislocation at giving up rural life for Kingston. The job schedule was also perfect because it ended at 2:30 p.m., giving me enough time to get to UWI for my first class at 4 p.m., Mondays through Thursdays. I soon settled into a rhythm and activated my search for a place to live in the city's housing market, which was more brutal than the transportation system.

---- ✂ ----

A leaky old refrigerator, an old newspaper, and my habit of reading anything that crossed my path came together late one afternoon around October 1987 to introduce new intrigues—new possibilities. I had survived another trip on the bus and the short walk home from the stop in the still unfamiliar and oppressive city heat. I stumbled into the kitchen parched, hazy headed, and blurry eyed, desperate for water.

As I reached for the refrigerator door, my eyes dropped to the pages of a days-old newspaper that someone had spread out to catch water dripping from the appliance. It was soaked, moments away from the trash. Barely discernible in the dulled gray text was an advertisement for a scholarship commemorating the hundredth anniversary of the birth of Jamaica's first national hero, Pan-Africanist Marcus Mosiah Garvey.

I picked up the paper and rested it on the kitchen counter, reading the criteria thoroughly. The theme aligned well with my nontraditional education and a personal value system that was only interested in the status quo from the perspective of dismantling it in the interest of the disenfranchised and the oppressed. Most importantly, I met the critical criteria to apply—academic potential and enrollment at the university as a first-year student.

It seemed like someone had designed the whole thing just for me! High-achieving students were generally from the traditional secondary schools. They aspired toward the Rhodes Scholarship as symbolic of the pinnacle of academic success and as a magic carpet ride to the best opportunities and the height of professional accomplishments. I was no less able, but that paradigm excluded me. I hope I would have chosen not to apply even if the system allowed me to. The Rhodes Scholarship did not align with who I was then, considering the dawning recognition of how oppressive and despotic figures used seemingly benign things like academic awards to immortalize themselves. The authentic liberation I was interested in required putting the awards in their proper context rather than mindlessly venerating them.

Philosophically, a scholarship honoring a fierce and tireless warrior for the liberation of Black people and tasking us with the responsibility of carrying his legacy forward was more valuable to me than one in the name of the racist imperialist who paved the way for apartheid in South Africa and the suffering of the Black majority, including icons like Steve Biko and Winnie and Nelson Mandela.

The deadline was days away—barely enough time to collect transcripts and recommendations, write a persuasive essay, fill out the application, and deliver it to the Faculty of Arts at UWI. I did so the day it was due after an intense effort. A few days later, I got a call from a woman acknowledging receipt of my application.

She was Harriet Bryan, a lecturer on the faculty. She also happened to be the wife of Patrick Bryan, chair of the Department of History—the same man who had intervened when the Ministry of Education decided to trash my entry in the essay competition at Cross Keys.

I had met them at the award ceremonies, but there was no email or cell phones then, and landlines were few and far between. I did not have the tools to keep in touch with Patrick even after learning how he had advocated for me. As life on campus became a reality, I thought I would eventually try to find him, say thank you, and establish, if I could, a real relationship with a respected professor, but I had not yet gotten to it.

He was proud of me, Harriet said. I had justified his faith in me by completing teachers' college and pursuing an undergraduate degree—the first student from Cross Keys High School to do so. Patrick was also chairing the selection committee for the scholarship I had just applied for!

A few weeks later, I hustled from my job in Cross Roads to the history department at UWI, where the interview would be held, trying to calm nerves frayed by the anxiety of teaching a class all day and having to rely on public transportation to get me to my destination in time to be interviewed by a panel of people I mostly did not know. I made it and sat outside the door, waiting my turn as each of the seven other finalists—drawn from a large national field—emerged.

Several of them spoke to me, telling me who they were, why they applied, and how they felt about the interview and their chances of winning the scholarship. Two took it for a lark, were completely unprepared, and were released early from their sessions. They ran out laughing, clearly unperturbed by the outcome. A third, Karen, emerged looking shell shocked, her eyes glazed over and brows furrowed, shaking her head from side to side. She seemed to need the scholarship more than all the others so far but did not think she would get it and was unsure she even wanted it after what she had learned.

"They want me to speak up for Black people," she said, her voice dripping with skepticism, "but I am not even Black!"

She seemed genuinely distressed at being on the receiving end of any such expectation, even though the scholarship was in the name of Garvey, one of the best-known advocates of Black consciousness, Black nationalism, and Black empowerment. The attitude is not uncommon: benefits matter, but not so much sacrifice or responsibility.

Compared to me or any of the candidates I saw, Karen was a "browning" with a medium coppery complexion and a dusting of freckles. She was not what comes readily to mind either when one thinks of a St. Elizabeth "red" person or an upper St. Andrew "Brown." There were no apparent signs of shipwrecked ancestors or direct evidence of how much White plantation owners exploited Black women. Where my DNA puts me at 13 percent European ancestry, she might be closer to 15 percent non-African and likely Indian. It was nothing that a few concentrated days in the sun could not fix, but she seemed proud of her pigmentation, supremely conscious of her privilege, and more than a little put out that the committee did not seem to recognize it. I tut-tutted sympathetically while she gathered herself and left.

Next to emerge was Adiva, a medical student from Trelawny Parish, Usain Bolt's birthplace. She was a good-natured, matter-of-fact woman who looked like she came from the same stock as me, with the same standard template. We connected right away. She needed the scholarship but was realistic about her chances because her profile did not quite fit. She was confident, though, that she would finish her degree one way or another and return to Trelawny to care for the people there.

The decision came down to the two of us, I learned later. Two super judges, the president of the UNIA (Universal Negro Improvement Association), Garvey's old organization in Jamaica, and the chair, battled for their candidates. The former was adamant that if everyone were like Adiva, with her passionate sense of righteousness and all-embracing view of humankind, there would be no need for Garveyism and its related social justice movements—no need for people like Grace Virtue!

The chair countered that since everyone was not like her, since society was so rife with injustices, including racism and the residual effect of plantation slavery, the country and the world needed people with the courage and the competence to advocate for the liberation of marginalized people, the same way I was equipping myself to do with my planned career in journalism and public service, and the same way Marcus Garvey had done.

That argument, the perception of greater need, my track record of civic engagement, and my profile as a dramatist, provocateur, and budding journalist aligned perfectly with the terms of the scholarship—exactly as I thought when I saw the advertisement. The Office of the Prime Minister awarded me the scholarship upon the committee's recommendation.

I learned one more of life's vital lessons: No matter how good you are and how well your qualifications and capabilities stand on their own, in any opportunity of a competitive nature, it helps to have an advocate in the room—someone who knows your story, is invested in your growth, and is committed to making space for you. Adiva was qualified, and her perspective on life, as interpreted by the UNIA head, had its persuasive value. Without Bryan countering with a more compelling argument, the scholarship would have gone to her.

I took away another crucial lesson—that the fellow aspirant is not necessarily a competitor, an opponent, or an enemy, as much as society has trained us to think in those terms. If it does not work out for them, they are not losers, just someone for whom a particular opportunity was not quite right at a time. The language we use and how we perceive the other determines how we relate to them. Hostile language and framing yield the same attitudes.

The scholarship again put me in the national spotlight. I heard my name repeatedly on the radio, that fascinating medium of my childhood, along with tidbits about my life as I walked to or from the bus stop. It was surreal and more so at the awards ceremony at Kingston's grandest hotel, the Jamaica Pegasus, a few days later. It was a formal breakfast this time, and all eight finalists had been invited; only Adiva came, giving me a warm, congratulatory hug. At the end of his remarks, Mike Henry, then minister of education and culture and the guest speaker, instructed me to "go and speak for the people."

There was no framework for what that meant and for the scholarship in general except that I was bonded to the country for three years immediately upon graduation, but I knew who Garvey was, the principles he stood for, and the methods he used: speaking, writing, and advocating on behalf of the downtrodden.

In the following months, I accepted invitations from a few Garveyites—a small, mostly marginalized group—to speak at UNIA-related events, and one year later, I wrote my first letter to the editor of the *Daily Gleaner*, the country's oldest and most prominent newspaper, founded in 1834, the same year slavery officially ended on the island. The letter protested the treatment of a young woman named Ruth Cammock, who according to media reports was pulled from the 1988 Miss Jamaica Universe contest by her sponsor, Dryad, because they thought her skin was too dark, expressly stating a preference for someone with lighter skin and longer hair.[9]

My letter decried the backward step the country seemed to be

---

9   Ruth Cammock currently lives in Jamaica. In a recent conversation, she denied that the company had dropped her sponsorship for those issues and suggested that someone connected to the pageant had planted those stories in the media to further their own interest.

taking, following the seventies when Manley and his wife, Beverly, discouraged those old colonial anti-Black attitudes so commonplace in the 1960s and early '70s and even tried to ban beauty contests. Years later, portions of my letter made their way into *Born Fi' Dead: A Journey Through the Jamaican Posse Underworld*, written by Laurie Gunst, a Harvard researcher, about the Shower Posse, one of the most ruthless gangs in the United States. The gang's roots lay in Kingston's violent political culture of the 1970s and '80s. Gunst made a connection between the lack of respect for a Black Jamaican identity decried in my letter and the violence that remains an unsavory part of the culture.

With scholarship money committed to me, I eventually tempered the hustle for survival to focus on my studies to become a journalist and on my life in Kingston. Living in the space, being one with this intense little city, and understanding its psyche and culture and how to navigate it were just as important as my labs at UWI.

Looming over my transition from country to Town was the dark, brooding presence of Edward Seaga, the man who led the opposition to Manley's effort at decolonization and his socialist policies of accessible housing, expanded secondary education, a national minimum wage, paid maternal leave, and a safer work environment.

Seaga looked like a White man—a good example, some would argue, of why our island adopted the motto "Out of many, one people" after independence. Depending on which side of the colonial fence one resided, Seaga's position at the top of the political system was either a good thing—since he was at or near a color spectrum that some thought was necessary for "good" leadership in colonial or White supremacist framing—or it represented continued oppression and disempowerment of the Black majority for those concerned with liberation. Over time, I learned that he was of mixed races, born in Boston, Massachusetts, US, to a Lebanese father and a mother of Indian, Scottish, and African descent. Ultimately, none of this mattered to me. What did matter was that he profoundly opposed the social policies of the Manley era and fought viciously to oust his government. It was significant, too, that the ruling elite saw him as their man. I interpreted that as a united front against the dispossessed and a dagger to the heart of the slow progress the country had started to make.

Naturally, I was not enamored. Had it not been for Manley's programs, my secondary education would have ended at age fifteen, and my father would not have been able to get a steady job and access a cheap loan to complete our house with proper sanitary facilities and water supply. The attempt to flatten the social hierarchy where the intersection of race and old money held sway, by making education free up to the university level, made room for people like me to dream and achieve. It had to be a measure of effective public policy that within a decade and a half, I would end up in classes with Manley's third child, Sarah.

Much time has elapsed, but I still believe the rise of Edward Seaga conflicted with what the country needed then—a leader uninterested in being a master, focused instead on the dignity of the individual, and willing to put in the work to chart a pathway to liberate across the entire social spectrum and build a society anchored in these principles. The collision of ideas and the conflict it generated heralded a frightening period of bloodshed and socioeconomic instability from 1976 to 1980, the bitter reality of a small country at war with itself. Manley and leading scholars of the day acknowledged that it had been a civil war, a proxy for the tension between the US and the USSR during the Cold War merged with the backlash from domestic protectionists who equated less profit with loss of status and privileges.

The election was seven years in the rearview mirror by the time I got to Kingston, but politics remained tribalized and tribalizing. I navigated the city with the full awareness that what felt like peace was as fragile as an eggshell; the hot war might have cooled, but there was little relief from the conditions that caused it in the first place and therefore no assurance against further eruptions, anytime or anywhere. The divides were stark and relationships so brittle that a deadly snap was an ever-present possibility.

On any given day, I was within a relatively short drive to Tivoli Gardens, the enclave that Seaga had carved out in West Kingston to secure effortless reelection to Parliament for as long as he wanted, as well as guarantee his eligibility to be either prime minister or opposition leader, the two most politically powerful positions in the country. Socially and physically cut off from the rest of the country to some extent, the area had become synonymous with violence, and it was the incubator for some of the nation's most sinister individuals.

The class divides were stark but painfully normal. The upper classes seemed like an unyielding morass of self-indulgence, and many people in the professional circles I was moving into did not seem overly concerned by the inequities or outraged by the desperate poverty and lack of opportunities among large sections of the population. They seemed more interested in how they could move up and protective of whatever connections they had to those already "above" them.

Life would teach me why this strategy, while clearly self-serving, is not necessarily evil. Self-preservation is the most basic human instinct, and in a small society like ours, or even big ones like the US, overtly challenging the system can lead to ostracism or marginalization. Purely by virtue of my background and social conditioning, perhaps, I was always among those concerned with who would make the change and how comfortably I could accept, revel in, and live off the sacrifices of others—like national hero Sam Sharpe, an enslaved Baptist preacher who led a massive rebellion from 1831 to 1832 in St. James Parish and was hanged for it; or Baptist deacon Paul Bogle, who led a revolt against an oppressive colonial government in Morant Bay, St. Thomas, in 1865 and was hanged as well; or George William Gordon, the conscientious businessman and outspoken critic of Governor Edward Eyre who was tried under martial law and executed; or Marcus Garvey, the outspoken advocate in whose name I was studying.

I grew up portraying one or another of them during our National Heritage Week Celebrations in October each year. Of the seven Jamaicans conferred the nation's highest honor, only one is a woman. Our teachers chose boys and girls to impersonate them. I cannot recall ever playing Nanny, but I did play Sharpe, and oh, how my spine tingled every time I had to repeat his full-throated, infinitely courageous, and now immortal declaration of the importance of total liberation for all people on his way to be hung: "I would rather die on yonder gallows than live in slavery!"

It is possible that the way we are educated impacts some of us more than it does others.

As if Kingston did not already seem completely foreign, the weather was also quite different from what I was accustomed to. Where Cross Keys, Mandeville, and Spalding were covered in lush vegetation or stayed breezy and cool most of the year, Kingston was a dense commercial space almost devoid of greenery and nearly always blanketed in a blistering, soupy heat. Depending on where one lived relative to the national dump, a persistent cover of black smoke from burning garbage brought stench and more unbearable heat. I longed for the countryside, where mornings brought crisp, clean air and dappled pathways through dewy fields of grass or untamed woodlands in the hills across from Hibiscus Place.

Most trying was the absence of Manchester's easy communal spirit and sensibilities. I no longer knew the people who drove the cars or buses I took or those with whom I shared a seat when I could find one. The people who waited at the bus stops with me in the mornings and evenings were stone-faced strangers. There were no cheery hellos, no one to call me by my name or Papa's name. I could not talk to my parents on the phone to ask how they or my little brothers and sisters were doing. I wrote them sometimes, but a letter is not the same as a voice or a body nearby. I felt vulnerable all the time, but I kept going; there was no future back home for a girl who was afraid of a sewing machine, and Papa did not have enough land for the orchard I sometimes dreamed of planting.

This aching loneliness and my natural gravitation to children led me to befriend a little boy I met on the avenue where I had rented a townhouse with three other young women once I found a job, buoyed by the knowledge that my scholarship check would eventually come.

Oaklawn Park was a residential area with neatly kept two-story, single-family homes typical of middle-class Kingston. Mid-level civil servants and small business owners presided over well-maintained structures with lawns barely bigger than postage stamps and neatly trimmed, ubiquitous hibiscus hedges with bougainvillea and crotons thrown in. I could only afford to live there by sharing a place with three roommates—two teachers and a nurse. They were like me, from Manchester and neighboring St. Elizabeth Parish, and had also moved to Kingston to pursue undergraduate degrees at UWI, the next step up the ladder for ambitious young professionals.

Slightly west and across the road from our white brick house, a poorly maintained dirt field gave way to an informal community of tiny houses hidden behind brown zinc fences. By the standards of Kingston, these communities bore the markers of urban poverty and were breeding grounds for antisocial behavior. A shortcut on the edge of the community took me to the nearest grocery store on the main road. I took this path cautiously in the daytime when I needed to but had no interaction with any of this area's residents. I had no reason to and did not go looking for any.

That changed one typically blistering Kingston afternoon as I walked down Essex Avenue toward my house, feeling drained from the heat and a little disoriented by a viselike ache that started at the top of my head and ended just below my brow. I was desperate to get inside, but walking toward me was a dusky-skinned little boy with short, curly hair. He looked about three years old and reminded me of my little brothers at that age. The gray T-shirt he wore was too big for him, the neck drooping down his arm on one side. He was chewing on a corner of it. I stopped, one hand on the gate, and waited as he approached. He did not look unloved or uncared for. Rather, he looked like the child of parents who did not belong to the middle classes and lacked the sense to care about where their child was, or maybe they were less paranoid than I was—more trusting of the streets of Kingston. He gazed at me from full, innocent brown eyes that tugged at my heartstrings.

"What is your name?" I asked him.

"Junior," he said, smiling initially before dropping his eyes to his feet, bare on the hot asphalt.

"Where is your house, Junior?"

He pointed toward the informal settlement across the field.

I talked to him a little more before making him wait at the door while I got him a drink from the fridge.

He struggled to drink the ice-cold lemonade, and I realized he was not used to it. When I was his age, my family had no refrigerator. I drank everything at room temperature. On the rare occasions when we got ice from somewhere, I struggled just as Junior did. I soon sent him on his way with gentle encouragement to go home to his mommy and watched him disappear across the field.

It became a daily thing after that. Junior figured out my routine quickly and would wait at the gate in the afternoons or early evenings. I made sure I had some cold treats in the fridge that he could enjoy or take with him. It was, for me, a pleasant interlude, a chance to connect with and care for—in a simple way—a little human being who needed and appreciated it as much as I did.

There would be unintended and unforeseen consequences. Junior soon brought another little boy with him, then two, three, and four. Before long there was a daily-expanding group of little boys waiting for me, and they began to bring bouquets picked from the neighbors' hedges. It had become an absolute annoyance for some of my middle-class neighbors, one of whom eventually paid me a visit to tell me what she and others were thinking. In essence, I was blurring the lines in the neighborhood—between the good people who lived on our side and the bad people across the field. In the interests of those on the good side, this was not allowed.

Around the same time, I realized that the high concrete wall behind our townhouse cut us off from a gully and another depressed community like the one visible across the field. Our well-organized, middle-class community, therefore, was flanked on both sides by pockets of material poverty. A good deal of Kingston looked much the same way, with affluence and deprivation existing within easy reach of each other.

"As young as you see them, they are criminals," my visitor asserted. "They are just waiting for the right opportunity to break into your house or any other house on the street."

Mostly caught off guard by the visit and how passionately she felt, I listened quietly.

"Don't harbor them over here," she finished with a stern warning.

I looked at her, carefully weighing my response. Her daughter had been in the high school English class I taught the previous year, and I had found the rental property through them. She was my liaison to this community where resident homeowners assumed a seriously superior posture over us—four young women working full- or part-time while pursuing degrees at the university. My prior association with this woman explained why she had been corralled to deliver the message that I could not entertain high-risk people in the neighborhood, even if the ones in question still had their baby teeth.

I understood her concerns to some extent. Urban violence was a problem, and people wanted to feel safe. Plus, some of the boys' behaviors were out of order, like picking the neighbors' flowers and hamming and yelling whenever I did not come outside to them. It had become annoying for me too, but I did not see them as criminals, not when the eldest of the group, a boy named Omar, was only six years old. I understood the issue as one of classism and almost impenetrable conditioning around who mattered and who did not and, most importantly, how attitudes toward or treatment of those children could have a Pygmalion effect, driving the behavior we fear or expect.

I eventually promised her I would talk to them, and I promised myself that I would never become someone who could be so disdainful of children bringing small amounts of stolen flowers in the hope of something to eat or drink, even if they got a little loud sometimes.

I had set my internal boundaries with Junior before he started bringing the other boys. I would talk to him on the streets, bring him out of the sun, and feed him sometimes, but I would not go in search of his parents. Part of me resented them for not looking for him, for seeming not to care enough, but I also understood that over time, they must have figured out where he was and assumed his safety in "proper" middle-class spaces.

I was insufficiently appreciative of the implicit agreement between those inside and those outside spaces of exclusion. This worked well in Jamaica, particularly in Kingston, as I came to understand it. People felt safer behind strong brick walls and wrought iron gates. Even without them, though, people are mostly conditioned to operate within their chosen or designated space. Any breach is usually and perhaps reasonably perceived as hostile.

My experience with the culture of exclusive spaces was reinforced when, just after finishing university, I moved from the house in Oaklawn Park after being forced out by the landlord's harassment. It would also mark the end of my contact with the young boy. I never saw him again. I still occasionally wonder if he made it safely into adulthood and how he turned out.

The older, well-established neighborhood I moved to was even more exclusive. It was expensive enough for homeowners to expect that only others as well off as themselves could afford to or should live there and even more rigid in its assumptions that human worth was calculated relative to how people earned their livings, the cars they drove, whether they owned or rented their homes, whether they had finished university and were already doctors, lawyers, or airline workers, and, most importantly, by the color of their skin.

Except for a Black couple directly across from me, a woman around my age married to a much older man, the neighbors were Brown, White, or other non-Black Jamaicans and expatriates. They treated the Black couple the same way they treated me: they would not so much as lock eyes lest it obligate them to a hello. I knew I was not imagining things. In my case, some of these neighbors served as the eyes and ears of our White landlady, reporting everything from a missed garbage pickup to how many visitors we had in a day.

Fortunately, I had stopped caring completely—if I ever did. I dug in on my rejection of those parts of society grounded in inequities, colorism, and class privileges. I was certain that worth was not defined by any of these things, and as present as they were, I would reject them. Maybe I was becoming the Marxist my classmates at Church Teachers College said I was. Or maybe I was not a label at all—but merely the adult the girl from Old House had grown into.

The university was reinforcing rather than disapproving of my adult self, thankfully. My classes in journalism, sociology, history, anthropology, and political sciences added new layers to my understanding, my identity and ideological grounding, and how I saw myself in the struggle for liberation from oppressive practices. Many people were oblivious to the struggle and saw me and my friends as among the privileged 3 percent who could access a university education, climb the socioeconomic ladder, or cement their place if they were already at the top.

Deeply connected to the island's plantation history, the university campus reflected the varied journeys of transformation from oppressive to more liberating spaces. At one time, it was a works yard for two sugar estates in St. Andrew, the parish that neighbors Kingston and constitutes most of the city's suburbia. A cut-stone aqueduct, which remains there today, carried water from the Hope River north of the campus to the old sugar mill. The iconic Mona Chapel next to the aqueduct was constructed from the bricks of a rum distillery in Trelawny Parish, removed by hand one at a time and transferred to Kingston to build a space of grace. World War II saw the site transformed into a facility known as Camp Gibraltar, home to evacuees from that British peninsula at the tip of Spain and, eventually, Jewish refugees from Spain and Portugal.

A royal charter in 1948 established UWI there under the direction of the University of London. When Jamaica became independent, the university became an autonomous degree-granting institution and incubator of radical progressive Caribbean thought, with which I was supremely comfortable. Some things did not need tinkering; they needed a sledgehammer. Theoretically, at least, UWI embodied this belief, and it was often a hotbed of activism. Administration was staid and traditional in the way they tend to be, but they understood the mission of the institution and were a part of it. The dominant ethos, therefore, was that of a people on a quest to forge a Caribbean identity that was high functional, impactful, and liberating. We did not have to be mimic men operating on a template forged in the image of others. We could and were creating our own image of equal worth or much better. It was highly impactful.

I began to meet or take classes with insistent proponents of a Caribbean way of knowing, of using our own framework for analyzing and synthesizing our historical and contemporary experiences: Edward Baugh, Mervyn Morris, Michael Witter, George Beckford, Derek Walcott, Carl Stone, and Aggrey Brown, among other social scientists and members of the literati. Rather than my being an unidentifiable student in their classes, journalism brought me face-to-face with all of them. Brown, who headed the journalism institue, became my mentor, and we shared an enduring, mutually respectful friendship until his death from cancer in 2011.

Beckford, the iconic author of the Jamaican classic *Persistent Poverty*, which, in part, explored the experience with structural poverty like my family endured, was the subject of my first feature article as a journalism intern with *The Gleaner*. Established in 1834, the year slavery formally ended, and published continuously since, the paper is so ubiquitous and influential that Jamaicans use "gleaner" as a generic term for "newspaper." For much of its existence, it was the only newspaper on the island and always the dominant one. At the end of my first year in the journalism program, my professor, Marjan de Bruin, fresh out of the Netherlands and bringing invaluable new perspectives, secured internships at the paper for the three print journalism students. I was soon off on a thrilling and impactful adventure, beginning with my interview with G. Beck, as he was known among his colleagues on campus. It was nicely written by the standards of the day but, in retrospect, an epic failure relative to the major reason for the piece in the first place.

Although I sat with him for about an hour and asked about politics, current affairs, and his academic work, and witnessed how frail and wasted he looked, I did not ask about the cancer that was taking him away in the prime of his life. The rumors were pervasive, and the knowledge that he was dying was mostly why I was interviewing him at that time, but neither my training nor experience had prepared me to overcome that taboo, which would have been as intrusive and impertinent as asking my mother why she did not use birth control. He lived long enough to see my flattering write-up, the last newspaper article about him in his lifetime.

I interviewed Walcott, the first graduate of the university and the second Caribbean national to win the Nobel Prize in any category, on his first trip to Jamaica after receiving the award for literature in 1992. Unlike the Beckford interview, this was short and unplanned. And unlike Beckford, he was globally renowned for his work. He was also blunt and forthright. I had seen it on display inside the packed-to-capacity Assembly

Hall earlier when, after a few tries, he refused to use a malfunctioning microphone and demanded he get one that worked, or he would not be speaking! He was their Nobel laureate, after all, and they had invited him to speak. The least they could do was get him a proper microphone!

I doubt UWI was prepared for such an outright confrontation. Walcott did not laugh, did not think it was funny, and he let them know. The smackdown rumbled through the Assembly Hall, where the audience applauded and resonated around the region—a lesson for the institution about proper execution and for everyone about the courage to be authentic even it creates awkwardness.

I had the dubious pleasure of asking him for a quote for my story after that. I was apprehensive, but I, too, have something of a rebel in me. I would at least try. He radiated pure grace, clearly recognizing that I had a job to do and choosing not to let me bear the brunt of any residual annoyance. I got my quote and wrote my story for the *Gleaner*, where I would eventually land a permanent job in the summer of 1991 after a brief stint at JAMPRESS, the national news agency then. Both positions opened vastly more opportunities to encounter people across all strata of society, including being in the Assembly Hall at UWI with Winnie and Nelson Mandela when they visited in July 1991, just a year after Nelson's release following twenty-seven years in prison, and meeting Queen Elizabeth II in 1994, during her fifth visit to Jamaica.

I often cite these latter two examples as defining moments in my life and crucial examples of the lens through which I process people and institutions. The queen represented the height of White power and was the direct heir to the fruits of ancestral suffering. From the perspective of history and the old, hackneyed paradigm of what constitutes news, she was an important figure. Beyond that, she was merely a curiosity to me, like an expensive item from a novelty store that one might save as a conversation piece but with otherwise no value. As an institutional figure, she was not an object of admiration—just a woman with centuries of intergenerational wealth, inherited privileges, and the accompanying celebrity. That was not meaningful to me.

I met her at King's House, the official residence of the native governor-general, who represents the monarchy on the island. After debating whether I should even attend the morning reception, I made the trip as a nod to history for my children. By this time, I was the mother of two daughters. My girls, toddlers then, had been born shortly after I left UWI. They solidified my commitment to work toward a more just and equitable world. Family support, cheap labor, and good childcare allowed me to continue my career without much interruption.

The reception was also an opportunity for a split-screen moment—to survey the arc of my life from Old House to King's House and evaluate how I was doing in my quest for experiences different from the circumstances in which I was born and infiltrating so-called elitist spaces to understand better how they work. I also saw an opening to exercise one little act of defiance: I looked her directly in the eyes and did not curtsy.

Comparatively, when Mandela entered the Assembly Hall, I felt a shock, like a swift-moving electromagnetic storm passing through. I recovered and stomped and cheered along with everyone else in the overflowing building. He was the greatest freedom fighter since Jesus Christ, earning adulation through his leadership and sacrifices on behalf of an entire nation and race, not a celebrity who inherited a position, wealth, and titles.

I applied this framework to my journalism work in Jamaica, cultivating little interest in the lifestyles of the idle rich, which publicly manifested as endless partying or other purely self-indulgent pursuits. I realized that many considered themselves to be on the high end of a meaningful and superior life, but I knew that preoccupation with social status or appearances would not move the needle on human progress. I vowed not to waste my education on trivial pursuits.

I was interested in how to fix the problem of so many poor, hungry Black people in Kingston, Manchester, St. Mary, and elsewhere in the country who were living in squalor or entering public hospitals suffering from diseases that could have been prevented, only to be treated as throwaways. Violence had a constant presence. Unsurprisingly, rage simmered just below the surface in what should have been harmless interactions that too often exploded, summoning guns and knives into play and leading to, for instance, the death of a brother because he ate someone's leftover dumpling or chicken leg.

Slavery's legacy of brutality was hardwired in the culture. This untreated and unacknowledged trauma could and needed to be changed over time with deep and consistent psychosocial intervention, cultural reengineering, and corrective policies and legislations—for example, regarding who was allowed to own or carry certain types of weapons. The possibilities for prevention seemed lost on the legislators, who did little more than lament the most gruesome acts of violence, and only for as long as the issue remained in the headlines.

I was at my best roaming the streets and searching for genuine interactions best found among the "lowliest," those unschooled in artifice, rather than covering stories from the assignment book. My comfort zone was always among people with real lives. I wanted to hear their stories of battles lost, won, ongoing; lessons taught and learned; aspirations and fondest dreams. I wanted their stories splashed across the front pages, to call attention to their plight and shame those who should be changing things but were not, or to celebrate their triumphs despite the persistent obstacles they faced. It worked as I intended, "stirring debates and making people think a little differently," as Carol Mayne, one of my supervisors then, said of my work.

Those stories were out there on any given day, just outside our building on North Street in downtown Kingston, because it was surrounded by some of the country's poorest neighborhoods. If I left the premises and headed east, west, north, or south, I would find hungry children who should be in school but were on the streets begging, hustling for themselves or their parents, or just loitering. There were homeless people at the bus stops; underfunded schools with broken fences and even more broken children; and sick people on the sidewalks, covered in flies, who needed to be in health-care facilities.

There were streets filled with potholes dug out by raw sewage and overflowing with uncollected garbage, and nearby, the old hospital creaked under the strain of too many stabbing and gunshot victims. The rusted zinc fences hid many of the nearby houses—those enduring symbols of circumstances that trapped their inhabitants physically and psychologically, for generations in some cases. Women bathed naked in trash-strewn gullies, uncaring, it seemed, of how exposed they were or whether what they were doing even made sense. I began to understand that urban poverty was acutely dehumanizing. It stripped the individual of their dignity in a way that rural poverty and the food insecurity of my teenage years did not, and for those who lived in such conditions, it became an undesirable subculture, unacceptable to general society and even more marginalizing for them.

I was still an intern one day when I secured my supervisor's permission to roam outside North Street. I asked the news car driver to drop me at the entrance to Kingston Public Hospital, a short distance away, and went inside, not sure what I was looking for. I decided to sit and observe.

Soon enough, a devastating pattern emerged. Every fifteen minutes to a half an hour, porters would come running in with someone on a stretcher, often drenched in blood from a knife attack. Knives routinely came into play in domestic disputes between siblings, between male and female romantic partners, gay men in relationships, or friends fighting over an unpaid debt. These attacks severely taxed the hospital's ability to cope with the nonviolent cases that presented in the emergency room. I wrote about what I saw.

I earned my first front-page byline with that story, though my supervisor said he had to fight for it. It did not align with the crude form of breaking news the decision-makers were accustomed to but sought instead to paint a picture of the chronic, pervasive violence in society and its impact on the health-care facilities and the medical practitioners faced with unending trauma.

My second byline came when I ventured into the smoke-filled urban slum of Riverton City: the national dump where reports said more than 10,000 people lived in abject squalor, in houses made from debris, breathing in the stench of burning garbage and smoke from morning to night. These were the most desperate living conditions I had witnessed, and I struggled to understand it. The women there helped me.

Martha had lost a leg and her old family home in a volatile Kingston community to political thugs during the political violence from 1976 to 1980. The no-man's-land where Kingston dumped its trash became her home, and there was zero hope of getting out. She slept in a hut she made herself and foraged for food amid the refuse, alongside wild dogs, pigs, and goats.

Patsy, a thirty-year-old mother of ten, was also a victim of Kingston's violence, which was as pervasive in the city as reggae music and street food. I sat beside her on her neatly made-up bed in her one-room house constructed from rusted zinc and plywood sheets and talked about her life. She had one consuming dream: to secure a prosthesis for one of her sons, who had lost a leg to gun violence.

Their conditions reminded me that in the same way Britain has yet to compensate Black Jamaicans for plantation slavery, those who suffered the damages of political warfare or state-sponsored violence have not been compensated—and deserve to be—by the Jamaican state. I committed to humanizing rather than objectifying Martha, Patsy, and everyone else living in those conditions. My story was titled "Laughter and Hope Amidst the Slum."

Despite the debilitating socioeconomic conditions and those spaces and metaphors of exclusion that demanded conformation or confrontation, I was falling in love with Kingston. Structurally well laid out and much of its architecture built on British sensibility, it teemed with the energy of ordinary Jamaicans: street vendors, carpenters, taxi drivers, street cleaners, bargain shoppers, and store owners, all boasting an unfathomable resilience and resolve to defy the stresses of their lives and carry on, day after day. Even more incomprehensible at times was the contagious joy and hopefulness on the streets of downtown

Kingston, among the people at the economic base of the country. This persisted among the vendors in Coronation Market, where Sa Bea had spent so many years hustling to feed her children. I connected with the market and saw it as a microcosm of the real Jamaica and a place where I could always find a piece of home.

CHAPTER FOUR

NEW YORK! NEW YORK!

A good teacher, diligence, intellect, and the grace of a good man opened a door for me with my essay win. That and a good amount of serendipity led me to a prestigious scholarship that would not only pay for my education but also unlock the gateway to the world. With thousands of dollars in my savings account and two years at the university still ahead of me, I applied to the US embassy in Kingston for a visitor's visa early in the summer of 1988.

I still remember the consternation on the officer's face when I handed him my application form, passport, and a bank statement showing over $25,000 in my account!

"Oh, come on, Grace!" he said. "You mean to tell me you saved all this money from your teacher's salary?"

With no other obvious source of income, he was correctly skeptical. The alternative for someone like me was either a healthy call-girl client list or smuggling ganja up the nether regions to New York or London. I had to speak quickly and identify an unlikelier source before he slapped "DENIED" in my passport, as had been the case two years before when I was a final-year student at teachers' college, applying with $700 in my Workers Bank account.

"I have a scholarship!" I said and pushed my award letter from the Office of the Prime Minister through the sliver at the bottom of the window. He picked it up, read it carefully, and looked me directly in the eyes.

"Congratulations! Come back for your passport at 3 p.m. today."

It was stamped with a one-year visa, meaning I could make as many short trips as I wanted during that period without returning to the embassy. This marked the beginning of my realization that people like me could be tourists, even in the United States. It was not a term reserved for White people who made the reverse trip in search of sand, sun, sex, or some other undefined quest.

I arrived in New York on a violently stormy night in July, the summer of the Tawana Brawley grand jury hearing and the suicide of Carter Cooper, Anderson Cooper's brother. Those two events and political campaigning for primaries preceding the November general election dominated the news cycle during my stay. It was a current affairs bonanza. The television was king. I was a willing subject.

The storm had forced the closure of John F. Kennedy Airport when I arrived aboard Air Jamaica, resulting in the plane circling the airport for what felt like a long time. I was ready to be back on the ground. When it finally landed, we sat on the tarmac for several more hours before disembarking. Half asleep by then, I exited Customs into a New York City night subdued by the passing storm.

The Yellow Cab taxis were lined up outside, thankfully. I remember little of the drive other than crossing the Brooklyn Bridge, which the driver helpfully pointed out after realizing this was my first trip to the United States or anywhere else outside of Jamaica. I must have told him that. It was entirely on him to get me across the East River to Aunt Priscilla's house on Avenue A.

Sheets of rain blocked my initial view of America's most famous city. It would be days before I shook off the novelty of life outside Jamaica, my first airplane flight, my arrival in one of the world's most iconic regions, and numerous television channels, unlike the one government-owned station I was accustomed to at home. Four days after I arrived, Carter Cooper, the twenty-three-year-old son of entrepreneur and fashion icon Gloria Vanderbilt and older brother to now renowned broadcaster Anderson Cooper, jumped from a balcony at his mother's Manhattan apartment to the street below. No one was talking about mental health then.

It was a fascinating human interest story for me: why would a rich, handsome young man with none of the problems of my world simply give up on life? More evidence, I thought, that no one is immune to tribulations and sorrows. They simply show up in different ways and are hardly ever of our own choosing. His death and the case of Brawley, a Black teenager who had accused four White men, including a police officer and a prosecuting attorney, of sexually assaulting her, showed up in every newscast. At the center of the Brawley case was a big, bellowing man named Al Sharpton, loudly advocating justice for her.

I sat on a stool in my aunt's canary-yellow kitchen, glued to the television set she kept on the counter, absorbing the intrigue of the city. Evenings brought a woman named Oprah Winfrey, whom I had never heard of before. I began following her then and would do so religiously for more than twenty years, until she ended the show. She was my anchor and inspiration at some of the worst times of my life in the United States.

I was fine those first few days with just sitting there in the kitchen, taking it all in, and contemplating how my world was slowly expanding—from Old House, where life was simple, quiet, and unhurried, through Mandeville, Kingston, to the University of the West Indies, and now to New York. I had made that journey with some pointed intervention but mostly by carving a path for myself. It was profoundly empowering—and satisfying. I still channel that feeling whenever I find myself staring up or down an obstacle and questioning my ability to do or withstand: *Yes, you can do it, kid!*

Within a few days, though, I craved more from this bustling city with more traffic than I had seen in my whole lifetime and none of it going anywhere I knew! The bus stop was just outside the side gate near Aunt Priss's two-car garage, but I did not feel ready to climb on, since neither the bus number nor its destination meant anything to me.

Eventually, I left the kitchen for the front porch and then headed diagonally across Remsen to a small Chinese shop on the other side of Avenue A. I bought orange juice and the *New York Post*, mainly to give myself something to do and assert a bit of independence. Minus the juice, that became my morning routine. Of course, reading the papers had great practical value. I got the news in detail and began to learn the names of places within and beyond Brooklyn and the Bronx.

Next, I ventured further east on Remsen Avenue, making mental notes of landmarks and where I had veered off and exactly how many turns I had taken, right or left, so I could find my way back home without asking strangers for directions. Cell phones or Google-anything was more than a decade into the future, and Aunt Priscilla, a registered nurse working the night shift, would go to sleep soon after arriving home in the mornings. Though I had seen pay phones on my route, I did not want to wake her to ask my way home. It would just be better if I did not lose my way.

As big and unwieldy as New York seemed, I soon began to run into people from Old House, Cross Keys, and surrounding communities. People, even some I did not know, called out my family name as I sat on the porch, watching the world go by, or took more trips up or down Remsen. Eventually, Brooklyn took shape as not simply a place where my aunt had made her home but one where thousands of West Indians, Africans, Asians, and people from everywhere in the world had done so as well and were all part of a loud, lively, and fascinating mosaic that is uniquely New York.

I had no real plans for the summer other than being in New York, so it was entirely coincidental that my first substantial trip outside the house was to see the Statue of Liberty, the iconic landmark that until then had only registered marginally in my consciousness—seen on posters, T-shirts, and stamps on the red-and-blue airmail letters my aunts sent my grandmother.

My cousin Junie, Amir's younger sister, thought it was a great idea. She was a few years my senior and had grown up in South Florida with her mother. Comfortably American and a traveling nurse by then, she breezed into Aunt Priss's house, as only she could, the week after I arrived and informed me that we were going to see Lady Liberty right after she got me sunglasses and sunscreen.

I do not recall the trip to Manhattan, but I experienced my first boat ride ever on the way to Liberty Island and fell in love with water travel. The heat was blistering, and the line of tourists at the statue's base was deflatingly long when we arrived. We joined them for a while but eventually gave up, bought ice cream, and caught the boat back, agreeing that we would try again another time.

I have yet to return, even now that I know the Statue of Liberty is one of America's most enduring symbols of freedom and understand why New York is the ultimate destination for so many who are fleeing oppression and looking for a hopeful new beginning. The welcoming ethos is captured in the poetic lines on a tablet at the base of the statue:

> GIVE ME YOUR TIRED, YOUR POOR, YOUR HUDDLED MASSES YEARNING TO BREATHE FREE, THE WRETCHED REFUSE OF YOUR TEEMING SHORE. SEND THESE, THE HOMELESS, TEMPEST-TOSSED TO ME, I LIFT MY LAMP BESIDE THE GOLDEN DOOR!

That glorious idealism seemed to persist everywhere in metropolitan New York—the ultimate hustler's paradise and the prototype of surviving from one day to the next on nothing but the drive to work, the desire to succeed, and whatever natural talents an individual has.

Time would teach me that Lady Liberty, authentically French and a gift to the United States after their brutal civil war to free enslaved people, represents something far more complex than freedom or democracy; she also symbolizes the dissonance that emerges when multiple layers of oppression exist in spaces where official rhetoric projects a liberating philosophy that broadly does not correspond to reality. That philosophy might be true for New York to a degree, but it is not so for the US in general.

I knew a lot about Aunt Priscilla, but I did not know her. She was a shadowy figure in the background of my life at Old House. Someone always brought her up in conversation, and they did so with as much veneration as they showed God. I thought of her with part wonder, part intimidation, and complete childhood adoration, even though I did not have so much as a photograph of her. I only knew she was a goddess who happened to be my aunt.

She left Old House long before I was born, and with more than a generation between us, we were never directly in touch in my early years or even while I spent most of my time with Mammy. Realistically, we could not have. I was a child, and adults communicated with adults. Whatever communication we had was through Mammy, like at Christmastime when she sent a few dollars for me, commensurate with my childhood standing. Family lore said she owned a successful beauty salon in Kingston, catering to the city's elites, before meeting an American sailor of Hungarian descent, marrying him, and migrating to the United States in the late 1950s or early '60s. They separated at some point but never divorced. He was a Catholic, and she had converted. By the time I arrived in New York, she had not been in touch with him for twenty years and had not even the vaguest idea of where he might be. She kept his last name attached to hers and sometimes referred to him by it.

My first real memory of her was of her visit home to see my grandmother when I was about eight or nine. Before that, I was too young to remember details, though I have vague recollections of the buzz that preceded her trips and lasted until she left again.

I was living with Mammy during that visit, keeping her company in the little bungalow her children had renovated and expanded. In the excitement of her eldest child's imminent arrival, she either did not notice or care that I stayed up, equally excited to see this esteemed relative traveling from an exotic place called New York. Along with my excitement, I was also apprehensive about what it would mean for us to be in the same small space, even for a short time—whether I would have to speak English all the time, walk instead of run, speak in hushed tones, or, God forbid, sit at the light-brown Formica table with her for dinner and use a fork and knife. Things are always different when influential strangers come calling, even if they are family. I wanted to feel her out as early as I could—to decide, for example, if I wanted to stay in the house with her or find some excuse to escape to Mama.

Aunt Priscilla did not disappoint. She came dressed in a black trouser suit with a white sailor-collar blouse, hair pulled back in a lush chignon at her nape, and a black beret perched jauntily over her forehead. I could not take my eyes off her, not that night or the whole time she was there. I followed her around, looking, waiting for something undefined—tangible evidence that she was my aunt and was even marginally interested in who I was the same way I was in her. She, in turn, treated me kindly, like a household pet. She would not hurt me; she would feed me milk or water or scraps from the table sometimes, but she took no interest beyond that.

I do not recall seeing her again until she returned around five years later for Mammy's funeral. That visit was part mourning the dearly departed and the passage of time spent away from them, part joyful reunion with others who shared the same feelings, and wholly challenging because of the confluence of emotions and experiences to navigate. In this case, five opinionated siblings who had separated in early adulthood had all come back together in their forties and fifties for the first time to bury their mother, who defied the tentacles of rural poverty and shepherded them to responsible adulthood.

Aunt Priscilla stayed in the corner near the casket, a striking presence in a semi-shiny black dress with a tight bodice and accordion-pleated skirt belted at the waist. She called my name gently, just once, extending her arms as I shuffled toward the casket to see Mammy for the last time. Overcome with grief, I turned and ran through the living room to the back of the house and cried until there were no more tears.

---- ✀ ----

Aunt Priscilla reached for me again that first night in New York, pulling me in from the rain, my pretty rose-and-black rayon skirt suit soaking wet from the brief time it took to retrieve my suitcase from the taxi's trunk and run up the steps to her front porch.

She was eleven years older than my father and in her late sixties when I stayed with her that summer of my twenty-third year. I knew there was goodwill between us. I looked up to her because everyone else did. She was my grandmother's favorite child and my father's adored sister. I knew she appreciated that I had kept Mammy company for the last six years of her life—that I had mostly been her hands and feet in the two final years especially, when she was too sick to do anything for herself. I was her messenger, too, running around when she needed me to, and carrying the final message to inform neighbors and friends when dawn broke that July day in 1977, just a few days before I graduated from primary school, and she did not open her eyes.

Aunt Priscilla and I stayed in touch loosely over the following years with infrequent airmail letters and messages and packages couriered by community members visiting from New York. In 1983, when I applied to teachers' college with no idea how I would afford it and asked her for help, she sent me $300—enough to cover my tuition for the first year and the highest I would ever have to pay in the three-year program. It saved me an abundance of angst.

I knew that she, along with other aunts, uncles, and cousins home in Jamaica, England, and the US, were proud of me too, as well as of my ten siblings—all of us defying our circumstances and bringing honor to the family name as teachers, journalists, and community activists. With no teen pregnancies or negative encounters with law enforcement, we had escaped the two leading indicators of adverse life outcomes for people like us. In these most critical ways, we had already won.

Still, my exposure to my aunt as an adult was too limited to form an independent opinion beyond my knowledge that she was everyone's idea of what it meant to be perfect, successful, and sophisticated. I was excited, therefore, but only partially looking forward to spending six weeks alone with her when there was as much distance between us, including generational and cultural, as there was goodwill. I also knew the attitudes and expectations around her combination of Jamaican Black and European heritage DNA, including diminished respect for people of African descent and their heritage and, in its place, an assumption that the latter owes deference to the former based on skin color alone. This was true even within families like ours. I did not accept it and was becoming less tolerant of those attitudes. I hoped I would not encounter those dynamics, but given all that I knew about my aunt and where our realties collided—as family members from opposite ends of a color spectrum that still mattered in our slowly evolving postcolonial society—those considerations held sway as I began my visit with her.

Days after my arrival, I received my first scolding from Aunt Priscilla after she overheard me speaking to my friends in Jamaican Patwa on the phone and had had enough of it already! Her shrill voice dripped with disdain as she addressed me from the top of the stairs.

"Grace! If anyone hears the way you talk, they would never believe you are a high school English teacher!"

Intuitively, I never spoke to her in Patwa because it is a language of familiarity and informality and my relationship with my aunt did not check those boxes yet, assuming they ever could. I kept her sensibilities in mind, but she was upset that I was using the language at all. Naturally, it irked me. I was long past internalizing that my race, gender, or social background, including the language I choose to use, in any way diminishes my personhood, and I was beyond giving credence to the notion that everything with White associations automatically meant more extraordinary evolution as a human being. I was also not interested in a brand of upward social mobility that required erasing my authentic self or putting distance between me, my parents, my siblings, or the people I played with as children. On the contrary, I treasured those relationships characterized by depth of familiarity and long-established loyalties rather than ones forged around a perceived elevated status in life—mine or theirs.

I knew how hard I had worked, but I also knew some of my good fortune resulted from dumb luck. More than anything else, that dumb luck included my grandmother's literary skills—her ability to write, read, comprehend, and navigate various spaces—which she passed on to my father. He took that gift and multiplied it for me, putting me well ahead of my classmates, some of whom reached adulthood without having mastered reading, much less English, at the level I had.

Choosing to use my mother tongue in conversations with them meant shared meaning, understanding, and memories. It was therefore a conscious choice, and berating me for it represented the loss of agency I fear in situations where people have control over the space I inhabit and are prepared to exert it in unnecessary and unreasonable ways. How long would it take to explain to my aunt that I interpreted her scolding me about how I spoke—inside the house, at that—as being grounded in class bias, belittling of me as an adult, and an attack on an essential part of my identity? How could I convey that I did not share her loyalty to a heritage that carried with it the dehumanization of my ancestors and their struggles and the view that Africa and all things Black, including our language and culture, was inferior to all things European?

I covered my irritation with a laugh and did not "talk back." Should I have? Almost four decades later, with new experiences and a self-assurance that I did not have then, the answer is an unqualified yes. I should have expressed my feelings, initiated a conversation, and heard her out. I wonder what treasure trove of understanding and insights I might have unleashed had I done that.

I quickly figured out that my relationship with Aunt Priscilla would likely always be a little brittle but would probably not go up in flames if I put effort into it. She was not warm and fuzzy, and she was infected with colonial-era prejudices that she tried to impose on me. I reminded myself that I loved her dearly, idolized her even, and learned not to "pay har too much mind" when it came to some things. After all, I was in New York partly at her expense, and life was unfolding in exciting ways outside her house. There were things to see, do, and understand.

For example, I saw a lot of White men dressed in top hats and black suits in the blazing sun walking past the house daily. That was a novelty for me. I learned they were Orthodox Jews. I did not know any Jews in Jamaica, even though I knew through history books and newspaper reports that some were there, among other non-Black ethnic groups, like the descendants of indentured Indians who came to work on the plantations after emancipation. The Indians were mostly burnished as dark as Africans by the tropical sun, and only hair texture provided any discernible difference between them and the Black population. Then there were the mixed-race people, "brownings" like Karen, many of whom took pride in their differentiation from Black people but would not pass the "brown paper bag test" in the United States or apartheid South Africa.

In general, though, my daily interactions on the island were with Black people and the occasional Chinese grocer in Mandeville, Spalding, or downtown Kingston. The Chinese had also come as indentured laborers but transferred to light commerce as soon as they could. They remain dominant in that space today, along with a wave of new immigrants arriving in recent years and working in the construction and engineering sectors, building bridges and highways.

My first significant interaction with White people had been at UWI, where five of my first-year professors, including my journalism professor, Marjan de Bruin, were White. I was perplexed, initially, by the German teaching me Jamaican and Caribbean politics with an accent I struggled to understand. How could this be? I fell thoroughly in love with the White, middle-aged, bald-headed Barbadian teaching one of my first-year core classes: Ideas about God, Humanity, and Nature. White people were slowly beginning to take shape in my mind as something other than whip-wielding slave masters or scions of extreme privilege, though being a professor at UWI was regarded as a high-status job too.

New York offered a paradigm shift, a grand explosion of experiences and possibilities that made such difference normal, dislodging some of the hardwired cultural practices I was accustomed to even as I knew they were socioeconomic contrivances fiercely protected by those who benefited from them.

Aunt Priss unknowingly set off a cognitive dissonance storm on her way out of the house one evening, casually telling me that someone would be coming to cut the grass in the morning, likely before she returned from the night shift at a nearby hospital. It was an FYI so I would not be alarmed should sudden noises awaken me.

I heard the first sputter of the lawn mower around 8 a.m. and looked through the front window. A heavyset man in his fifties was pushing the mower, and a younger one was trimming the hedges with what looked like a giant pair of scissors. Two White men! Clearly, the eleventh commandment did not say Black people must always work for White people and never the other way around! Clearly the twelfth commandment did not say White men cannot get their hands dirty!

Pardon my shock at what now has long been normal for me, but I had never witnessed White people existing outside of privileged positions in Jamaica—never saw them doing yard work or living ordinary lives of the day-to-day hustle, like selling water coconuts from an old fridge or a crudely made lean-to at the side of the road or jerk chicken from a half drum in Cross Roads or Spanish Town Road. I never saw a White person selling (or buying) tomatoes and yellow yams in Coronation Market, pushing handcarts down King Street, or driving a taxi or a bus. I had never seen them working as bellhops, housekeepers, or waiters or waitresses in restaurants or hotels; or working as nurses, secondary school teachers, policemen or women; as conductors on city buses, or as gardeners or maids to anyone. I never saw them in any situation that could be considered a role reversal—a Black person in a position of authority over someone White.

Socially, Jamaica is not constructed that way. With limited exceptions—and primarily outside of Kingston, such as in St. Elizabeth and Westmoreland Parishes, where the descendants of Scottish and German indentured servants and survivors of a shipwreck had settled—White or Brown people inherited spaces of social and psychological dominance or exclusivity, reliably supported by the media they owned, which could be counted on to weave spectacular narratives about the nobility of their character and how it fuels their successes as gurus, captains of industries, socialites, beauty queens, or other positions that communicate the superiority of Whiteness and its corresponding privileges.

The numbers matter. Black people make up more than 90 percent of the population in Jamaica. This partly explains why one can go for days, weeks, or even months without encountering a White person. It also explains why it is a less racially hostile place than the US. However, it does not explain the overrepresentation of non-Blacks and the underrepresentation of Blacks in positions of privileges. That is about biases and historic privillege.

Of course, the situation perpetuates itself. Many Black people accept the status quo because it was all they know. Others relate to the mantle of superiority around White or Brown People from a position of disciplined hostility, putting up with it because they have little choice in a small island economy. Still others see them as equals, no more or less human, and entitled to nothing above or below anyone else. I fall into this category with the caveat that I believe equal rights are commensurate with equal sacrifices and responsibility, that White supremacy exists, and that Black people deserve to be compensated not just for hundreds of years of free labor on sugar and cotton plantations but also for the discrimination and trauma following emancipation. I believe this to be true of the United States, Jamaica, and anywhere Africans were enslaved and treated as subhuman.

As the men wielded their shears and made light work of the tiny lawn, I slowly processed that in a big, White-majority country like the US, it would be typical to see White people cutting grass, selling snow cones in Flatbush, or among the homeless population in New

York City—as much part and parcel of the environment as were the doctors, lawyers, or bus drivers.

I tried to explain the culture shock to a Fulbright panel in Kingston the following year as I sought funding for graduate school in the US. The blank looks on their faces said I was not connecting to them with my story. Maybe I had done a lousy job explaining what I had experienced and what I regarded as a lesson in anthropology or sociology and a real insight into how race presented differently in the US than it did in Jamaica. Maybe it was not the appropriate answer to their question, which I cannot now recall. Or maybe they were among those who did not want to hear anything that felt even marginally like questioning what they saw as the preferred order of things—anything that might start a conversation about racial biases in Jamaica. It was and remains a fraught subject.

At its core, my observation was about racial or ethnic-based privileges in Jamaica and how the system preserves it; the psychological burden it represents for generations of Black people; and the impact on productivity when a skewed norm is hammered into the collective psyche to the point where many simply accept it as the natural order and immutable, like sunrise or sunset. I understood too that like many Jamaicans at a certain professional level or social standing, their opportunities for upward social mobility depended on their proximity to centers of privilege, which were still mostly non-Black. For them, "Out of many, one people" was the motto—no questions asked, no deconstruction required, no examination of how systemic and cultural biases still privileged a small minority and disadvantaged others.

Slightly north of Oaklawn Park, where I had met little Junior on the street, were some of the city's most exclusive neighborhoods. Michael Manley lived in a townhouse within walking distance—a modest space that contradicted any idea that his goal was to be exclusive; everyone needs a place to live. Sometimes, while I waited for the bus to UWI, I saw him driving himself home after his early-morning jog around the Mona Dam. I occasionally walked into some of those neighborhoods for exercise and to enjoy the trees and shrubbery that were less abundant in Oakland Park. In the mornings, I met the maids and gardeners walking to work. In the evenings, I met them going home. The only people I saw on the streets were Black.

My aunt and her White gardeners had exposed me to a shocking new reality, and there was more. Her basement, another concept I was unfamiliar with, had been converted to office space. Her longtime tenant was Dr. Schmidt, a Jewish doctor. I saw him sporadically—a tall, robust man who seemed to wear the same cream-colored shirt and red kippah—entering or leaving the building from the side gate on Remsen Avenue.

I never spoke to him or asked my aunt how he came to be her tenant. The stereotype of the Jews in Jamaica was that they were all rich. I knew something of their history, but I had never seen them outside the paradigm of power or persecution—who they were as real people. Now there was one occupying the space beneath the kitchen where I watched TV, writing my aunt a check every month because the house belonged to her and not the other way around. Years later, I would learn so much more about the Jewish people, particularly through a dozen years of deep friendship with a man named Mayer Resnick. Nothing about my Jamaican experience allowed me to see that possibility, less than a decade down the road.

This multiculturalism was part of a glorious New York reality. It was a blissfully confounding place, in the best sense of the word—a laboratory of social experience for which I had no reference point. It stood counter to the more familiar frame baked into old plantation societies like Jamaica, where the dominant narratives attributed the social structure and the advantages held by others to their ancestors' hard work, diligence, and frugality, without mentioning the proverbial elephant in the room: the advantage of skin color or how powerful families sometimes collude to exclude those not born into privilege.

For women, beauty contests—absurd, cringeworthy competitions revolving around hair length and texture, skin tones, and body types—have long been used to send anti-Black messages. Only recently have the "queens" started to look more like the majority, albeit in response to the global social justice movement rather than a native rejection of the biases embedded in our colonial past. This is episodic. The contests continue to be accorded more attention and importance than they deserve, and the default is still to choose the Eurocentric or hybridized women as standard bearers. I have always rejected them as overt symbols of misogyny, racism, and the embodiment of unhelpful biases and unearned privileges.

Aunt Priss had more thought-provoking lessons for me, communicated as innocuously as her FYI about the gardeners. A dry-cleaning service would be coming to collect the big, intricately embroidered bedspread from the guest room the next day, and they would likely get there before she returned home.

"If the men who come are White," she said, "you can open the door and give them the spread. If they are Black, do not open the safety chain. Just tell them to come back Saturday."

"Okay," I said, even as my stomach tightened with anxiety.

I feared she did not understand me even a little. I was with her in New York less than a year after being awarded the Marcus Garvey Scholarship in honor of a man persecuted for his strident opposition to anti-Black racism in Jamaica and the United States. I was not then, nor was I ever, in a space to accept the paradigm of Black people, of myself, as naturally bad or untrustworthy, which was how I processed my aunt's comments—the same negative way I understood her reaction to my use of Jamaican Patwa inside her house.

All the men I knew were Black: my father, six brothers, uncles, cousins, good friends, and lovers. I had no frame of reference for Black men as more dangerous or undesirable relative to another race, and I did not question their humanity and assign them a value less than others. On the contrary, my normal template for what it meant to be human then was Black, but my aunt was telling me that she saw Black men, at least, through a prism hugely different from mine, even though she had three Black brothers and a mother who, despite some evidence of racial mixing, would not come close to passing the brown paper bag test.

Not even during the 1970s in Jamaica, when violent deaths became as casual as stray mongrels and I lived in fear that it could reach our doors, did I process any of it as Black men committing crimes. I understood it as the result of unscrupulous people fighting for power and using those who existed in distressing and dehumanizing social conditions as pawns to perpetuate it. In a Black country, it was a given that both victims and perpetrators would be primarily Black.

Clearly, there was a clash of perspectives. Aunt Priss was talking to me as a privileged, light-skinned Jamaican woman, and I was receiving her as a Black Jamaican woman. Knowing that allowed me, once again, to be indifferent to her comment; so, when two Black men maybe a few years older than me rang the doorbell the following day, I ran upstairs for the bedspread, opened the door, and handed it to them. They thanked me politely and were on their way.

A few days later, when Amir, her nephew, and my cousin, came to visit, Aunt Priss demonstrated that not even her relatives were immune to her deep-seated biases.

"Don't let him in the house!" she shrieked when she spotted him approaching late one Saturday afternoon. Before I could say, "Who?" she fled up the stairs with a litheness that belied her sixty-odd years. "He is so dark, and that red shirt he is wearing is too harsh against his skin. Just keep him outside for me, please!"

She seemed genuinely terrified, like Blackness was a deadly virus that might escape Amir's skin and settle on her and the furniture. I did not understand it.

Amir was my mammy's oldest grandchild. He had an abundance of swag, multiplied a thousand times when he became the owner of that little red transistor radio, the first in our family and most of the neighborhood. I took his place keeping Mammy company when he was sent to Kingston at fifteen to become an apprentice at a car repair shop.

Although he was several years older, we were best buddies. I looked forward to holidays when he would come home, especially after he bought his blue Ford Cortina and would take me driving through the neighborhood, his stereo blaring country music. Things changed when his mother filed for him to join her in the US in his early twenties. By then, the mother–son relationship had become irretrievably strained, so after a brief sojourn with her in South Florida, he headed to New York and settled in the Bronx. He was responsible for putting the idea of my visit in both my head and my aunt's and helping me with the logistics for my first flight out of Jamaica. He was dearer than a brother.

I had been heartily looking forward to welcoming my first visitor—my favorite cousin and someone closer to my age—and offering him juice from the refrigerator, reminiscing about our childhood, and determining how Brooklyn stacked up against Old House. Instead, I was unexpectedly caught between my aunt's prejudice and protecting Amir's dignity.

I tried to prolong our conversations on the porch but otherwise did not attempt to keep him out there. What else could I have done besides tell him baldly what Aunt Priscilla had said? When he wandered into the kitchen, I followed nervously. Happily, there was nothing to do there; we soon returned to the porch. That was where Aunt Priss found us chatting and laughing riotously when she came back downstairs, unable to stay away much longer without conveying shamefully bad manners or downright hostility.

Three weeks into my visit, I was ready to be on my way. Aunt Priss's anti-Black prejudices, particularly her reaction to Amir, were disappointing, and the novelty of life in New York was wearing off already, replaced by a growing and uncomfortable dissonance. I valued the newness, but some elements were severely discombobulating, translating into what most people in my position would feel: extreme culture shock, homesickness, loss of autonomy, and near desperation to return to Jamaica, far away from the breathtaking speed and jangling noises of New York; back to the familiar chaos of Papine, the little township near UWI where I often caught a bus home late at night or stopped in the market on Thursday or Friday afternoons; and to Mandeville, close to home and the first big town I ever visited, my hand tucked firmly in my father's. With all its contradictions and difficulties, and dispensing with some of its worst side effects of an oppressive history, Jamaica was home, with a particular magnet that would endure forever.

I decided I could survive in New York a little longer when I learned that a family I knew from my primary school days lived a block away on Remsen.

Miss Little, the matriarch, had run a small shop in Cross Keys where we sometimes bought candy or bulla cakes on our way to and from primary school. She was a higgler like Sa Bea, and they often rode the truck together to Coronation Market. At those times, Barb, her daughter, ran the shop. Her granddaughter, Sydonie, was my classmate and good friend at the new primary school I was transferred to. They connected me to her.

They looked, talked, and ate like me. Spending time with them tempered my debilitating homesickness. I ate oxtail and yellow yam from Miss Little's pot—no more spaghetti and meatballs with Italian sauce, thank you!—and joined Barb on frequent errands to Queens, Far Rockaway, and Long Island. As the sprawl grew less scary, I began taking the bus to Flatbush and the train to the Bronx to see Sydonie, who correctly insisted she would not pick me up; I had to learn the transportation system. I did, and New York opened further. We went to the Bronx Zoo, and I found my way to the Brooklyn Museum, less than half an hour away, and Kings Plaza Shopping Mall, where I identified things I would buy if I had money.

I saw much more of lower New York outside the densely populated boroughs and gained more realistic insights into the experience of immigrant communities than those I gleaned in my youth when people returned home to Old House and neighboring districts from the United States, Canada, or England. Then, it seemed they put on a determined show of affluence. They wore sharp new clothes advertising "foreign" from a mile away, loud, multicolored makeup, and jangling jewelry rounded off with accents so deep that it was often difficult to understand them. In New York, it slowly dawned on me that the visits home were these expatriates' only real opportunity to engage in the fantasy of life abroad as anything other than a grind—a profound daily struggle to make ends meet on uncertain schedules with employment agencies operating in smelly fourth-floor walk-ups with staircases strewn with trash and cigarette butts.

Vacation clothes could be bought on credit and paid for over time. Until New York, I had no concept of what a credit card was or that clothes could be bought on hire purchase like a bed or a stove. Sydonie let me in on the trick: some people habitually wore and returned clothes to the store after their trips abroad. I had no idea that could be done either.

Nothing of what I saw in the harried, uncertain lives of many of the people I met seemed like a persuasive reason to migrate, but I knew firsthand the difference their struggles made to communities back home. From their sacrifices, the pit latrines turned into flush toilets, children were going to school with lunch money, and old people were being taken care of at home instead of ending up in poorly kept faraway government infirmaries or on the "pauper roll." The coming-home show-and-tell was likely a much-needed respite from the tensions inherent in the choice to forge a life in a new country while taking care of another one abroad. Also, the culture expected it. Why leave home for a foreign country if life would not materially better there? Dressing to prove that point made things simpler than explaining how hard life was even in New York, and it left the hope door open that one day affluence could become a reality, even if the odds were as long as winning the lottery. In the meantime, clothes on credit bridged the gap.

My parents made different choices. They did not see migration as a route for them, and, somehow, I was making sufficient progress at the time of my visit not to see it as necessary for myself. I had beaten the odds and made it to UWI, and I was merely on vacation in New York. I was living in my aunt's guest room in her professionally decorated townhouse, reflecting the fastidious elegance for which she was known, and with just as careful attention paid to the small space outside.

Occasionally, when we ate together, we did so at the kitchen table, not in the formal dining room adjoining the living room. That room and the living room, with a plush, deep-rose-colored carpet, were off limits for anything other than cleaning furniture that was never used. Anchoring the living room was a stylish rose sofa a shade lighter than the carpet and a pair of exquisitely carved custom end tables with genuine Tiffany lamps on both sides. Materially, Aunt Priss was doing better than many of the people I encountered from the community. I was not surprised, and I confounded myself by being proud of her.

I wondered what that meant and whether I was not as resolutely socialist or egalitarian as I thought myself. Perhaps I was also possessed with the human need to be "better than"—sometimes, at least, or in relation to some people who I thought were big show-offs. Or perhaps the bonds of kinship were so strong that I simply wanted my aunt to do well, sans comparison to anyone; or it might have been a recognition of how well Mammy's children had done for themselves, given where they had started. Maybe it was some of everything.

Years later, I began to understand other potential layers to my aunt's warning not to open the door to Black men. The normalized fear of them as purveyors of violence was not peculiar to her, and the 1980s was a remarkably violent time in metro New York. Genuine concern or fear could have driven the directive she gave me. However, my perception of her did not derive from just one thing. It resulted from the spoken and unspoken prejudice I experienced while living in her house for six weeks. Just like Mammy, Aunt Priss was an amazing woman with many flaws. My brother once told me that I reminded him so much of both!

Eight years after that first trip to New York, I left Kingston again, this time for Washington, DC, to study for a year. I found no favor with the Fulbrighters, but the Inter-American Press Association recognized that my work in journalism was making an impact as intended and awarded me a fellowship because of it. It stipulated two semesters of study in the United States, not necessarily leading to a degree. I decided to pursue a master's degree at Howard University anyway, since I could complete it within a year.

In the interim, I visited New York one more time, among a small group of journalists accompanying the late Gordon "Butch" Stewart, Jamaica's leading hotelier, as he collected a global hospitality award at a gala event at the Loew's Hotel in Manhattan. He flew us back first-class aboard a rented Air Italia airplane operating as Air Jamaica, which he owned then. I had good legroom and another sneak peek into how the other side lives.

Two personal trips to South Florida also made the US a little more familiar. The pace, the expanse, and the chaos of big-city USA remained far from my normal tempo, but I felt drawn to the space as an intense cultural melting pot with far more room for cross-fertilization of ideas, relationships, and experiences than were available to me at home. Island culture was infinitely rich, but opportunities were limited in that small, stratified society, and a good deal of relationships percolated within rather than between social class and ethnic groups.

Eminent sociologist M. G. Smith, with his plural society thesis, succinctly captured this aspect of Jamaican and Caribbean life with his observation that we "mix but do not combine."[10] But growth often requires greater access and different environments beyond the narrow, comfortable confines into which we are born or our "assigned" spaces.

---

10 M.G. Smith (1965) posited that cultural, social, and/or racial differences and separateness were strong features of the society sustained by parallel institutions that did not overlap. The education system reflected this to a good degree, as previously described.

Cable television had come to Jamaica during that time; those huge, metallic "satellite dishes," once indicators of individual wealth and neighborhood affluence, were no longer the only access to overseas media. Suddenly, people with average budgets like me could afford an endless array of US programs, initially pirated by pioneering local individuals and sold to subscribers who knew nothing about international trade or intellectual laws as the government struggled to keep pace with the developments in broadcasting. The US eventually extracted conformation, which included licensing of operators and government oversight. Cable was formalized, and foreign programming became the norm.

I worried about the significant risks of distortion or erasure of the fragile native culture now absorbing exorbitant amounts of material from dominant cultures. I wanted desperately to preserve my own culture even as I yearned to experience others, but eventually I too was navigating between local and American programming, watching the *Today Show*, enjoying its multiculturalism, and believing that it was an authentic slice of America like I had seen in New York and South Florida.

The new service also brought America's ugly underbelly to the forefront, exposing the reality that fueled Baldwin's insatiable rage and haunted and inspired Martin Luther King's dreams. I watched the beating of Rodney King, an African American man, by Los Angeles police in 1991 and the riots that ensued when the four White officers, tried for using excessive force, were acquitted. Three years later, the O. J. Simpson case again exposed America's racial fault line. Simpson, forty-seven, a Black all-star football player, was arrested and charged with the murder of his wife, Nicole, a White woman, and her White companion, Ron Goldman, outside her home. His trial mesmerized the US and much of the world, with support and dissent starkly divided along racial lines. From the newsroom where I worked, I watched the verdict along with the entire staff after the monthslong trial. The whole newsroom cheered when it came back not guilty, except for one man, who remained motionless, his face flushed a deep red—a White Australian sports journalist who was temporarily working at the newspaper. In our own newsroom, across the sea, the racial divide was as stark as it could get.

But the verdict was not all about race. The Black jury did not simply let Simpson go because he was a Black man. The lead detective turned out to be a racist and was discredited for lying about his use of the word "n****r." Simpson's team also effectively cast doubt on the quality of the DNA, then an emerging tool in crime fighting. Finally, Simpson's attorney, Johnnie Cochran, rebuffed the prosecutors ill-fated attempt to link a glove found at the crime scene to the former NFL running back. As Simpson struggled to get his hand inside the glove, Cochran delivered the fatal blow to the prosecution's case: "If it doesn't fit, you must acquit," he said. The jury agreed.

Still, I thought studying in the US would enhance my work and understanding of a system of governance that, from the outside, appeared more effective than what Jamaica had. I wanted to advance my career with education rather than by connections and ever-present biases and use my knowledge to improve our systems, to the extent that I could. I was older, and I would not be living in my aunt's house. I also had my children to return to as a matter of urgency. I could survive two semesters unscathed by the racism America could not seem to shake.

I began studying at Howard University in August 1996, intrigued by what lay ahead amid the nation's most potent symbols of racism and the struggles against it.

CHAPTER FIVE

GREAT EXPECTATIONS

I rode the Red Line train from Glenmont Station in lower Montgomery County, Maryland, to Howard University most days for what turned out to be four and a half years as a student. I had finished my yearlong master's program with a deep sense of dissatisfaction that it was incomplete and intermediary in some regard. To truly benefit from the opportunity to study in the US, I needed further study, work experience, and more exposure to life outside the boundaries of Howard.

Providence was on my side, or so I thought. A Rotary Foundation scholarship I had applied for had been approved, but unbeknownst to me, the notice sat in Jamaica for almost a year. I retrieved it with just enough time to communicate my acceptance before the deadline expired. It provided generous funding and a support system for me to pursue doctoral studies. This meant extending my stay and allowing for new possibilities.

Rotary had one demand, however: I must leave Howard University and take up the scholarship elsewhere. There were too many complaints, they said, from previous scholars about Howard's challenging administrative processes and their dissatisfaction with the program overall.

This was not news to me. One scholarship recipient from South Africa had opted to return home rather than complete the program. I suspect she might have been one of the chief complainants. By then, too, a part of me yearned to experience US academia and its political and social constructs from other perspectives, but this required more effort and, even with my scholarship, more resources than I wanted to expend to relocate further north, especially since Boston University kept coming up from Rotary. I prevailed on them to let me remain at Howard and used the opportunity to bring my young daughters to the United States.

I wanted them to be with me because that was where they belonged, and I wanted them to experience life in a more cosmopolitan space. I also wished for them to experience school in the American system and explore parks, museums, and so much of what we either did not have in Jamaica or could not afford. Remaining at Howard gave me the latitude to do that and, with its large Caribbean community, reduced the sting of being away from home.

Living in the US revealed a lot of what we did not have relative to technology in Jamaica, for example. The internet was becoming popular and revolutionizing communication. I knew it was a harbinger of dramatic social changes; I was studying mass media and international politics and deconstructing the implications as the technology expanded into public use and consciousness. I also supervised the computer lab in the School of Communication and explored it at leisure. I thought it would be a useful tool for my children to master, allowing them to take these skills back home in three years when I finished my doctorate.

I spent my commute reading the *Washington Post*, preparing for classes, and sometimes absorbing the dynamics between fellow commuters. In those early days, I was struck by the absolute and disciplined lack of human interaction between people who sat with their bodies touching. The majority stared straight ahead, seemingly in an earnest effort not to acknowledge the person sitting next to them. This mode of transportation and the corresponding culture was light-years away from rural Jamaica, where we knew by name the few drivers who operated taxis or minivans from Cross Keys to Mandeville's town center. Often, we knew our fellow passengers too. Even in Kingston, one could become familiar with certain taxi drivers or conductors over time. Metro travel was nothing like that. It was a starkly cold, impersonal space and downright scary in the early days when I had to switch trains at Gallery Place and Chinatown at rush hour.

As a student at Howard, I found that race and racism assumed vastly more importance than they ever had, even with my long-standing interest in the subject and the Garvey scholarship. The subjects dominated my thoughts as I navigated my early life in the US. On the train, for example, I often wondered about the White person I sometimes sat beside. What were they feeling or thinking about a Black person sitting so close on those cozy two-person seats? Were they hardened enemies or passionate segregationists who would prefer I did not exist? Or were they a potential friend? How weird would they think I was if I attempted to start a conversation? Was I even thinking rationally or just being a victim of paranoia?

Even with the relative recency of the King and Simpson cases, race relations in the United States in the 1990s appeared better relative to the 1960s when Rosa Parks was jailed for not giving up her bus seat to a White male passenger in Montgomery, Alabama; when Black people, led by Martin Luther King Jr., Malcolm X, Kwame Ture, and others like them marched day and night for fundamental human rights in the United States. Both King and X would be murdered for their agitation for racial and social justice. This history was a constant refrain at Howard, the self-proclaimed repository of the Black experience in the United States. I could not easily forget, even if I wanted to. Watching the interactions among passengers on the train was an attempt to connect the college discourse with the reality of day-to-day life to some extent. At least Black and White people could sit next to each other. They did sometimes, however uncomfortably.

There was progress, but the US was not a happily integrated society. In DC, some areas of the city destroyed in the riots following Martin Luther King Jr.'s assassination in 1968 remained in a state of social and economic distress. Old burned-out or abandoned buildings were still part of the landscape, with several communities, including some close to Howard University, showing obvious signs of that long-term blight.

It took me a while to recognize that these were the equivalent of Kingston's ghettos, or close to them. While the physical characteristics differed, with comparatively better housing stock, for one, they were on the fringes of the broader society, trapped by intergenerational poverty, violence, and social exclusion much the same as the ghettos in Kingston. As was the case there, the inhabitants were poor and Black.

People mixed where necessary, like on the train, but peace was a facade that would hold only if each group stayed on their respective sides of the fence. It did not matter that segregation was no longer the law. The norms and mores with which people were comfortable dictated their behavior; much of it was self-segregation. A genuinely multiracial, multicultural society was clearly more aspirational than actual in the US as the twentieth century ended.

The mere existence of Howard, the nation's foremost historically Black university, amplified the reality of the racial divisions. Without a great racial divide—racial inequities and hostilities—why would separate universities and colleges for Black people exist?

I had chosen Howard because of its leadership role in the civil rights movement, which reflected sound ethical principles, courageous actions, and the foresight to correct morally reprehensible behavior. I expected a space where people were liberated from oppressive ideologies and practices. For me, that meant a community comfortable with multiculturalism as an antidote to Whiteness, White supremacy, anti-Black racism, misogyny, nativism, ethnocentricity, and all forms of oppressive ideology. After all, it had been practicing for almost a century and a half, and that would be entirely in alignment with Nelson Mandela's philosophy that freedom is not merely to cast off one's chains but to live in a way that respects and enhances the freedom of others. A genuinely multicultural space would also align with the views of novelist William Faulkner, who argued, "We must be free not because we claim freedom, but because we practice it."

Howard was not there yet. It was ethnically diverse due in large part to the presence of students from African and Caribbean countries. Otherwise, it was most striking as a homogeneous space where much of life was processed through the lens of anti-Black racism rather than broader oppressive philosophies and practices like classism, nativism, or sexism, which cuts across all races.

One of my earliest wake-up calls to the presence of nativism occurred during orientation week in my first year, when I had to attend a mandatory accent-reduction workshop. It could have been useful as awareness training because accents can be hard to understand, but the workshop was shockingly nativist in tone, suggesting that those of us from elsewhere could only be accepted to the extent that we could shed the markers of our "otherness," and accents were essential to that.

As if I were not incensed enough, the session soon morphed into anecdotes about people from Africa who did not shower or use toothpaste or deodorant, resulting in unpleasant body odors. I got the message: Black foreigners like me were not good enough. I needed to sanitize the signs of my primary identity if I wanted to be acceptable to Americans, even those at Howard University combating and challenging the same expectations and biases from White Americans.

It was the beginning of a more profound understanding that by moving to the United States, I was up against not only racism but also an incredibly nativist culture that presupposed the inferiority of immigrants from the Global South. Just like that, I had dropped further down on the scale of human value. Nativism was one form of marginalization I did not have to combat in Jamaica. I belonged.

In the ensuing years, I struggled to process rival feelings of comfort and discomfort in the same space.

The most striking thing, though, remained the stark Black and White divide in the US, embodied, significantly, by the institution that had become central to my life. Some of my new friends and colleagues did not always understand what I meant when I voiced surprise about how segregated life was until I started rattling off "Black neighborhoods and White neighborhoods; Black churches and White churches; Black schools and White schools; Black sororities and fraternities and White sororities and fraternities; White media and Black media," and on and on.

My outsider's eyes were wide and focused when I visited the NBC studios for a job interview shortly after I first arrived in DC in the fall of 1996. Six weeks prior, this had all seemed far away. It was my first professional engagement away from Howard, and it gave me an opportunity to see the historic Tenleytown neighborhood and compare it to the communities around the university. The unexpected trip also opened a window into greater America and the racial dynamics that were slowly unfolding.

The *Today Show* had long become the soundtrack to my morning routine as I prepared for work as the international news editor at the *Gleaner* in Kingston. The cast—Katie Couric, Bryant Gumbel, Matt Lauer, Al Roker, and Ann Curry—had great synergy. I talked and laughed with them, with no inkling that I would ever be anywhere close to their world. It was not, in fact, something I yearned for nor a possibility I considered. There was no such emotional investment. I simply liked the show as great morning entertainment combined with the utility of frequent news updates and appreciated the multicultural cast as a symbol of comfortable heterogeneity.

From deep in the belly of chance, my department chair at Howard prodded me to go to the studio and explore the possibility of working there for a semester, in response to a request from NBC. It represented too big of a chance for me not to be curious, excited even, about what it would be like to see inside or work with a high-profile global brand. I also knew this opportunity would shift me to an extra-high-value category when I returned to the news desk in Jamaica. Still, I hesitated. I did not desperately need the money or want to commit to a twenty-hour-a-week work schedule along with my studies. I was more invested in completing my degree and returning home to my career and my family. I explained at length.

"Just go," she said, with a gentle pat on my shoulder. "We want them to know that we have qualified people we can send."

I did not quite understand, but she was older and kind to everyone—one of those individuals with a deep sense of humanity that I would meet at Howard—and part of me was intrigued by this unexpected collision between a distant, mediated world that had long been a source of fascination for me and this opportunity to experience it as reality. I also processed that she was more invested in me representing the school than in me getting the internship. I acquiesced.

So it was that my first professional engagement outside of Howard University was an interview with the National Broadcasting Company, one of the world's premier media organizations.

The BBC 8 a.m. newscast of my childhood, my political science classes at UWI, my work as a reporter and foreign news editor at the *Gleaner*, and my daily *Today Show* routine made for easy conversation with the HR manager, a warm, comforting African American woman, likely in her forties.

I did not see through her little ploy at first as she asked questions and pretended to forget the names of important people and places, allowing me to fill them in—names like Benjamin Netanyahu, the new Israeli prime minister; Chancellor Helmut Kohl of Germany; and President Alberto Fujimori of Peru. It was all in a day's work for me. She found it impressive, as she did my "unflappable" demeanor.

"You would be great for the newsroom," she said, assuring me the internship would allow me to work there or in the advertising department.

When I told her I was interested only in the newsroom, she flipped, discouraging it because I was overqualified, which might make the reporters uncomfortable. This was my first experience with a human resources professional in the US and the fine line they straddle between truth and something that only resembles it. It would not be my last.

"The unions would be here before you can say what!" she said.

Again, I found myself not entirely understanding an explicit comment. I was very much in Jamaican mode with little context for the American workplace. Why wouldn't they be happy to have an overqualified person as an intern? Would it not be to their advantage that I knew my work well? What was it about hiring me to work for a semester on a school program that could potentially trigger an adverse union response?

I was curious enough this time to ask for clarification.

"If we bring in people like you as interns, the argument could be made that we could potentially replace the whole newsroom with interns and pay them much less than our staff. Reporters would not be comfortable with that," she explained.

Ted Koppel, host of ABC's *Nightline*, put it slightly differently when I interviewed with him sometime later for a fellowship established in honor of Lionel Chapman, an African American producer who had died suddenly in 1997.

"You are coming out of Kingston already well prepared. I do not see what this internship would do for you. Plus, the guys are going to have a hard time asking you to get the coffee."

Koppel was genial and respectful. He loved the application essay I had written about *Nightline*. Following the interview, he allowed me to stay with him in his studio while he interviewed the former leader of a guerrilla group involved in the Bosnian War.

It was an insightful and pleasant sojourn with one of the public affairs titans of the time. Had I known better, I would have tried harder to convince Ted that while I was well prepared, I could use the experience as a bridge from Kingston to the American newsroom, and I certainly would not have minded making the coffee. It might have looked like a step back compared to where I was then, but it would have been a considerable step up relative to some things I had done to survive in the past. I have never discounted the dignity of honest work, no matter how menial, and I still do not. The clarity came after years of hindsight. Ted waved me on with a confident prediction.

"You are going to do something great with your life," he said. "I will be on the lookout for you."

I think of him with a sigh whenever I feel like I have fallen short in important ways.

I loved the adrenaline rush of the newsroom. My mission in media resided there and nowhere else. I could not even feign an interest in advertising, the corporate money-making side of the news business, to the NBC HR manager. I recognized its importance but saw it as belonging to a fundamentally different lane than my own. I did not say as much, but I did not need to.

The manager treated me to a tour of the facility, including the set of the *Today Show* and the newsroom, after the interview. Like my old one in Kingston, there was an intense buzz in the room, with dozens of people entirely absorbed in whatever part of the business lay in their purview—chasing news, gathering it, packaging it, and tossing it back into the world. People were conferring and hurrying back and forth with a great sense of purpose and urgency. White people.

Other than the woman with me, I did not see another Black person or minority. Notions of a sophisticated, multiracial organization soon went up in flames. Howard University was less than twenty minutes away, and the law school at the university's Van Ness campus was just five minutes away, but there was barely a Black presence at the leading broadcasting studio.

I was not overly disappointed when I did not hear back, but in the days and weeks following, I occasionally wondered what it would have been like to work in a newsroom that was as White as Howard University was Black. Over time, I realized that each institution explained why the other existed to some degree.

My growing awareness of the lingering segregation in Washington, DC, also helped me understand Howard's preoccupation with race and the contradictions of a society stubbornly holding on to worthless or problematic ideas about humanity. I was at Howard in part because of my own apprehension about anti-Black racism in the US, but I did not believe that a racially liberating environment had to be a racially homogeneous or exclusive space, purposely or accidentally.

I believed social progress meant a cross-fertilization of ideas and people coalescing around needs and interests without consideration of race—that I would find many more nonracist White, Hispanic, and Asian people among a diverse student body. After all, White supremacy is an ideology, not a race or skin color. Black people can be White supremacists too, and many of them are, and not every White person is a White supremacist. Skin color does not ideology reveal.

The professional schools were more racially and ethnically diverse, but there was no obvious overriding philosophy or praxis of liberation outside the opposition to White American racism. Plus, what existed too often excluded Blacks outside of the African American community. I hoped for a grander, more expansive vision of freedom and human dignity, untethered from the paradigm of the plantation. But even some senior administrators openly referred to the institution as a plantation. Corresponding to that, I learned the expression HNIC, or "head n****r in charge," there. It is a term used to ridicule Black people who manifest the same slave-master syndrome they decry in White people.

A colleague, an accomplished African American woman, introduced it to me one morning after an unpleasant interaction with a senior administrator, whom she met on the elevator in his office building. She greeted him by his title and name, followed by a quick "How are you?" He screamed at her, angrily reminded her of his status, and instructed her never to speak to him unless he spoke to her first. It was a potent demonstration of an ingrained belief in hierarchy; devotion to authoritarian ideas and structures that support it, and an ethos that is oppressive and disrespectful of those without the kind power possessed by those at the top.

Central to the culture was a pecking order serving one essential purpose on the plantation: to communicate that the worth of an individual was proportionate to their place in that order, however it was attained. This was codified in titles held by individuals without regard for the fact that, quite often, the primary qualification was loyalty to individuals and the system and privileges they wanted to preserve, however unhelpful. Those principles and ways of relating to the world mimicked White supremacy and seemed out of alignment with the institution's vision and mission.

I try not to fixate on people purely because of their appearance, so I did not just like Bryant Gumbel because of his appearance. I thought he was effortlessly smart, professional, likable, and an excellent foil for the rest of the cast, which was part of the *Today Show*'s appeal—the dynamism of diverse peoples interacting in a space where race was not a dominant factor in how they related to it.

But when Howard University announced Gumbel as the 2001 commencement speaker after I completed my PhD, I was ambivalent about the choice. Like many of my colleagues who had labored to complete the arduous requirements for a terminal degree, I felt that we deserved Secretary of State Colin Powell or some academic leader of great standing.

Then Gumbel spoke with raw vulnerability and forthrightness about what he thought mattered most in life: true love, friendship, family, loyalty, good health—the simple but profound things we are too often inclined to take for granted in pursuit of status, fame, and money. By the time he began his gentle admonition not to lose ourselves in the quest to achieve material things, the class was in tears. I sent him a thank-you note. He sent me the original text of his speech, which he wrote himself, complete with his markups. I still have it.

I took the satisfaction of becoming Grace Virtue, PhD, along with my life experiences to date, aspirations for future impact, Gumbel's imminently sensible advice, and the sweetness with which he delivered it, into my first job after graduation: a consultancy with a small nonprofit that had received a large grant from the Ford Foundation to fund anti-oppression work relative to the United Nations' fourth World Conference against Racism, Racial Discrimination, Xenophobia and Related Intolerance (WCAR), scheduled for Durban, South Africa, in September 2001.

I was tasked with gathering information from members of marginalized groups in Africa, Asia, Europe, South and Central America, and the Caribbean for a publication intended to force attention on the myriad ways in which bigotry and oppression existed around the world, condemning too many individuals and groups to a painfully marginalized existence for issues that were outside their control and had no bearing on their humanity. The goal, ultimately, was to support the conference's vision to "shape and embody the spirit of the new century, based on the shared conviction that we are all members of one human family."

The project was as intense as the goal was auspicious. It represented a pivotal moment, a bridge between my life in Jamaica at the intersection of classism, racism, and sexism—and nativism, once I moved to the United States—and this much bigger world where people were suffering for those and many other reasons. The experience was illuminating from my very first interview with Oliver, an activist from San Andrés. This small, English-speaking Island—a protectorate of Colombia—is located off the coast of Nicaragua in Central America. Islanders known as Raizales numbered about 25,000 then and are predominantly Black descendants of formerly enslaved Africans taken there by British Protestants in the seventeenth century.

Life on San Andrés appeared to mimic many of the sights and sounds of Jamaica. Prior to the project, I was ignorant of the island's existence, but they were fully aware of Jamaica. Oliver expressed a general and deeper affinity to us and the broader Caribbean than to Colombia, where Raizales were separated by race, language, and culture and treated as second-class citizens by the government. He was attending the conference to find a platform for his concerns and to seek protected status for the group that was rapidly being outnumbered by Colombians descending on the island in search of economic opportunities. He felt that the growing population from the mainland threatened their status as Indigenous citizens of San Andrés as well as the island's designation as a protected space by the United Nations.

Another interviewee, an Arawak woman from Guyana, was a reluctant warrior forced into activism by the sheer magnitude of the disadvantages facing her people in that South American nation. They were at the bottom of the pile, living in communities deep in the Amazon rainforest, physically separated from the center of life and socially, economically, and politically on the margins of society. They needed food, soap, and blood because in times of medical emergency, people died from lack of access to blood.

A Dalit from India was committed to the death in the fight against his country's caste system on behalf of approximately 240 million people. Dalits, or untouchables, he said, were regarded as so inferior that they existed *outside* India's rigid four-tiered caste system, suitable only for menial tasks like cleaning toilets or collecting trash. A Dalit's shadow crossing the path of someone from a higher caste could result in a limb being severed as punishment. Some of the harsher punishments had diminished, but they still occur.

An anthropologist from St. Lucia was engaged in a dual battle for slavery reparations for Black people and freedom from discrimination against his ethnic group. He was a Carib, part of an Indigenous group that fiercely resisted European colonization. He beseeched me to understand what life had been like for him in the Caribbean.

My mind went straight to my third-grade reading book, where the Caribs were described as fierce and warlike cannibals and the Arawaks, or Taíno, who were annihilated by the Spaniards, as gentle and quiet. The anthropologist turned that bit of history on its head and helped focus my attention on how narratives are manufactured for certain purposes but do not necessarily have any bearing on truth or reality.

I finished the project with a greater consciousness of contemporary liberation struggles worldwide, a sense of commiseration with those trying to dismantle and transform oppressive systems and culture, and an urgency and imperative to remain on the side of the oppressed—to resist, whether the oppressors were individual actors like Ubel, the man who terrorized my family in my early childhood, or historical or political structures inimical to the dignity of people without political or economic power. The intent of this conference seemed closer to Dr. King's Beloved Community than other organizations' typical narrow focus on race; it was what I had initially expected to find at Howard. The world still begs for structures and space to tackle the wide scope of oppression, with less focus on dueling notions of victims and perpetrators and more on the need to eradicate it as far as possible, in whatever form it appears.

Weeks later, I landed another exciting job offer in the rural development unit at the World Bank—a good place to potentially make a difference in communities like Old House. It would have meant heading to Nepal immediately ahead of a high-level delegation from the unit. I salivated at what it would signify beyond simply having money to take care of my children, but Immigration and Naturalization Services said it would take at least thirty days to complete the paperwork to change my status from a student to an H-1B worker. The bank moved on. I marinated in the bitter taste of a much-desired opportunity going up smoke. The fire that followed burned the US, scorched the world, and shaped the trajectory of my life in the US, as it did many others.

A semester teaching at Bowie State University in Maryland, a historically Black college, was the next best thing. That was where I was on the morning of September 11, 2001. My 8 a.m. class, scheduled to end at 9:30, was winding down when a breathless Mary Lampe, the dean's assistant, arrived to tell me the president wanted the student body in the auditorium.

"Our country is under attack!" she said urgently, in response to my nonchalance.

I dismissed the class five minutes early and ran toward my office, stopping to watch a nearby TV as CNN replayed images of two planes—suddenly looking like sleek monsters slicing through the air—crashing into the World Trade Center, turning the towers into a colossal ball of red flames and black smoke. In time, we learned than nineteen men from Saudi Arabia had hijacked four airplanes, two of which were used to launch a daring attack in New York. A third crashed into the Pentagon in Washington, DC, and the fourth, believed to have been destined for the White House, crashed in a field in Pennsylvania after passengers overpowered the hijackers.

Life became harder after that. Hostilities raged against not just Muslims in the United States but against all immigrants—and especially people on student visas, after it was falsely reported for a long time that the hijackers were all Saudi nationals in the US on those same visas. Reports revealed later that only one of the hijackers came to the US on a student visa.

The broad-brushing included people like me, a powerless, vulnerable pacifist repulsed by the idea of killing people for any reason and constantly working to extend that care to the breadth of the animal kingdom. I was learning, though, that it was one thing to be Black in the US and a whole other issue to be Black and an immigrant from the Third World. To many, this automatically translates to being third-rate humans with third-rate mental and social capacity, and deserving only of third-rate treatment. Any kind of difference is interpreted not just as evidence of inferiority but as deviance. This thought process is interwoven with White supremacy and American exceptionalism: the idea that White people are superior, America and Americans are the center of the universe, and all others are satellites, subsidiaries, or subordinates. The attack on America had compounded the existing challenges and made it much harder for those of us looking for jobs and requiring sponsorship.

A professional connection, a member of Howard's venerable Board of Trustees, recommended me for a communications job at my alma mater. Five months after 9/11, with much of the country still shell shocked and angry at immigrants, I was offered a full-time position. I seized the opportunity with both hands and embarked on a new journey, seeing the institution from different angles.

After my years as a student there, I already knew it was a comfortable place for Black people as far as racism is concerned. The institution's role in the civil rights movement was evoked constantly, a reminder of its own claim to greatness, of the sacrifices made by others, and of how life and career choices should be motivated less by the need to profit at the expense of fellow human beings and more by our desire to serve.

Every law school graduate knows, for example, that a lawyer is either a social engineer or a parasite on society, a belief that speaks to the need for education that serves the common good and for the educated to be people of character who will do more than uphold oppressive norms. Equally, medical students know that their duty is to serve underserved communities and to do so in the most holistic way possible, seeing their patients as full humans like themselves, to whom they owe a duty of care beyond their medical training. The faculty, which reflected genuine racial and cultural diversity, largely consisted of committed and good examples of professionalism and warm, embracing humanity.

Recognizing the difference between performative posturing and actualizing a glorious vision seemed more of a heavy lift for administrators. When I became a staff member, they became my primary contacts, exposing me to their thinking, idiosyncrasies, work habits, and lack of worldview alignment.

They valued my work, but they were surprisingly keen adherents to their own exceptionalism, regardless of any evidence to the contrary. My Blackness as a Caribbean native was certainly measured differently from that of African Americans, with varying degrees of acceptance. Some administrators did not want women who looked "too Afrocentric"—those who wore dreadlocks or braids—in public-facing positions, for example. This was at a time when professional Black women were fighting for the right to wear their natural styles on the job rather than being forced to chemically change their hair. Those biases were present at Howard too.

So was colorism. There was a preference for lighter-skinned people among sections of the community. This was not new. In fact, campus lore says Franklyn Jenifer, the university's fourteenth president, faced substantial pushback because he was thought to be too Black to serve as the institution's chief executive officer. The first Howard alumnus to serve as president, Jenifer had been only the fourth Black person appointed president of the nation's premier HBCU, and the darkest. He was ousted after only four years at Howard and went on to serve as president at the University of Texas at Dallas for eleven years!

Understanding the thinking of university leadership helped me realize why African or Caribbean scholarship and personalities did not feature prominently in institutional narratives. Marcus Garvey, in whose Pan-Africanist advocacy some scholars situate the Harlem Renaissance, did not show up. Neither did Claude McKay, Achebe, Ngũgĩ, or Senghor. Not even Walter Rodney, whose seminal work, *How Europe Underdeveloped Africa*, was the first to be published by the Howard University Press in 1972 and remained its bestseller until the press closed in 2010, had a place of eminence at this major Black institution. Yet the work remains a staple in development studies in and about the Global South.

As a still recent humanities graduate and a senior member of Howard's communication team, I wanted to do some things differently. I quietly designed a portfolio of activities, soliciting the support of interested departments and the Ralph J. Bunche International Affairs Center, to create spaces for academic discussions relevant to the African diaspora and advance, be it ever so slightly, a Pan-Africanist approach to Black experience, Black culture, and Black scholarship. At the least, I could broaden the definition of Blackness and Black experience in the world.

The year 2005 would mark the twenty-fifth anniversary of Rodney's assassination in Georgetown, Guyana, a cataclysmic event for the Black diaspora in the Global South, at least, and to UWI. Rex Nettleford, alive and well in the Caribbean, assumed similar stature in many ways. Awarded the Rhodes Scholarship in 1957 and going on to study at Oriel College, Oxford University, Nettleford was one of four prominent scholars worldwide to receive a doctor of civil law, honoris causa, from the Rhodes Foundation as part of its centenary celebration in 2003. In addition, he was awarded thirteen other honorary degrees from universities worldwide, yet he had never been invited to Howard in any capacity, even though students from the Caribbean typically made up the second-largest ethnic group after African Americans.

Despite my feelings about the origin of the scholarships and who they were named for, I recognized they remained a significant measure of academic achievement, which Howard respected enormously, judging by how intensely its own two student recipients up to that point—Carla Joy Peterman in 1999 and Maria Ofosu in 2003—were marketed. Mark Alleyne, a third, received the scholarship in 1986 but was not usually included because he was Barbadian. That Nettleford was also from the Caribbean explained the disinterest in his work and ideas, despite the regard in which he was held by the foundations and the academic community worldwide.

Working with a small and dedicated committee of professors, and later student volunteers, I planned a three-day conference to examine Rodney's legacy in the global Black diaspora, including Jamaica, where he was declared persona non grata in 1968 for his activism on behalf of the Black working class. This conference was also an opportunity to examine the progress and continued problems facing these same communities globally, and I knew no one could do that as well as Nettleford. I wanted to bring him to the university. A major tertiary goal was to place a noteworthy academic event on the university calendar, where the annual homecoming so often dominated attention and typically brought negative media attention, not only because it reinforced negative perceptions among many but also because of the predictable skirmishes that turned into shootings at events "near Howard University"—a constant source of frustrations for those charged with protecting its image. I liked the energy of the annual Yard Fest: the pounding drums, the rhythm of students stepping on the yard, and the colorful booths with handmade jewelry or jerk chicken each year, but I too found the obsession with homecoming an unserious representation of what an academic institution ought to be, especially one that served the constituency Howard had staked out as its own: those underserved in education, health care, housing, transportation, and every facet of American life begging for serious research, public discourse, and advocacy.

Mission accomplished on all three fronts.

Several professors who participated said the conference was the best in their recollection at the institution, which in some cases spanned over thirty years. There was no interest from the senior administration in meeting or welcoming Nettleford or the other visiting senior academics from the University of the West Indies in Jamaica, the University of Guyana, Brown University, Syracuse University, or the University of California, Los Angeles, who participated. I was not surprised, just more certain of the institution's insularity and the narrowness of the definition of both diaspora and liberation.

A formidable orator, Nettleford dazzled as usual during the opening evening of the conference, and the next day I had the pleasure of spending one glorious hour with him on a meandering walk from the Blackburn University Center on the main campus to the accounting department on Tenth Street and back. We talked about our lives as dark-skinned Black people from humble circumstances in Jamaica, navigating spaces unintended for people like us, clinging to our essential selves, and dedicating ourselves to advocating for others like us the best way we could. Among other nuggets of wisdom, he shared how he never allowed people to label him, nor did he label himself, because to do so would constrain him in ways he never wanted to be. Our perspectives were aligned, and it made my heart sing.

My finest moment came when the dean of the College of Fine Arts, who had served on the committee, met me in the faculty lounge at the Blackburn Center about two weeks later and asked, "How much of your money did you put in the conference?"

"Why do you ask?" I countered.

"Because everything was so good, I knew you had to have put some of your own money in it."

I learned a lot at Howard—about the necessity of justice as an ideal and, ultimately, how difficult it is to achieve without deliberate effort, selflessness, a deep and expansive view of humanity far beyond what is in our best personal interest or that of our tribe, and a commitment to unvarnished truth. In the thirteen and a half years I spent there, I learned much about the importance of distinguishing between the immutable reality of race and skin color and cultural differences or learned behavior. I learned about the insidiousness and intentionality of racism; the normalized oppression of non-White people in the United States over more than three centuries; and how minority communities have been traumatized, disenfranchised, and disadvantaged as a result, just like the Black population in Jamaica. Confoundingly, the institution was both a manifestation of the importance of social justice, the rejection of bigotry, and the diversity of human experience, and a contradiction of those principles.

In my view, social justice, including racial justice, should be a goal of higher education that cannot and should not be predicated upon segregation or exclusion of other races, whether de facto or de jure, but instead on the belief that people can and should live and work together comfortably and productively with no greater or lesser weight being placed on skin color, ethnicity, or any other variable over which people have no control. This is what liberation from White supremacy means. It also means that, broadly speaking, race as an attribute ought not to be converted into currencies of power for some and a disadvantage for others. Otherwise, society remains trapped in a never-ending dogfight, and multiculturalism will be nothing more than ticking a time bomb with the ever-present promise of implosions to come.

Oliver Otis Howard, the White Union general who started Howard University and whose daughters were among its first graduates, had a vision of a genuinely multicultural, anti-oppressive institution. It withered in part because of a population's desperate need to protect itself from White supremacy. It has been an incubator for many positive changes that should continue to evolve because a social justice agenda cannot mean reengineering systems of oppression to benefit a different group of people, even if they were previously marginalized.

Rather, it should mean a deconstruction and dismantling of oppressive ideologies and the apparatuses that support them. It should also mean reconceptualizing personal and organizational power as the capacity to implement change that, one, is liberating for all its constituents and, two, attempts to reconcile the conflicts inherent in spaces intended to be safe for a racially oppressed group but by virtue of their culture or construct are themselves exclusive or oppressive of other groups. It also requires a less narrowly defined understanding of oppression and liberation and universal respect in everyday interactions. This perspective requires expansive self-assessment, but that was not a part of the calculus then. The social climate now makes it more necessary, more urgent, and vastly more difficult.

In surprising ways, Howard reminded me of Old House. We were comfortable in our folkways because they made sense in the context of our lives. There was value in the simplicity, in being deeply rooted in a physical, psychological, and cultural space and grounded in some enduring values of faith, family, and community. Despite some less palatable aspects, these spaces still hold sentimental value to me.

It was also true that a good deal of our acceptance of life stemmed from the limitations imposed by circumstances outside our control. We knew little of what else existed. That protected us to some extent, but progress necessitates new experiences regardless of our fears and uncertainties.

CHAPTER SIX
HOPE AND CHANGE?

The weight of the anti-racism conference faded over time, but the principles stayed with me. Occasionally, the participants and their struggles still crept into my consciousness as my interest in oppressive structures deepened. Working for the university president—and his executives to a lesser extent—as principal writer and researcher deepened my understanding of the African American experience and how it differs from that of Black people in the Caribbean. Where our experience was horribly inhumane and psychologically debilitating, some level of real freedom came after emancipation. Many planters fled to Europe and the formerly enslaved to the hills to eke out a living without a whip over their backs. Freedom for African Americans came a generation later, and still it was not full freedom. Segregation was soon legalized, and with it normalized discrimination and cruelty.

One small but meaningful assignment was writing a biography of Walter Washington, the first Black mayor of Washington, DC, for the *Legal Times*. Washington had been a year into his tenure as the District's first and only mayor-commissioner when Dr. King was assassinated, and to him fell the responsibility of managing the fallout. His determination that no more blood would be shed put him on a collision course with FBI director J. Edgar Hoover, who wanted him to shoot looters and rioters on sight. Washington was adamant. "Sir, we cannot build a nation on a river of blood!" he said.

I had not heard of him before, and a mix-up in the president's scheduling office resulted in my having only a few hours to write the article for half the tabloid's page. I locked myself in my office and, with the help of the internet, delved into the assignment, carried along by the smart, engaging personality I discovered through material written about Washington during his tenure. The article appeared in the *Legal Times* on schedule with not a word changed or a comma added. The same thing happened when I wrote a *Brown v. Board of Education* fiftieth anniversary commemorative op-ed for *Currents*, the premier publication for CASE (the Council for Advancement and Support of Education), under the president's name.

From my earliest sojourn, I had been adding value—strategizing on crisis communication for both the university and the hospital in some instances, backstopping self-study reports, developing standards, advising, and working on issues outside of my purview so much so that a high-level administrator acknowledged that if I were not there, they would have had to hire consultants to do much of the work I did. Yet I was not advancing sufficiently relative to my contributions and ability and earned only professional minimum wage, just enough to keep a roof over our heads in the Maryland suburbs as my children were coming of age and needed more support. Truth is, I was doing good work, but I was not the prototype of a Howard administrator.

I did not, among other differences, attempt to shake off the markers of primary identity, because I did not want to, and I did not see why I should at an institution like Howard. Where race did not identify me as different, my accent did, and I do not mean that I spoke Patwa; it was standard Jamaican English. I simply did not attempt to sound more "American" because I was not. This meant no matter how well I performed, I was still a third-rate human being and not deserving to reap generously of the fruit of my labor like others.

The view of Black people from Africa and the Caribbean as inferior was not universal. There were faculty and some administrators who were loving, immensely respectful, and protective of us, but among others, it was as embedded as resentment of Whiteness. These and corresponding assumptions explain why a supervisor once asked me to use my voodoo to remove a spirit from an office she thought was haunted.[11] It also explains why a colleague once laughed at me when she saw me warming my milk in the microwave. "Oh, that's such a Third World thing," she exclaimed derisively.

She did not know that in my earliest days, my milk came straight from Uncle Alvin's cow—not from cartons bought at the grocery store. My parents knew that scalding, or bringing the milk to a slow boil, was necessary to kill bacteria from the cow or transmitted in the process of extracting it. An offshoot of that is that culturally, many people from circumstances like mine prefer warm milk without consideration of necessity. It saw her attempt at a put-down as a symbol of ignorance and a metaphor for the lack of cultural competence prevalent in many workplaces.

I knew these small ways in which I was "different" accounted for some of the tensions I experienced at Howard, particularly in relation to the administration. Since it was all anchored in mindless biases, I laughed at them, but I was cognizant of the ways in which they were hurting me, and I was disappointed that this was a part of my experience at Howard.

I longed every day to return to Jamaica, but I wanted to set my girls up for success and help them figure out their next move much the same way I had done a few years previously when it was time for high school.

Schools had come a long way since "separate but equal," yet the data I found was incontrovertible: Predominantly Black schools in the District of Columbia were failing by all designated standards. Schools with mixed demographics were in the middle. The predominately White schools in wealthy suburbs were the best, consistently scoring the highest on the standardized tests and graduation rates. The so-called elite colleges then used the scores to filter out Black and Brown children, contentedly reinforcing cycles of privilege and inequity. Despite some exceptions, the

---

11 Voodoo: an amalgamation of African diasporic religions that began in Haiti in the sixteenth century. The use of rituals to cast or cast out spells is common to voodooism. It is practiced in a limited way in Jamaica, but the author has no association with it.

organization of the education system was connected to income, and race by extension, with the most adverse outcomes for people who happened to be poor and non-White. It intensified my distaste for the system and those who perpetuated it under the guise of professional competence.

The advantage I sought for my children meant finding ways to circumvent systemic biases and deficiencies. I enrolled my older daughter at a private Catholic school in Maryland. I had my younger daughter tested for the gifted and talented program in Montgomery County Public Schools in middle school. Her success resulted in a seamless transfer from the humanities magnet program at Eastern Middle School to Richard Montgomery High School in Rockville, which consistently ranked in the top five high schools in the country. Within those overall excellent schools, issues of race, inequality, and the disadvantages faced by immigrant children, particularly those for whom English was a second language, would become clear to me as well. I realized that a template was firmly in place, and unless the creators were convinced that change was necessary, it would remain that way.

I knew things would not change for us. My best hope for my children, and increasingly to make remaining in the US worth it for us, was to navigate the system as best I could to get the most out of it. It would be a challenging process but a triumphant one as well. My daughters, ultimately, did well in a system not designed with them in mind and matriculated into some of America's best universities.

Against that background of an ever-evolving understanding of the depths of racism, in 2007, I had no sense of the United States as progressive enough to elect a Black man as president anytime soon. But then rumors began to swirl about Illinois state senator Barack Obama possibly running for office in 2008.

The language around issues of multiculturalism was condescendingly about tolerance—as if the fate of oppressed people depended solely on the benevolence of the powerful "tolerating" those they considered weaker, inferior, or just failing to measure up in some way to the default setting of Whiteness and the corresponding superstructures of Western society that are inseparable from it.

Tolerance, of course, connotes the unequal power relationships at the heart of the problem, in contrast to the value of respect, for example, or the need for equity and justice. Framing the issue in terms of tolerance made me profoundly uneasy. I did not care for anyone "tolerating" me then in the same way I do not care for them "including" me now. A thoughtless, superficial shift in semantics does not seem like a difference-maker to me. I remain fixated on the message that someone has the power to decide whether to tolerate me or not—to include me or not.

Three years prior, in 2004, Obama had made an indelible impression on the nation's consciousness as the keynote speaker at the Democratic National Convention, when he introduced then senator John Kerry as the nominee for the presidential election later that year.

I remember being mesmerized by Obama's magnetism. His unlikely story as the son of an African man born in a shack in Kenya and a White woman from Kansas and his rare status as a Black senator was spellbinding already. His audacious decision to run for president was one more reason to admire him; yet I wondered if he was running to make a statement, the way some Black activists of the past, like Jesse Jackson and Al Sharpton, had done, or if he was running to win. He was endearing, but even with his brilliant cameo at the convention, we still knew Sharpton and Jackson much better than we did him, and he would have to deal with racism.

The buzz grew louder. Then, in the fall of 2007, he came to Howard as the keynote speaker at the opening convocation. Suddenly the event was restricted, and the tickets for 1,500 seats in Cramton Auditorium became a hot commodity. I fought to get one for my older daughter so she could witness in person this man plotting to make history with so many odds stacked against him.

She sat in the front row, snapping pictures as he sat on the platform a few feet from her and later while he stood at the podium for his address. He was an electrifying presence as he promised to prioritize criminal justice reform, among other concerns. His platform resonated with an audience that was no stranger to the inequities in the justice system.

Slowly and deliberately, he reeled them in, denting the reservation that some people had about his lack of street cred within the community: he was biracial, attended Ivy League schools instead of HBCUs, and grew up in Hawaii and Indonesia. He earned himself a five-star rating and got the momentum he came for.

By early 2008, Obamamania was in full swing. Amid the intensifying euphoria, my esteemed trustee friend strolled into my office one day in early to mid-spring. He was successful enough to become a member of the Howard University Board of Trustees, or part of the godhead, and was well connected among many prominent African Americans. A veteran of the civil rights movement, he was thoroughly imbued with the rebel spirit of his Jamaican and African ancestors and inspired by the Black Power movement of the 1960s—hence my shock at his unhappiness over Obama's meteoric rise, surging poll numbers, and the increasing possibility that we might see a Black president in our lifetime.

"Mi nah drink de Kool-Aid, you know, Grace," he said in a tone that conveyed perplexity, disappointment, and agitation. "Mi nah drink it all. Mi nah drink it all."

Mutual friends had introduced us, and he had recommended me for the communications job when the university was about to launch its first capital campaign. Qualification, or even the fact that I was a recent graduate, fundamentally did not matter. I needed that personal connection, and he was it. He made a habit of stopping by my office in the old Howard Hotel whenever he was on campus for board meetings or other events, and I looked forward to the camaraderie. We talked in Patwa, laughed hard, got food from Negril, and caught each other up on Jamaican and American current affairs, politics, and whatever.[12]

I thoroughly enjoyed that my office was a place that colleagues

---

12   Negril is a Jamaica restaurant near Howard University named for one of the island's popular resort areas.

treated as a little center of deep conversations about what needed to be constructed, deconstructed, or reconstructed at Howard or in society generally. International students stopped by in search of assistance or advice, typically on their immigration status or how to find scholarships or other forms of financial aid, or purely for support and encouragement.

By the time my trustee friend visited, the Obama campaign had overtaken everything else as a topic of conversation. Those who stopped by, native and foreign-born alike, were equal parts wary and hopeful as Obama's stealth campaign seemed set to derail that of the widely presumptive nominee, Hillary Clinton. For so long, everyone had assumed she would be the nominee. Psychologically, we had been preparing for the prospect of America's first woman president. Very few had in mind an equally or more exciting scenario playing out. Hopes, loyalties, fears, gender and racial justice, and just plain wonderment collided.

My friend had significant personal reasons to be concerned. He was a Clinton supporter, close to her campaign, and confident he would have a meaningful place in her administration if she prevailed. That coupled with the fact that he did not think Obama, whose name was as unrelatable as his exotic heritage, could win was a source of severe distress as the campaigns charged ahead.

For him, Obama had no apparent connection to the civil rights movement, even though he would have been young at its peak. Neither was he publicly part of any national institutions binding African Americans together. While his wife was Black—a real sistah—she too had shunned the HBCUs in favor of double Ivy League degrees from Princeton and Harvard. So, even though Obama had already torn through Super Tuesday, my friend was concerned that if he won the nomination, it would result in a throwaway election for the Democrats and a waste for the Black community.

"Grace," he said, imploring me to understand why he could not throw his support behind the erudite legal scholar seriously threatening to smash through the paradigm of Whiteness. "Hillary can do far more for Black people than Obama, even if he wins the election. American racism will not allow Obama to do anything for Black people. Black people are mistaken if they think he can."

By then, I had lost all reservations. Obama was clearly the best candidate of the entire campaign, and his multicultural background, personal magnetism, and the newness he brought were highly persuasive. The internet was now ubiquitous, and the rational part of the country was beginning to transform the anger from September 11 into a desire to know the rest of the world better—a world that Obama's hybridity represented. I tried to sell my friend on his many fine qualities over his persistent objections.

"If he gets the nomination, I will support him," he finally said to my great relief, because I could not imagine a Jamaican like him not supporting the first Black man with a serious chance of becoming the nominee for the Democratic Party and winning the presidency. "I would have to, but I am not ready to drink the Kool-Aid just yet."

That conversation would play over and over in my head years later as I watched the campaigns of Kamala Harris, Corey Booker, and Julián Castro in the 2020 presidential campaign. It seemed they were too often trading on identity—comfortable that race or ethnicity would guarantee support from certain blocks—without fully understanding how hard Obama worked to win Black support.

The patronizing approach earned them no plaudits from me. I have seen, from multiple angles, how Black people in the US are often treated as a monolithic and infantile demographic by even other Black people, politicians in particular, but nothing could be further from the truth. As a deeply marginalized community over centuries, with little connections to the corridors of power, Black people are particularly invested in good governance, and that means supporting political candidates whose policies are morally sound and practically attainable.

Of course, it helps if we find all of this in a likable candidate, and more so if they happen to be Black because of the glass ceiling it would shatter and the new path it would chart for others, but it is never the only consideration. Black people tend to be especially discriminating, a fact that is often lost in a society that segments people into racial and ethnic blocks.

By Election Day 2008, I was fully immersed and reveling in the unlikely story of a man whose father, like me, came from the Third World as a student and now looked set to become the first Black president of the United States. I was not yet an American citizen. I had the right neither to vote nor to be actively engaged in support of any candidate, but I could cheer like hell from the sidelines, and I did!

I gave Obama all the screams, shouts, thumbs-up, and positive psychic energy I could during the campaign and on election night when he was declared the winner. Naturally, I wanted to be at the National Mall to see him inaugurated two months later, but the forecast called for bitterly cold weather. Getting a good spot would likely require camping out overnight. I did not love him enough for that. I planned to give it a shot on my own terms, and that did not involve heading downtown just after midnight.

Minutes before 9 a.m. on January 20, 2009, I pulled my black Toyota Camry into the only available spot on the lower level of the parking garage at the Wheaton metro station in lower Montgomery County, Maryland. I took it as a good omen that someone pulled out of a space as I entered the garage, saving me time and allowing for quick entry into the metro system.

I felt the cold in my bones already, yet it had warmed up considerably since my daughter left home at 3 a.m. to travel with her Ghanaian friend and her family to the National Mall to await the midday swearing-in of the forty-fourth president of the United States.

Yes, I was far behind the truly faithful, but I left as early as I could tolerate and as late as possible before the whole escapade became an exercise in futility. It came close, as it turned out, with things getting much more competitive as I drew closer to the event.

Alighting from the train at Union Station, one of my favorite DC landmarks, I joined a mighty pilgrimage heading toward the National Mall. I would end up walking in circles, looking for an entry, before a police officer told me the area was at capacity. No one else was being allowed in. Terrified that I would miss seeing the ceremony live, I ran toward the nearest building—Rayburn House, home to the offices of 169 representatives, as it turned out—hoping to find a TV in the lobby at best. To my shock, they let me in the building with a basic security check and directed me toward an auditorium with bright-red carpet and an enormous television. There were fifty or sixty people in there already, lots of empty chairs, and it was warm!

It was the best possible outcome for me, mainly because I could watch the proceedings simultaneously on the west front lawn through the auditorium window and on the screen, and I could hear the audio with complete clarity while comfortably ensconced inside a US congressional building.

I was at once calmly reflective and beyond euphoric at the reality that just over a decade after I had arrived in the United States, and while still processing it as a segregated society, a Black man had cracked the most intractable glass ceiling of all, disrupting more than two centuries of White ethnocentricity, and was on his way to the White House, the iconically named presidential mansion, built in part by slave labor, and the seat of the most powerful person on earth.

There was a lot to deconstruct, but it still felt like progress. I had the pleasure of writing the cover story for *Howard Magazine* and attempted to capture the community's sentiments and the enormity of the moment. More than a decade and a half later, there is only so much one can now add to the infinite number of words and images that already exist. But for myself, the people close to me, and people out there who might want to know what the moment felt like for people like me, I must still record the pride I took in Obama and his victory; in the campaign he ran; in his glorious audacity for believing he could and dragging along people like me, who were hopeful but doubtful at the start, and for putting in the enormous work required to blunt the destructive mold of racism; and finally in the character and decency he revealed thereafter. He was, for a moment, a grace figure for the world.

Outside of personal achievements and those of my children, few other occasions in my lifetime will measure up to the satisfaction of Obama's victory. His election was not just about Black people; it was about oppressed communities worldwide who saw it as symbolic of their own aspirations to break free of the structures keeping them on the margins of society over hundreds of years.

For the little girl from Old House, for the Dalits in India, for the native peoples of New Zealand, Australia, and the Americas, and for the people of African descent throughout the Americas or Europe, Obama's accomplishment marked the dawn of new possibilities in the struggle against oppression. He was an American president serving with the freedom and demands of the position, with the usual constraints it imposed and the added constraints of his identity. Throughout his administration, he exhibited equanimity, stability, capability. I trusted him and his leadership.

As long as he was president, the future seemed hopeful, even though his election did not necessarily signal a new racial unity. The circumstances of his victory were much more complex than that, involving factors like America's rapidly changing demographics, the enthusiasm of people of color and young voters, and the fact that he was a far more compelling candidate than his Republican opponent, Arizona senator John McCain, a stiff older man wholly lost in the digital age where Obama and his campaign dominated.

The election was also a backlash to the presidency of George Bush, which many people considered a disaster after the invasion of Iraq and Afghanistan following 9/11. The war profoundly damaged America's international image at the start of the new millennium. With his expansive view of the world, Obama was not just trying to be the antithesis of Bush-era thought processes; he was. Regardless of why people voted for Obama, the outcome was the same: America got its first Black president, and just as surely as it uplifted and inspired those who prayed that day would come, it also smoked out those for whom it was their worst nightmare.

By the time his second election came around, the racial attacks were unrelenting. Rumors persisted that he was born in Kenya and therefore not qualified to be president of the United States, forcing him to release his birth certificate. He was accused of being a Muslim—as if that should be disqualifying—despite repeatedly explaining that while his parents were primarily agnostic, he accepted Christianity as an adult. He was frequently depicted as a monkey, a shoeshine man, and, of course, an Islamic terrorist.

I found Arizona governor Jan Brewer pointing a finger at Obama's face in 2012 insulting, belittling, hostile, and disrespectful. It was one of those things that I looked at as a Black person and saw stark racism. Her entire posture carried a resistance she likely would not have found necessary in an encounter with a White man. It weighed on my spirit enough for me to write to President Obama to tell him how disgusted I was with the system and what they were doing to him and that I did not feel like I could continue to trust it. He wrote back and told me to guard against cynicism.

Years after his presidency ended, and contemplating some of the animus that followed, Obama mused that he did not think America had been ready for his presidency. I agreed, but the critics struck again. How could that be? He was elected, after all! Why did he hate America so much?

By then, he had come to recognize the depth and breadth of the enmity, the extent of the bitterness, and the backlash that had prompted my letter to him, even if he had no recollection of it.

"How are we going to manage without you?" my colleague wailed when I told her I was leaving my job. "You are the conscience of this university!"

Well, her affirmation was better than becoming a vice president, the provost, or even the president, except that it did not come with money, security, or comfort in a resistant space.

It was time for something different from the "Howard Way"—with its exhausting and too often unproductive ethos and too many people content with the narratives of a past drenched in unquestioned splendor, a present as grounded and immovable as the pyramids at Giza, and a future as certain as death. Where was the incentive to grow?

Efforts like the Rodney conference and bringing Rex Nettleford, the Black Rhodes Scholar extraordinaire, to the campus were meant to confront that stagnation by doing something that was perfectly normal for colleges and universities but occurred much too infrequently at Howard. The same was true of a smaller but just as impactful effort—premiering the English-language version of *Lifting the Weight of History*, an ethnographic film by University of Colorado professor Katherine Brown. This documentary showcases the experiences of women entrepreneurs in the French Caribbean island of Martinique as they navigate barriers of race and gender in a culture where postcolonial attitudes are still prevalent in business.

Brown said she wanted to demonstrate the strength of Caribbean women and reveal how they were claiming their space in the economic life of the island as Afro-Caribbean people. They could have easily been my cousin, Sa Bea from Old House, or any Black woman in Mississippi, Alabama, or Southeast DC.

We had a hard time wrapping up the event. The student attendees, all young women, asked one question after another. None of them had known there were French islands in the Caribbean—outside of Haiti—inhabited predominantly by Black people. One had been contemplating traveling to France to learn the language because she thought it was her only choice; she suddenly saw new, less expensive, and more personally appealing possibilities.

Another program I planned with the Ralph J. Bunche International Affairs Center and the Inter-American Development Bank (IDB) in 2008 to discuss the implications of a looming global economic recession in weak economies like Jamaica and Haiti attracted Richard Bernal, a former Jamaican ambassador to the US and then a vice president of the IDB.

I was thrilled to see him because I had not extended an invitation—had not thought he would consider it worthy enough. His presence validated the importance and timeliness of the discussion, which, as usual, was robust, well attended, and insightful.

It would also result in a collaborative effort in Jamaica. Immediately after the economics event, a student contacted me, wanting to know if she could help with some of the conditions I had talked about in my opening comments. I agreed to see her and was mildly surprised to see a tall, blond, well-dressed woman walk through my door for the appointment.

Florence Maher was from a small, all-White town in the Midwest and had grown curious about worlds different from her own, she told me. She applied and was accepted to Howard to pursue a bachelor's degree in social science. She lived at the International House at Dupont Circle.

I shared with her some of the projects in Jamaica I was interested in.

Together with Adnan Kummer, a Johns Hopkins University student and a resident at International House, we submitted a grant to the Davis International Peace Program and used the $10,000 we received to set up a computer lab at Hanbury, a home for orphaned and abandoned children just outside Mandeville, Jamaica, where I attended college. Unable to participate in the handover, I put Florence in contact with my brother and the Rotary Club of Mandeville and sought their help to connect the facility to the internet.

We thought there would be great value in connecting children on the margins of society to the wider world so that the most current technology could inspire them the way radio inspired me during my childhood. I am confident this was one of the earliest facilities of its kind to be connected to the World Wide Web.

The project made national news in Jamaica, though I had done no media outreach. I was happy about the coverage, but it prompted an unnerving shift in my thinking; the report referred to me as Jamaican-born instead of Jamaican, and in that lay the idea that I had been away long enough to warrant a shift in how I was identified. I did not see myself that way and was far from ready for it.

A terrible Christmas Day accident severely injured my father just over a year later, putting an exclamation point on just how much time had passed since I left Jamaica, how I was missing from family celebrations when they occurred, and the responsibility I had to my parents as they aged. In that profound space of existential reckoning, I quit my job as senior writer and executive communication manager at Howard University in 2011.

I was comfortable with my positive contributions within and outside the scope of my job at Howard, but swimming against the tide was tiring and downright treacherous at times. I did not enjoy having to push back so often, but I usually felt I had no choice. Pushing at the structural underbelly to get even basic things done was like squeezing molasses through a pin-sized hole, whether it was challenging a blatantly abusive supervisor or constantly navigating egos among some administrators. I would miss my friends, miss many things about the community, but it was time to put this significant chapter of my life behind me.

I decided to use the break before taking up my new job—one at a faith-based institution closer to home—to visit my father, who remained in the hospital. The facility was on the campus of my old university, and I booked a room in the lodge nearby.

I looked forward to waking up with the sun creeping over the Blue Mountain and walking by my journalism school alongside the old stone aqueduct that carried water to the old sugar mill. The trip would take me halfway around Ring Road, always lined with intermittent bursts of bougainvillea hedges on the fringes where the partying arm of the student body lived their best lives in blissful revelry at the annual university carnival.

The doctors had said Papa was doing well and would be released in a few days. I planned to await his discharge and take him home to Hibiscus Place.

I boarded the airport shuttle at 4:15 a.m. on my way to Ronald

Reagan National Airport, September 8; the hospital listed this as his time of death. I got the news from my sister while I waited in transit in Miami.

The airport was bustling with end-of-summer crowds, and the jet I boarded was full, but I doubt I will ever feel as alone as I did on the eighty-minute flight to Kingston—or as devastated as when I went to the hospital to see the bed where my father had spent the last months of his life, and later to the morgue with my youngest brother, watching as they pulled out a tray and lifted the shroud so I could see his face. My father looked so much smaller than I remembered him. His eyes were closed. I could not see the twinkle that was always there. His smile was missing too. His cheek was cold to my touch. I held on tightly to Marlon, my heart shattered in a million pieces.

Always in my thinking had been the desire to spend lots of time with my parents, taking them on road trips and showing them parts of Jamaica, they had never seen, and, when that time came, taking them to their doctors' appointments and making sure they were getting the best care and attention possible in a system not known for that. It came before I was ready. Mama survived for only a year after.

I felt fully grown, suddenly, and alone in many ways. Bereft of their presence, I clung hard to their memories, feeling that no matter how hard I had tried, how many letters and checks I had written, how many times I had visited, or how many phone calls I had made—Papa and Mama had individual mobile phones by then—I fell short of doing and being enough for them. I questioned what part of this odyssey in the United States had even been worth it.

I would ask that question constantly over the next two years as I began my new job while navigating the loss of my parents within less than thirteen months of each other.

The patterns of abuse at this school were infinitely worse than what

I had left behind. My circumstances forced me to pay closer attention to my faith beliefs and my field of endeavor. While my work was informed first by my training as a journalist and later as an academic, with honest and ethical communication as a hallmark, many people involved in the same fields were entirely dedicated to manufactured reality, whether by spin or disinformation, I realized.

The position delivered nothing it had promised. The institution itself was like my childhood home in Old House, absent the warmth of family and the charm of the natural world. It was dilapidated physically and populated by rats and snakes, some assuming human form. As I sought to understand what I was dealing with, I found accounts of numerous women before me who had come and gone, victims of personal and institutional abuse. I found out, too, how many EEO (equal opportunity employment) complaints had been filed and settled with nondisclosure agreements, how normalized the abuse was, and how pointless it was to complain to anyone internally or externally. It was a thump in the face.

In that setting, I was forcefully reminded that I should not expect a commitment to high ethical standards or moral correctness just because I was working in a faith-based institution. The administration operated within a context of duplicity, where nothing that was said was meant and what was meant was often not said at all. My most strenuous task was not running a communication department with no budget but distinguishing between truth and falsehood. It was disconcerting.

My daughters were both in college, one at the University of Maryland at College Park and one at Princeton University. Like any good Caribbean parent, I still felt an obligation to keep life stable for them, including ensuring they had a place to come home to during the summer months or anytime they needed to be somewhere other than campus. I was floundering, uncertain how much longer I could hold on—until one of my daughters gave me a Sara Bareilles album with my marching orders:

Say what you wanna say
And let the words fall out,
Honestly, I wanna see you be brave.

The pivotal clash came when the institution refused to sign off on the paperwork for one of my graduate assistants, who required H-1B sponsorship to remain in status. They had committed to doing it and even tasked me with preparing his job description. Understanding the urgency of his situation, I worked with HR and turned it around quickly.

The young man's situation was dire. His parents were missionaries who had left their native country with him as a toddler, making several stops in Asia before arriving in the United States and qualifying for green card status. By then, he was over eighteen and did not qualify to be included on their application. He remained on his student visa and later transferred to optional practical training (OPT) for the one year allowed by US Citizenship and Immigration Services (USCIS) at the end of an academic course.

I became his supervisor just as his OPT was coming to an end. I knew what it was. I too had been on OPT. I knew that without the transition to the H-1B, which immigration policy provided for as long as he had a job offer, he would be out of status within thirty days of his visa expiring. He had two choices after that: upend his life and leave for a country he did not know, or drop out of status, become undocumented in the US, and destroy his future.

I understood the lack of dignity inherent in the process and the frustration for the person on the receiving end. There was no reason why the young man had to be staring down a nightmare. It was not particularly expensive, and immigration laws provided for it. I clashed with the administration repeatedly over their footdragging and refusal to give a straight answer, eventually recognizing that they had no intention of signing off on the H-1B filing. My immediate supervisor, a man of exceptional grace and equanimity who remains a treasured friend, recognized the bizarre no-win situation and gave me cover, shielding me with his presence so I could exit with as little harm as possible. With no prospect in sight, I quit the position after two years, with my dignity and reputation mostly intact.

Among other lessons, I processed that experience as valuable insight into the archaic nature of the workplace; the deficiency of the labor laws; the prevalence of bullying where White people are not always the perpetrators; the brokenness that people in power often bring to the workplace and public spaces; and the deceptive and destructive marketing practices that lure the unsuspecting as clients or employees into toxic situations. I learned how little recourse employees have and that employers will always have the upper hand by a long shot.

I realized that the workplace is the most obvious example of human existence as a series of power relationships. It is where all forms of bigotry collide, and—rather than the empty rallying cry of DEI—insistence on and adherence to the highest levels of ethical conduct, along with dismantling embedded hierarchies, is necessary to create the liberating space required for innovation and productivity.

The role of HR also became clearer. No matter how it is constructed and marketed, this department serves the interest of the organization and not the employee. There is no difference to split or balance to strike; the rank-and-file worker is always the vulnerable entity courtesy of their dependence on a paycheck and benefits like health care, which until the Affordable Care Act (ACA) was more difficult to obtain outside of employer-assisted programs. HR personnel are the primary gatekeepers.

I spent the very challenging time between jobs writing a highly impactful social justice opinion column for the *Jamaica Observer* and significantly influencing government policy in several areas, including education, a ban on plastic bags, and changes in animal control law. One column decrying the plight of an elderly man living in the woods under inhumane conditions made the Google top-ten list of most-read articles that day and garnered more than 400 comments.

The Obama critics in my orbit were especially trenchant then—demanding to know how I benefited from his presidency, mainly because the last two years had been the most difficult of my life at a personal level. I did not think any of it was Obama's fault, even though I saw the need for more workplace reform policies. Furthermore, one of his most substantial achievements, the ACA, served me well in that period. I suffered, but it felt infinitely better to have stood up rather than simply let an injustice stand. I believed then, as I do now, that pushing back against oppressive, dehumanizing behavior is my duty. Otherwise, my education, my life, is of no value.

In the twilight of Obama's presidency, the seething undercurrent of racism in the United States became open and visceral. Despite the struggles in my own life, I took enormous pride in the intangibles of his administration. The wealth of the world's capitalist empires combined could not equal what it meant to me to have had this man disprove the many biases and stereotypes to which we are often subjected, and stand proudly for all of us.

However, progress is not linear, particularly as it relates to bigoted attitudes and social movements. White supremacy made its discontent with a Black presidency known. I soon reverted to wondering who was friend or foe the way I used to when I had just arrived in the US and rode the train to and from Howard University from the Maryland suburb where I had settled with my children.

White supremacy loomed in my consciousness again, but I did not know how it would manifest. Then, on the evening of June 17, 2015, Dylann Roof, a twenty-one-year-old, walked into the Emanuel African Methodist Episcopal Church in downtown Charleston, South Carolina, and sat down with worshippers in a Bible-study class before using a handgun to kill nine parishioners.

They looked like my family. But for the randomness of history, they could have been my mother, sisters, uncles, brothers, or children. How could I not wallow in grief, despair, rage? It reinforced the trauma of race-based violence against Black people in America, each a reminder of countless others and one more jolt on a roller coaster of pain.

There was, for example, September 15, 1963, when a member of the Ku Klux Klan detonated a bomb at the Sixteenth Street Baptist Church in Birmingham, Alabama, just before Sunday-morning services. Four Black girls—Addie Mae Collins, fourteen; Carole Robertson, fourteen; Cynthia Wesley, fourteen; and Denise McNair, eleven—who were in the basement, preening in their Sunday best, were killed. More than twenty other people were injured, including twelve-year-old Sarah Collins, Addie's sister, who lost an eye. In the riots that broke out after, two Black boys, Virgil Ware, thirteen, and Johnny Robinson, sixteen, were also killed. From the White House, September 16, 1963, President John F. Kennedy lamented:

> If these cruel and tragic events can only awaken that city and state—if they can only awaken this entire nation to a realization of the folly of racial injustice and hatred and violence—then it is not too late for all concerned to unite in steps toward peaceful progress before more lives are lost.

Two months later, Kennedy himself would be assassinated. Shell shocked, Black people went full throttle on civil rights, and their vigilance ensured the passage of the Civil Rights Act of 1964. In the years I spent writing speeches at Howard University, I made numerous references to these incidents. It felt like déjà vu all over again.

After the Charleston, South Carolina, shooting, I attended my first and only Black Lives Matter event: a gathering at the U Street Cardozo metro station in Washington, DC, a few blocks from Howard University. I went to pay respect to the dead and commiserate with like-minded people mourning their loss, all of us desperate for an end to racism, bullying, and violence.

It was my only direct exposure to Black Lives Matter, the group that started agitating for racial justice following the murder of seventeen-year-old Florida teenager Trayvon Martin in 2012 by a White supremacist neighborhood watch coordinator—who would later be acquitted of Martin's death. Heartbreak for families like that of Sybrina Fulton, Martin's mother, hardened my resolve to be even just a pebble creating the tiniest ripples in the stream against injustices, if that was all I could be.

White people seemed to form the single largest ethnic group among the eclectic mix, which included Latinos, Blacks, and biracial people, who showed up for the event. I was satisfied that the outrage transcended race in a big way.

There were speeches, poetry, and songs, but no unifying goal was articulated beyond reacting to the incident of the moment. I did not think this was either good or bad, but I yearned for a clear message and ideas on how to forge a path forward to challenge and defeat oppression and injustice. I felt like the audience was ready and hungry for marching orders, the next step, but those orders were not forthcoming.

My mind went back to Kwame Ture, the freedom fighter whose given name was Stokely Carmichael and whom I first heard about on our little transistor radio in Old House. A fellow West Indian, hailing from the twin-island republic of Trinidad and Tobago, he was the chairman of the Student Nonviolent Coordinating Committee, a prominent civil rights group during the 1960s that advocated the kind of organic urban uprising against racism that Black Lives Matter seemed to be attempting. Ture had been a gifted leader—militant, focused, passionate, and determined to make a difference.

The moment seemed to call for Ture, but he was long gone, dead seventeen years prior in Conakry, Guinea, where he had fled American racism. A year before, while he was on a visit, our paths literally crossed when he ran past me in front of Founders Library on the Howard campus. On that day, his presence went unnoticed and unacknowledged. There were no reflections on his life, lectures, or communications with my office. I should have run him down, stopped him to say hello and thank you, but I did not. He died soon after.

Satisfied with my attendance at the event to show solidarity with the victims of the church shooting, I edged away from the crowd. The clouds were brooding and restless as if absorbing the emotions of the moment, and a thunderstorm seemed imminent. As the first raindrops splattered my right arm, I took the elevator to the metro platform and boarded the train back home.

Resistance to what Obama represented expressed itself in incidents like in Charleston and the routine killings of young Black men by American law enforcement—like thirty-two-year-old Philando Castile, whose death in 2016 resulted from a purportedly routine traffic stop in Falcon Heights, a White suburb near St. Paul, Minnesota. I learned that unshakable grief is part of the burden that weighs minority people down in oppressive societies.

CHAPTER SEVEN

THE AMERICAN DREAM?

Sometimes it seems like only a handful of summers have passed since my arrival in the United States, when I first fell in love with the well-kept neighborhood parks we did not have in Kingston and with taking long walks in the woods, invariably triggering a quiet intonation of Robert Frost: "The woods are lovely dark and deep, but I have promises to keep, and miles to go before I sleep." It seemed apt in so many ways.

It feels like only a few seasons ago that I realized the true meaning of fall—that the leaves do fall entirely off the trees, leaving them bare and fallow for half the year. The futility of trying to keep the yard leaf-free before all the trees had fully shed took me a while to grasp, reinforcing some big life lessons about accepting things I cannot change.

Even my first encounter with a few chilling snowflakes remains fresh in my memory. Oh, the wonder! Oh, the magic! And oh, the absolute recognition that I was in a space where I could never entirely belong! Every other discovery reminded me that this experiment in the United States was supposed to be time-bound and I needed to head back home. Soon. Soon should have been a long, long time ago! In 2016, I realized in a profound way that it had been two decades since I left Kingston. A whole chunk of my life had passed.

There were multiple reasons why I remained in the US rather than returning home. None of them were because life was easier or more meaningful, even though there were amenities and opportunities here that were not available at home and still are not. At the core of my decision was my children's education and what I could achieve for them here, despite the challenges, compared to what I could do back home with limited resources. I would find, too, that the longer I stayed, the more intense the tension grew between remaining in the US, becoming a citizen, and giving my daughters the benefits of that life, or returning to my native land.

The choice was agonizing. Jamaica, particularly the hills and valleys of South Manchester, would always be home to me. Home was about birthright, belonging, culture, vibes, and soul—those deeply metaphysical bonds that connect us all to the places where we were born; to the food; to the landscapes of trees, flowers, and shrubs; to oceans, seas, and skies; to a rhythm and tempo of life that is seared on our consciousness early on and stays with us forever; to folkways—songs, stories, speech, habits, and ways of being in our families, communities, and the world; to real laughter and real tears; to our normal template. Those things seared on our brains in our earliest years become our default, our reference point for everything else that follows. They stay with us for life.

My template was shaped in South Manchester, among rural people who lived ordinary lives close to the earth, guided by the rhythm of nature, the bonds of family, and the needs of our communities, and was burnished for eternity when my papa buried my umbilical cord—which he had saved along with my siblings'—at the root of an orange tree near a window at Hibiscus Place, his own house on his own land. I am enormously comfortable in the marketplaces, among the vendors who remind me of Sa Bea, and in the woods among the birds and goats, more so than I am in performative spaces, no matter how luxurious. I know now that those spaces, the most authentically Jamaican, also connected me to my African ancestors, which explains the restlessness I feel whenever I have been away too long. I made peace with never experiencing the same sense of belonging in the United States. The spiritual estrangement and cultural disconnect were too great even as I adjusted to daily living and comfortably navigated diverse social, political, and cultural spaces.

The good thing is that belonging was not a necessary goal. I was one of generations of Caribbean and African people seeking opportunities rather than a sense of cultural or psychological belonging; because we already belonged somewhere else. This paradoxically is part of what allows us to endure the rootlessness of marginality, and even abuse, better than some African Americans—Africans without memories and Americans without rights, as the saying goes. How comfortable can any Black person feel in the daily struggle for the right to exist outside a paradigm of oppression and servitude?

The goal, for me, had always been to gain some experience and return to Jamaica—to continue to combat oppression where it exists and push against the structural inequalities working against the people who began life in the same position as my family.

Those desires were not aligning well with material reality. I had turned up no viable career leads there, and given my thorough understanding of how difficult it is to assimilate as an adult in the United States, I saw the value of sending my children through the American education system rather than taking them home on the cusp of their teen years only to return five years later to repeat the worst of my own experience. As time passed, I began to process life through their eyes more than mine.

The desires seem contradictory. I am sure the same is true for many emigrants from the Global South. Much remained the same at home. There was little socioeconomic progress, the inequities were graver, violence was escalating and looked even worse from afar, and governance was weaker than before. I remained attached to home, looking back, even as I tried to move forward in the US.

My children, the older one especially, had routinely asked to be taken back home in their earliest years in the US. As they grew older, they became more content with their lives and their circles of friends and stopped asking. I felt both more and less guilty and doubled my effort to have it both ways.

I thought I could straddle Jamaica and the United States and raise my children to be grounded in what was right about their native culture and identity and a sense of belonging there. I took them home at summertime and Christmas as often as I could. I knew it was not the same, but these visits allowed them to remain connected to family and what it means to be Jamaican. They knew and adored their grandparents, aunts, uncles, and cousins—the most important thing to me. I also knew that regardless of the difficulties, there remained great value to the American experience. The US remained the most cosmopolitan country in the world, the most technologically developed, and within easy reach of the Caribbean. It was not a bad idea to have a foothold here.

By then, I also had an acute sense of how one's status on arrival in the United States dramatically impacts life's trajectory here. People who come in as "landed" (or permanent) immigrants or on green cards can immediately take advantage of many of the same opportunities as citizens, and within five years, they are qualified to apply for citizenship. This category is usually the result of so-called chain migration, where family members who have attained citizenship can petition for the entry of close relatives such as parents, spouses, or children. Perhaps because true love is elusive, marrying a US citizen is the fastest way to American citizenship.

Outside of the green card, all other visa categories are highly restrictive. This was true of the F1 (student) visa, on which I studied for four and a half years. I transitioned to the H-1B after graduating from the university. For all intents, it is the professional equivalent of the farmworker's visa—designed to keep seasonal workers tied to whatever plantation hires them in Florida or elsewhere. The key difference is that the H-1B puts the holder on a path to permanent residency and citizenship with a maximum of six years to transition to the green card, with the employer's consent and cooperation. The Office of International Students at Howard treated the process like patronage doled out by Third World politicians in exchange for votes or personal loyalty. It became a brutal experience for me.

On the brink of my last permit expiring, just as my children were approaching their final years in high school, I applied for and was granted a visa for immigrants of extraordinary ability by Citizenship and Immigration Services. It gave me another three years, enough time to choose between my abiding aspiration to return to Jamaica or deciding to "pledge allegiance to the Flag of the United States of America and the Republic for which it stands, one Nation, under God, indivisible, with liberty and justice for all."

I pledged. It was the only choice that made sense. I wanted to support my children and be free from constantly filing paperwork to remain in status, and I wanted to participate more in national life in a space where I had already spent decades of my life. In this regard, a man named Donald J. Trump became my biggest motivation. I applied to become a citizen in March 2016.

By then, it was clear that the perpetually red-necktie-wearing reality TV host from Queens, New York, who had been a thorn in Obama's side, would likely win the Republican nomination. He was sufficiently vacuous, sufficiently corrupt, and sufficiently racist to qualify. I did not want to be a mere bystander to history and let such an undeserved aspirant go unchallenged. Equal to the intensity of the grave concern I had about Trump was the desire to support Hillary Clinton, should she get the Democratic nomination. It would clearly be a choice between her and Bernie Sanders, and in many ways, I would have been comfortable with either.

By September, I had my date for the citizenship test. With quiet resolve and casting all doubts aside, I finally began to look ahead more than I looked back. I felt a sense of peace that one of the biggest challenges of my life in the US—filing visa applications and structuring my life around them—was finally coming to an end and that I had finally reconciled my realities: I was and always would be Jamaican, and my passion for my native land burned as brightly as it ever did, but I was also an American. I was on my way to becoming a Jamerican, but only after one final unexpected and dramatic challenge.

I took the Red Line from Wheaton to Union Station on the test day and caught the MARC Train en route to the USCIS district office in Baltimore. I had taken the train for a whole semester to Bowie State University, where I taught from August to December 2001, and not once did I encounter a problem. But twenty minutes into the ride of my life, the train slowed to a stop just beyond the New Carrollton station in Prince George's County, Maryland. I waited, unperturbed, expecting it would move momentarily as they usually do. But it stayed and stayed and stayed. There was no movement and nothing from the intercom to explain why. A growing dread slowly replaced the hopefulness with which I had left home.

With every passing minute, my spirit sagged lower under the weight of weary certainty that I would miss the appointment. Is there a worse feeling than being stuck on a train on the tracks or an airplane on the runway with the doors closed and cross-checked but unmoving and no one explaining why? Other than a mission to save someone's life, what could be more critical to an immigrant than the trip to take the citizenship test? What could be more devastating than missing the test after twenty years of rootlessness and exploitation? I pondered the implication but ultimately resigned myself to the theater of it all—the appropriateness of this one grand convulsion at the tail end of all I had gone through. I eventually learned that a tree had fallen on the track ahead, and we had to wait until it was cleared.

The fear of interacting with the black hole that was the USCIS to try to reschedule my appointment and explain why I missed the first one, along with a cultivated belief in the value of moving forward instead of turning back, prompted me to continue with the journey to the office once the train was running again. Maybe there, I thought, I could speak to a real person, in crisp, clear English at that—a facility that has so much currency for so many people—and beseech them with my eyes and let them know that I was not on island-people or colored-people time but was late because of something entirely outside my control.

But in a wonderfully unexpected turn of events, my appointment remained on the calendar. I took the test nearly two hours after my originally scheduled time!

The officer, a military veteran whose name I wish I could recall, sat across from me at the table, holding a ream of paper containing my twenty years of correspondence with the agency as I explained why I was late and how fearful I had been about missing the test. He said he thought I was on my way since I had not rescheduled the appointment up to the day before. He brought forward other appointees already there and bumped me to later slots until I showed up.

It was a delightful and desperately needed application of grace and common sense that took me by surprise, given the context. I fully expected to be penalized, or at least treated with coldness enough to leave me appropriately chastened for showing up so late. Instead, for a fleeting moment, he turned a central idea of American culture on its head—a break from the notion of time as a commodity, measured in minutes, seconds even, and the obligation to punish lateness regardless of the reasons. His approach calmed my spirit and reaffirmed my belief that someone was looking out for me—that my many hardships were lessons to be learned and whenever it truly mattered, the Divine would intervene.

"Who was the first president of the United States?"

And I, Grace Virtue, PhD, the quintessential news junkie, promptly froze on the first question, as if my hard drive had been completely deleted or the files in my brain corrupted by anxiety. Evidently, I still needed to recover. Nothing was downloading. I could not distinguish between Abraham Lincoln, George Washington, and Thomas Jefferson.

I stared at the officer. He looked back at me with kind, steady eyes, waiting for the answer he knew I knew.

My heart was beating so loudly that I wondered if he could hear it too.

Inside my head, a clock tick-tocked away, sounding like giant thunderclaps.

Time was running out.

Then, across time and space, I saw Mammy and Mama and their struggles, and my own in the last two decades. As usual, I had put in the work and stayed on the straight and narrow. I had pulled out that damn little book every time I had a free minute and practiced the test repeatedly! Of course, I knew the answer: George Washington was the first president. Abraham Lincoln was the sixteenth. He led the nation through the American Civil War and freed enslaved people. Jefferson was the third president and principal author of the Declaration of Independence. He fathered six children with Sally Hemmings, an enslaved woman. I released a deep breath and let the answer roll off my tongue. I answered the next four questions correctly too, and just like that, it was over!

Two weeks later, I returned to Baltimore for the swearing-in ceremony with a recorded welcome message from President Obama. I registered to vote on my way out and signed up with the Montgomery County Board of Elections later that day to work on Election Day. A few weeks later, I received my certificate of citizenship in the mail under the signature of Barack Obama, the first and only Black president of the republic to which I had just sworn my loyalty. I tucked it away among those papers I must keep for the rest of my life and began earnestly looking forward to Tuesday, November 8, 2016.

CHAPTER EIGHT

RED NECKTIES

The only thing more exhilarating for this new American citizen than processing the first voter at Highland Elementary School in Silver Spring on Election Day 2016 was casting my own vote at Wheaton Fire Station, which I had done a few days prior—for Congressman Jamie Raskin; Senator Chris Van Hollen, who had helped me correct an egregious error on my green card application, resulting in USCIS kicking out the submission and costing me one more year in limbo; Clinton–Kaine for president and vice president; and downballot Democrats, whether I knew them or not. It might not have been the most critical approach, but my thinking was that merely running under the banner of the Republican Party with Trump as the standard bearer was disqualifying.

This was my second time serving as an election-day worker. The first was decades before in Jamaica. There, too, I had signed up to work as a poll clerk as soon as I came of age. Civic responsibility was a family tradition I learned from my father, who voted and worked during every election for as long as he could. The day I worked the polling station at the courthouse in Cross Keys, my father and my two older siblings toiled at other locations in similar roles.

My father was the overseer, managing the entire process at his precinct on behalf of election officials rather than the party he supported. It was a measure of his integrity in a country where political parties have long been elevated to the status of ancient tribes and great atrocities have been committed in the quest for power. He was a committed Socialist and party loyalist, but everyone trusted him to execute the responsibilities of the office faithfully and fairly.

Although he had passed five years earlier, he was on my mind when I showed up for work thousands of miles away in Montgomery County, Maryland. I knew he would have been so proud that I was finding my feet in a new land, more so that I was not merely sitting on the sidelines but engaging in a process I believed was an essential civil responsibility. I was also supercharged by what I saw as a certainty: that my first effort in the United States as a citizen would help give us our first female president. I started at the check-in desk and remained there for about an hour before moving to the scanner, where I spent the next ten hours or so working alongside a man named Christopher.

We worked effortlessly together, making small talk in between voters bringing their ballots to the machine. The rules forbade us from discussing politics, and we did not, but in the intermittent lulls, I learned that Chris was a lawyer trained at Georgetown University and married to a Trinidadian woman. He was savvy about island cultures and shared enough family anecdotes for me to conclude that, like me, he was a Democrat. It was not much of a stretch. After all, we were just outside Washington, DC, where loud laughter had erupted in one of the training sessions when a facilitator asked for volunteers to role-play a Republican poll worker. No one wanted to.

The exercise was a necessary part of the training because a worker might need to identify their political affiliation—if, for example, party representatives are needed to sign off on a document or provide oversight for a voter who needs assistance marking a ballot. People eventually came forward, but the initial response was telling, providing a moment of levity among an otherwise reflective group.

Along with the other workers, Chris and I remained at the precinct for another two hours after the polls closed at 8 p.m. We tallied the votes one last time and posted the results outside the building as required by Board of Elections rules. I quietly exulted as Hillary and the Democrats romped home with more than 80 percent of the votes.

I was hopeful this was a bellwether for a nationwide Democratic sweep.

Our final task was to break down the room and load the trucks with equipment to be immediately returned to the Board of Elections headquarters so the space could be a gym again for the students arriving for school the next day. Finally, minutes after 10 p.m., fourteen hours after I arrived at the precinct, I was ready to go home to watch the votes come in and celebrate a decisive win for Hillary Clinton. Chris agreed to drop me off at my house, less than ten minutes away, and we left together. He turned on the radio as we got into the car, and for the first time that day, we learned what was happening in the rest of the country.

The traffic light was red as we approached Amherst and Arcola Avenue in Wheaton. For no reason I could explain rationally, I felt a sudden panic deep in my stomach. In radio land, the pundits were not pronouncing Hillary Clinton dead yet, but the commentary sounded like it was leading up to her obituary rather than expressing the elation I expected.

"What the hell is going on?" I asked.

We still had not outed ourselves as firm Democrats, but by then, we knew.

"I don't know," Chris replied, "but whatever it is, it sounds pretty scary."

"Can you switch to 103.5?"

I did not know what channel Chris had his radio on, but I knew which one it was not. CBS would help me make sense of what was going on—tell me that Hillary would be declared president before midnight and not create unnecessary drama like that other station was by making it look as if Donald Trump had a chance. He did as I asked, and I was reassured for a brief while. But this reassurance was soon replaced by perplexity and a return of the panic I felt at the stoplight. Hillary was not as far ahead as she should have been, and it did not matter which radio station I listened to.

Heaped on top of the end-of-day physical exhaustion was a growing sense of impending doom. The journalist and social scientist in me recognized by then what the radio stations were hinting at but loathed to say clearly: Hillary was too far behind in the Electoral College, and the trajectory was not in her favor.

I made the disquieting observation in a Facebook post at home. A friend and fellow Jamerican in Atlanta wrote to me privately, imploring that I not despair. I responded bluntly: Wisconsin had gone to Trump, and Michigan and Pennsylvania were also moving significantly that way. We were losing blue or purple states and not winning any red states. Where, then, was the hope? Without waiting for a response, I switched off the television and went to bed. I fell asleep immediately.

At 5 a.m. on November 9, I got out of bed and, from my upstairs hallway, switched on the big TV in the living room, one level down. A still photo of Donald Trump took up the entire screen, with text running across the screen, declaring him the president-elect of the United States. I went back to bed.

For the second time in my life, I wept at the outcome of a general election. The first was in 1980 when Manley, the visionary leader whose social justice agenda lifted my family and countless others out of extreme material poverty, was defeated by Seaga. Like Donald Trump, Seaga had an authoritarian bent that automatically meant a diminished respect for individual agency. He believed in the supremacy of his own actions, allowing nothing to get in the way of what he desired.

The reason for my sadness was the same in both cases: The people had two clear choices, and the worst one won out. The results gave a massively flawed individual tremendous power over people's lives, including mine, and the opportunity to do great harm to society. In Trump's case, I knew his election would have ugly consequences beyond the borders of the United States.

I understood what happened in Jamaica to a degree. Violence had taken a toll. People were weary of the chaos driven by internal and external forces, and the relentless propaganda incited by the political opposition convinced a majority that the country had been on the edge of a communist takeover. No one wanted that. Manley and his government were voted out.

Accusations about communism were a hoax. Manley said he was not a communist, and Papa said he was not, and young as I was, I knew that the social changes he was making were vital, regardless of the label people used to describe him and them. My tears were for the reversal of those programs—the social justice agenda that was so essential to the dignity and prosperity of the descendants of enslaved people, to inclusive socioeconomic growth, and to the development of a small country with limited resources and opportunities.

By comparison, I could not register why patriotic Americans would give Donald Trump the reins of power and the privileges of the Office of the President when he showed himself, over months, to be lacking the intellect and the character for such a high office. I had not understood that the animosity toward Obama ran deeply enough for many to willingly sacrifice America's finest ideals in favor of their race-based discontent.

I knew Trump would be bad news for people like me but did not fully appreciate the extent to which he embodied the White supremacist ideal or that he had found a critical mass of support to propel him to the presidency. I cried for the embrace of a leadership pathway that would be incredibly destructive to the progress of the slow-moving American experiment and, by extension, to the most vulnerable communities.

I was off kilter over many days, thrown by the dissonance, disappointment, powerlessness, and anxiety over what the future held. I feared that whatever he served up, I would get a quadruple dose of it for being born Black, for being a woman, for choosing to be an immigrant in the US to give my children a chance at a better life; for being born a descendant of formerly enslaved people, without an inheritance, and having to claw my way from the bottom of the socioeconomic ladder; for being the prototype of the oppressed in the US and the world, with immigrating to the US being the only deliberate action on my part.

I also felt disappointed in the United States for its continued backwardness on women's rights. Clinton's election would have been a leap forward to bring the United States—the world's leading democracy, it calls itself—to number eighty-two among countries in Europe, Asia, Africa, and the Caribbean that have already elected or appointed a woman to the highest office one or more times. Even majority-Muslim countries like Turkey, Indonesia, Bangladesh, and Pakistan, America's perceived archnemeses precisely because their women are oppressed, have elected women as head of government.

My support for Clinton went beyond the election campaign and way back to life in Old House, where I was surrounded by competent women contributing positively to the community and shaping how I saw myself in the world. I had taken this awareness to my career as a journalist in Kingston, starting a women's desk at the newspaper just as First Lady Clinton was courageously blazing a trail to free a new generation of women from old, useless templates of femininity and womanhood. At the Beijing conference in 1995, her declaration that "women's rights are human rights" helped me place my advocacy within a larger international framework and learn the pitfalls from men who felt threatened and women dismissive of this "women's issues nonsense."

I continued to follow her career after I moved to the United States, even through her support for her husband, whose tryst with a young intern while he was president threw his leadership into disrepute and led to an impeachment trial. I knew not what transpired behind the scenes or what political calculus factored into her decisions. I saw her honoring the marriage vows she made, for better or worse, and choosing her family, perhaps influenced by what she knew to be her own imperfections. None of it conflicted with the feminism I subscribed to, which is about women's right to their own choices.

That emphasis on choice as a cornerstone of feminism helped me process my feelings during the campaign when I briefly had doubts about Hillary's candidacy. Specifically, threads of entitlement and inevitability had started to rankle, the dirt thrown at her from all directions had become wearying, and by then she seemed like the embodiment of the establishment compared to Bernie Sanders, who wanted to take a sledgehammer to it. I thought a fresh start might be in order and campaigned briefly for Bernie, knocking on close to a hundred doors in Falls Church, Virginia, on a bitterly cold January day. Once Hilary was chosen as the nominee, though, I reinvested in her campaign and was raring to see her go. The prospect of the first woman following the first Black man into the White House was intoxicating. It was not to be.

The gut punch was unbearable, more so because she had comfortably won the popular vote, yet the archaic contortions of the Electoral College handed a victory to an unqualified candidate and an awful human being. As a new citizen, I rued an America that did not seem to care that leading the world cannot be solely about technology, military, or even economics but should also concern morality and ethics, even to just a recognizable degree. The marginalization of women over centuries was unethical, and so was the elevation of a criminally reckless and incompetent man, capable of doing great harm, to the most politically powerful office in the world.

The Montgomery County Board of Election unwittingly gave the knife a final twist a few weeks after the election when I received a tiny commemorative pin for my work on Election Day. It was a perfect memento that I could have and would have kept and handed to my daughters at the end of my days as an heirloom to pass down to the women in our family had Hillary won. With her loss to Trump, it was out of place: a symbol of something too painful to commemorate. Wordlessly, I handed it to my daughter. She let out an anguished wail.

I knew who Donald Trump was before I moved to the United States. He was often on the cover of glossy magazines and on cable TV—rich, arrogant, idle, entitled, obsessively devoted to self-gratification, and always in his signature red necktie. I likely saw him on the news at least once on my maiden trip to New York in the late 1980s, the decade of his meteoric ascendance in the city and beyond.

I watched television incessantly as his 2016 campaign accelerated, increasingly repulsed but unwilling to miss new information that could decisively sink the campaign and spare the world the toxic Trump effect. There would be many disqualifying revelations, yet by late summer, he had become the Republican nominee with the tacit support of his party in his attack on minorities: Muslims, immigrants, women, the disabled—anyone or anything that did not comport with his twisted view of the world in which the law of natural selection favored wealthy White men or women whom he rated a "ten" and worthy of being grabbed by the crotch. All others were merely qualified to wipe his shoes.

Aided by the media in their ruthless quest for ratings and his stealth theft of populist elements of Bernie Sanders's campaign, Trump's ascent accelerated. Russian propaganda pushed him over the edge. Whereas I had joyously attended Bill Clinton's inauguration in 1997 and Obama's in 2009, not even for history or family lore would I consider attending Trump's.

Bill Clinton's second inauguration came a few months after I first moved to the United States. It was novel and exciting to watch up close. It would also be my first visit to the iconic US Capitol. I made my way to the entrance of the Rotunda, walking past Jesse Jackson and his wife, Jacquelyn, as well as NBC's Tim Russert, and Maria Shriver—names and faces I was already familiar with. More than a decade later, Obama's inauguration was endlessly joyful because of what it represented for Black people and marginalized groups worldwide.

Trump's, meanwhile, was the continuation of a horror show and symbolized a rising threat to non-White people in the United States. I had no desire to help legitimize him. I knew I was only one insignificant person, but I would resist however I could. Happily, I was far from the only one, as the day after his inauguration would reveal.

On January 21, 2017, the day after Trump's inauguration, I joined hundreds of thousands of people on the National Mall and millions nationwide to protest him and his agenda loudly and resolutely. I was officially part of the resistance. The energy was potent from the time I boarded the train in Wheaton to when I joined scores of women, many clad in pink pussycat hats, singing, "We shall overcome." The event became my punching bag, my release from the disappointment of Clinton's loss, the exhaustion of Trump's win, the belief that a hostile foreign power contributed to his victory, and the recognition of how vulnerable the United States was and our seeming helplessness in the face of it. To see his public rejection just over two months after his election was immensely cathartic, not the least because the world was seeing it and hopefully understanding that most Americans were not behind their new president.

It was the ultimate thumbing of the nose at the nation's forty-fifth leader, whose inauguration crowd the day before amounted to a smattering of people compared to the protest the next day or to either of Obama's inaugurations—or to any other presidential inauguration in the modern age. So thick and tightly packed was the crowd that I urged my friend, whom I had met at Union Station with her six-year-old son, to move out of the middle of it and onto the sidelines. I worried that even a balloon popping could trigger a stampede and result in tragedy.

Taking it inches at a time, we made our way to the edge of the crowd and moved further and further away until we were headed home. I was confident that if the women of America stood together, we could be the bulwark of opposition against his worst instincts and the protectors of our democracy.

I also nurtured the hope that Trump's presidency would not survive four years—that whatever force propelled him to the presidency would unravel, and Clinton would be recognized as the legitimate president.

Surely justice required no less, and didn't the United States establish it as an ideal in the preamble to the Constitution?

> We, the People of the United States, in order to form a more perfect Union, establish Justice, insure domestic Tranquility, provide for the common defence, promote the general Welfare, and secure the Blessings of Liberty to ourselves and our Posterity, do ordain and establish this Constitution for the United States of America.

I hoped, too, that the women of the march would be a unified and consistent voice toward that end. Unfortunately, the movement sputtered after that and rapidly diminished as an organizational force.

Nine days after Trump's inauguration, I took my first trip abroad on my American passport. Other than calm acceptance of my status as a new citizen and the travel freedom embodied in the dark-blue passport compared to my red Jamaican one, I paid little attention to the document as I left Ronald Reagan National Airport on a work trip to Paris, my first visit to Europe.

Exiting the US is never difficult unless one is a fugitive, I would imagine. It is reentry that is always tricky for noncitizens because every attempt serves as a reminder that a visa is a permit and any immigration officers, for whatever reason, can choose to revoke it at any time and put the person seeking entry on the next flight back home. Every immigrant knows this. Hence, there is always a degree of stress involved in clearing Customs, even if one ends up on the elite O visa like I did before becoming a citizen. An American passport, therefore, was the ultimate freedom. And now I had one. I experienced what that felt like on my return when I joined the US-citizen line and got a genuine "Welcome home" from the immigration officers—my fellow Americans!

Still, it was without much conscious thought that I scrutinized my passport as soon as I boarded my return flight, an action triggered by the fact that I had been detained for "extra screening" at the security checkpoint at Heathrow Airport in London. I had no idea why, since I was fairly used to flying internationally by then and had not so much as an outstanding traffic ticket anywhere.

I glanced around and noticed I was the only person of color trying to get through the security line and the only one detained. Suddenly, all the agitation I felt after Trump's election, and everything I had experienced since, flooded back, ballooning into full-blown rage. My throat tightened. My heart pounded. My hair stood on end.

"Move back!" a woman agent screamed as I stood slightly sideways of the conveyor belt, waiting for my bag or for someone to tell me why it was detained. I had been standing there for a good thirty minutes as the clock ticked toward departure time for my flight. No one seemed to care except me.

"No!" I yelled back. Short. Sharp. Firm.

Our eyes locked.

"I have been standing here long enough," I said. "I do not know what you are doing with my bag, but I am not moving one inch until you give it back to me!"

I had no game plan—not a single idea what would have happened if they decided to escalate for whatever reason. I just knew I had had enough of being targeted for no reason other than my appearance, because that was what it felt like. The week I had spent in Paris, enduring what felt like the hazing from some coworkers at my new job and preoccupation with Trump's win by others, had worn on me. The knowledge that I was returning to his America also weighed heavily.

Surprisingly, my pushback was enough to calm the agent down, and she went searching for my black-and-beige Ralph Lauren tote, a gift from my sister Loretta, who was named for my grandmother, that

I carried everywhere. She brought it out and dusted it with a white powder before transferring the contents piece by piece to one of the plastic bins on the table: the new phone I was using and an old one I had taken because I had not learned how to set the alarm on the new one; two microcassette recorders from the media-training workshop I ostensibly led in Paris; and a copy of Ta-Nehisi Coates's *Between the World and Me*, my in-flight reading material.

The items were innocuous tools of my job, and the book was standard for long flights. Suddenly, I was seeing them through the eyes of anti-Black bias and wondered what stories the workers might conjure up about a middle-aged Black woman with a braided updo staring defiantly at them and oozing impatience at their casual disregard for my things and my time. I snatched the bag the moment she released it and scrambled to catch my flight. I barely made it and boarded the aircraft with my passport still in hand. As the plane taxied down the runway, I began flipping through the pages for the first time since receiving it.

It was not just a travel document, I realized. It was a call to patriotism, filled with quotes from the Constitution and America's most iconic citizens: Abraham Lincoln, George Washington, Daniel Webster, Martin Luther King Jr., and others, including this, at the very center, from John Fitzgerald Kennedy: "Let every nation know, whether it wishes us well or ill, that we shall pay any price, bear any burden, meet any hardship, support any friend, oppose any foe, to assure the survival and the success of liberty."

My thoughts immediately turned to a woman named Yuliya, a Ukrainian colleague and one of my dinner companions on my last night in Paris. As soon as the conversation turned to Donald Trump and the US election, she began to cry. She could not grasp what was happening, she said, and was worried about her country's continued vulnerability since the United States could not be counted on to support them against Russian aggression.

I felt as stricken as she looked but frankly did not know enough about the situation to offer her words of comfort. It took a few years before her fears were realized, due in no small measure to the climate stoked by Trump, who embraced and supported Russian leader Vladimir Putin and undermined the Ukrainians and their quest to join the North Atlantic Treaty Organization. However much of an affront or even a threat the Russian leader perceived, the international system recognizes the right of nation-states to self-determination. The invasion of Ukraine that followed is counter to that. I understand now why Yuliya cried.

High above the Atlantic Ocean, I read through my passport repeatedly, wondering where American patriotism and integrity had gone—the glorious idealism captured throughout the document and embodied in the very last quote from prominent Black sociologist and liberation activist Anna Julia Cooper: "The cause of freedom is not the cause of a race or a sect, a party, or a class. It is the cause of humankind, the very birthright of humanity."

Back home, I attempted to settle into life under a president who felt entitled to grab women by their genitals and deemed people like me, and Barack Obama's father, to be from "s**thole countries." That logically meant we were s**tholes too. I was entirely certain that targeting his predecessor was the point of the message. Suddenly, the whole United States felt like the worst parts of Old House, with Trump as Ubel, stalking people he did not like and raging at us for no reason at all.

With a heightened sense of what it means to be marginalized and an equally strong conviction that Trump was both an ugly scar on the national conscience and a malevolent presence on the international scene, getting through those early days was difficult. I engaged in a game with myself, trying to figure out precisely what he was, what possible force of nature created such a walking conundrum, this thing that appeared biologically human but was bereft of all it meant to *be* so.

In so many ways, he contradicted everything I had been taught as universal truths: what my grandmother taught me in Old House about right overcoming might, good triumphing over evil, and that living without integrity would not get anyone far in life. My teachers promised, too, that the cream would always rise to the top, and I grew into adulthood believing that people who had responsibility for the well-being of many others would be competent and at least more decent than not.

Even after moving past those simplistic frames, I came to believe—somewhat naively, I soon realized—that the United States, for the most part, was working its way toward a perfect union. I believed that the rule of law, social and political norms, and a commitment to ethics and decency would have protected the United States from someone like Donald Trump. It did not.

Instead, I had to process that not only could Trump stretch existing norms pretty much as wide as he wanted, but legislation was either nonexistent or insufficient to hold him accountable. I realized too that his election was, in large part, a backlash against the centrist, disciplined, dignified, and patriotic Obama because he happened to be a Black man. Those qualities stoked the rage of those who believe that elevated offices should be the exclusive preserve of White men or White people. Normalizing Blacks in high office was a threat to their belief system, and they were not having it. They wanted to put us back in our places.

The climate at the anti-poverty nonprofit where I had started working one week before the general election helped me to understand and process White supremacy much better. My life would be a study over the next two years into how some seemingly well-meaning White folks could not transcend the belief that they were innately better than people of color and how they lived out their belief, that in all matters personal and professional, their views, their wants, their desires, and their needs took precedence, and nothing short of complete acquiescence was good enough for some of them.

Much like aspects of Jamaican society, I was again in an environment where White people entirely occupied the spaces of influence and privilege, which they considered their natural right. Anyone who they perceived as a challenge to that paradigm found themselves in the fight of their lives. Even a clarifying question, which I am prone to ask because of my journalism background, would be enough to draw someone's ire, but I was not interested in undermining or replacing anyone. I wanted to understand how they work and the thought processes that go into what they do, which was not always evident. I turned up there—in response to their hire—as a foreign-born Black woman with significant competence and lived experience in the field, but I realized that it did not matter. They wanted my presence in order to show that they were adding "diverse" staff. Otherwise, they wanted me to be obedient and grateful that they had chosen to "include" me in hallowed spaces. And just like that, I was living under the brooding malevolence of Donald Trump and combating White supremacy within the organization where I worked every day.

I was ecstatic at the beginning to finally be working in international development, where I had wanted to be after graduate school if I could not go back home—and making up a tiny bit for the World Bank offer I had missed. But this nonprofit promising to combat global poverty was doing so outside of any recognizable framework. I did not recognize anything that said they understood underdevelopment at all, much less from the perspective of dependency theorists, for example, or anything deconstructing the capitalist superstructure that both causes and sustains global poverty. In the same way I had loosely assumed that the American president would be a halfway decent person, I thought anti-poverty, equity-focused nonprofits must necessarily be interested in the root causes of inequities and guided by principles of social justice or other frameworks beyond a mechanistic exercise driven by racialized benevolence.

I soon realized that my perspective was based on some naivete and an incomplete understanding of how inextricably capitalism and White supremacy are intertwined in ideology and culture, leading to a deep and pervasive conditioning of the mind that those schooled in their influence are unable to deprogram. Equally, I began to understand better the extent to which some international nonprofits were a part of the problem, and why the enormous impact they claim to have in their marketing material and grant proposals translates to only negligible gains, if any, in the communities they claim to serve.

I had some sense of this before. Critiquing the role of international nonprofits had been part of my humanities studies at UWI and Howard, and it came up often enough in media reports. But now I was obtaining firsthand experience by working within a nonprofit organization that would have gotten less than a B in one of our analyses, and not because the people were wholesale evil. There were some sincere happy warriors, and I am certain they were having some effect, though not as much as they claimed. The problem was the White supremacist perspective and culture, the arrogance that went along with it, and, correspondingly, the lack of awareness or understanding of its own deficiencies.

I saw the signs as soon as I entered the organization and realized that while its partners and clientele were partly in sub-Saharan Africa, the DC staff was almost exclusively White, just like the NBC newsroom had been when I arrived in the United States twenty years prior. Further, the few people of color, who could be counted on one hand, occupied the most junior positions, all with White supervisors, though they were among the most qualified in terms of lived experience and degrees from the London School of Economics, Columbia University, and George Washington University. I joined their ranks to become the only person in the institution with a terminal work-related degree, grounded in the thinking of non-White postcolonial development theorists like Gunder Frank, Beckford, Rodney, and Nettleford.

To my outsider's eye, accustomed as well to a society built on a plantation model, the patterns were glaring; they were vastly more so through the eyes of a social justice advocate, a journalist, and a scholar of the humanities. Driven by curiosity and inspired by those perspectives and an obligation to further my understanding—because this organization was engaged in anti-poverty work in the Global South, where racism in the international system has historically and contemporarily played an enormous role in the poverty of nations—I eventually asked a senior leader in a one-on-one conversation why nearly all-White staff had important-sounding titles regardless of their roles and why all the associates of color were strategically organized to report to them, even when the person in the subordinate position had better training, more experience, and was in every obvious way more suitable for the leadership role. Why was it that not even in one case was the dynamic reversed?

He said it was the organization's practice to pair less experienced staff with more experienced counterparts. I never asked how he defined experience or at what point the non-White staff would be deemed worthy because I did not buy it. I saw and experienced an organization entirely locked into a White-dominance and Black-subjugation framework where the descendants of enslaved people were largely cast into positions upholding the same old plantation paradigm. Unable to transcend its deep-seated cultural disposition and biases, the organization could not conceive of a relationship in which the dynamics were reversed or this paradigm was not the force behind its ethos.

This model explained why my days were filled with microaggressions and mindless meetings about how to work with the team, including the most memorable of all: my supervisor summoning me to her office to discuss why a coworker, a White woman who had shown the greatest animosity toward me, was not sleeping well—at home in her bed at night, far away from me! Somehow, that became something I needed to respond to. I tried to protect the supervisor from her inexperience and convince her that I did not belong in that meeting, but she was not having it. Clearly, she lacked the experience to understand why such a meeting should not happen or that it was an act of personal and professional abuse. So, there I was, brought to book for someone's insomnia.

Living with oppression and so often having to choose between ignoring and enduring or pushing back against racism, sexism, elitism, nativism, or other element of the toxic stew that diminishes people like me, resulted in an immense existential weariness that quickly overtook my passion for the job. This treatment had nothing to do with my talent, ability, humanity, or the rich experience I brought to the field. It was bigotry and a good deal of attempted bullying.

I made those observations while forming meaningful relationships with some of my colleagues and trying to contribute to the workplace as I was accustomed to doing. This was how it came that halfway into Black History Month in 2018, I invited my colleagues to join me for a lunch-and-learn in the conference room. Despite the nature of our work and their professed anti-poverty mission, the organization up to that point, February 13, in the heart of Washington, DC, had not so much as mentioned the annual observation designed to promote understanding of Black culture, Black oppression, and the primary reasons behind Black poverty and inequities in the United States. Plus, the director whom I had asked about the office structure, to his credit, had encouraged me to engage and share my experience with the staff. "Be an evangelist," he said. I sought his and HR's permission to conduct the informal lunchtime conversation.

I began with a video presentation titled *Race, Trauma, and the Doctrine of Discovery* by Mark Charles, a Native American theologian, in which he traced a fifteenth-century papal doctrine stipulating that any land not inhabited by Christians could be claimed by European explorers and explained how this doctrine has been applied practically and the effects it has had on non-White people in the United States. He explained further how the persistent subjugation of Blacks in the United States was traceable to the core belief of White Americans—once enshrined in the Constitution—that Blacks should be counted as three-fifths of a human being for taxation purposes. He ended with a poignant observation that oppression hurts both the oppressors and the oppressed, a familiar and persuasive theme to me. I thought it was a good choice, especially liking the compassion and spirituality that Father Charles brought to his observations and the fact that the presenter was someone outside of the Black community who was analyzing racism through a historical lens and connecting it to broader oppressive practices.

The ensuing silence suggested the presentation had obliterated all life in its path, but that was a typical reaction in the office whenever any situation called for frankness or on-the-spot original thinking on matters of race. I deduced that minority staffers were reluctant to speak, fearing their views might be poorly received or negatively impact their careers. White staffers often did not engage for one or a combination of three reasons: they did not accept the historical truths of slavery or the impact of ongoing racism; they saw anti-racism efforts as finger-pointing and a call for them to accept some responsibility because they were beneficiaries of ill-gotten privileges, which they also rejected; or they did not accept the credibility of Black people to speak on anything, not even racial justice issues, except in the cases where they had achieved celebrity status for work unrelated to racism. This would include people like Oprah Winfrey, Michelle Obama, or the late Maya Angelou.

No one had either a question or comment to begin the stimulating discussion I longed for and expected in any space pretending to search for answers or reasonable positions on some of society's pressing issues, like global poverty: how to define it and how to end it. Reactions eventually came in the form of a demand for me to apologize for showing the film and charges of anti-Semitism because, in a brief aside of about ninety seconds, Father Charles had criticized the US's relationship with Israel, which he described as an unhealthy codependence. It was nothing I had paid attention to because it was not directly relevant to my reasons for sharing the video. The value for me lay in the historical context it provided for racism against Black people, Native Americans, and other groups of color. I respectfully declined to apologize.

I had seen significantly more enthusiastic participation in so-called social justice discussions when White colleagues led them. This would be the case at another brown bag discussion near the end of August, centered around an article titled "Fake Equity: We can't train our way to racial equity," written by Heidi Schillinger, a diversity consultant based in Seattle, Washington. I found it to be an apt description of what I was experiencing. In part, she said: "A predictable pattern of systemic racism gives White people the benefit of the doubt while requiring people of color to show proof and evidence. This double standard plays out in who organizations hire and promote based on perceived potential."

The last of Schillinger's five recommendations was to change the decision-making table to include more people of color.

I initially did well on my commitment to simply listen, uninterested in unwittingly stoking the hostility that had followed the event I organized. Reactions to it had left a senior administrator in tears, unable to deal with the bullying from staffers demanding I be forced to apologize for the video I had shown. The ringleader was the woman who wanted me to account for why she had not slept well since I started working with the company. However, when another senior staff member commented that Black people should be patient with White folks who are still racist and not yet convinced that equity and justice are values to which they should subscribe, I asked for clarification.

"For how much longer?"

The question tripped off my tongue, prompted by the pompousness and impenetrable arrogance that often shows up when a White woman decides to take over a conversation about Black oppression. The woman, a self-styled reverend, tied herself up in countless knots in her attempts to respond then and in follow-up emails. I responded to a few, then let it go.

Those events and the response to them demonstrated that my nonprofit was not anti-oppressive, even though they said they were. They merely wanted to brand themselves that way and pretend to support "diversity and inclusion" without any interrogation of Whiteness or privilege. I saw no genuine interest in creating a just and authentic space supporting the anti-poverty work it claimed to be doing. In fact, I was directly instructed not to use the word "justice" because that might be perceived as political; and somehow politics and ongoing critical deconstruction of structures of injustice were deemed mutually exclusive and any opposing perspective was seen as subversive. It is a conundrum for a workplace culture to want highly educated, credentialed, and experienced people merely to comply and conform while talking about diversity.

Unwittingly, I had stumbled into the "everything is normal," garden-variety "nice" racism—a space of abundant discomfort for someone whose template is grounded in something very different.

Life has been too much of a battle for me to go looking for fights. With no initiation from me, racial tension simply became an unexpected and uncomfortable part of my reality. One way or another, I was consumed by it, and it made life infinitely more exhausting and got in the way of the goal in which I was invested: to end poverty, which I discovered was a concept superficially and insincerely constructed by the organization I worked for as well as by many others in the nonprofit community. The pressure was impossible to escape in a confined environment.

Other than devising ways to cope, I was invested in understanding and processing the many ways in which White supremacy exhibits and sustains itself. This is a necessary precursor to its dismantling, which is so vital to social progress and lasting peace. It is also necessary to help organizations that are insufficiently knowledgeable about the world they seek to change and cannot process life outside the paradigm of some people as superior and all others as inferiors based on racial and purely material constructs. The truth is that many NGOs, particularly small ones working in the Global South or in marginalized communities in the US, lack the comprehensive cultural knowledge they need to make the differences they claim to want to effect.

Over time, I recognized that White supremacy, toxic as it is, is grounded in a fragile sense of superiority and the deep insecurity it breeds. Centuries of exploitation, however, ensured that it is embedded in the superstructure, such as in the workplaces where more Black and other non-White people are attempting to integrate. By their nature, workplaces are the foremost purveyors of White supremacy and other forms of oppression, and a profoundly consequential reality is that most organizations either ignore or deny this quality. To work actively and sincerely to dismantle oppressive cultures and structures would mean a loss of identity and ego, both of which are central to holding the personality and psyche intact.

I was processing all of this in the shadow of the Brett Kavanaugh hearing in September 2018. Nominated to the Supreme Court by Donald Trump, Kavanaugh faced numerous reports of misconduct, including sexual assault and other unethical behaviors. I was plugged in—interested in the news as always and in this appointment specifically because it indicated the spiraling consequences of handing great power to an unscrupulous person.

Trump's choices would impact my life as much as what was already happening in my workplace. They would also affect my two daughters, whom I regard as Jamaicans and third-culture people but more American than anything else. The multicultural democracy that is America needed to get that one right, I thought.

I knew that the court should not be politicized and that the way the Senate handled the hearing would impact its image and character for generations to come because of the messages sent about our norms and mores, our integrity, or the lack thereof, and the degree to which power without ethics would be seen as our operating paradigm regardless of the rhetoric.

Trusted, politically impartial leaders, and institutions of stature, are essential to good order and social progress, and in the US, the Supreme Court needs to be that. I hoped and prayed that the Senate would send a positive message about honor, ethics, and integrity worldwide. In Jamaica, for example, where government corruption is problematic, I feared they would take their cues from anything resembling the same in the US system and throw it back at people like me and others who attempt to hold them accountable. I have never stopped paying attention to Jamaica. Whatever the US deems acceptable will influence behaviors there, for good or ill. The rest of the world watches what the

US does and jeers at its contradictions and inconsistencies.

I arrived at work one day in late September, feeling wearier than usual. Summer had cooled, and the leaves were falling gently but resolutely. Fall no longer triggered anxiety about impending cold weather. Instead, it meant slowing down, long evening walks at Brookside Garden or the Northwest Branch trails with my friend Mayer, and enjoying the woods in their myriad shades of gold, rust, and brown. In some essential ways, I had adjusted to life in the US.

The weariness was neither about heat nor cold nor the unsupported workload, nor the energy it cost me to push back on all kinds of absurdities instead of working on behalf of the so-called "global poor." It was about Donald Trump, my new daily reminder of Ubel, just a little farther from me and without the actual machete sharpened on both sides. It was about the sneering, privileged Brett Kavanaugh; Mitch McConnell, Trump's enabler; the other dodgy old White men in the United States Senate; and everyone else pretending to be upright people but manipulating the investigations into Kavanaugh's conduct to get the outcome they wanted. It was about depraved and unconscionable people with the power to impact my choices on the most intimate and vulnerable parts of my life. It was about my powerlessness to stop any of it.

Throughout Obama's presidency, I had watched McConnell wield his power as Speaker of the House with incredible vitriol, laser focused on blocking all initiatives to make life better for average American citizens. In his own words, his one goal was to ensure that the president failed! McConnell, then third in line to the presidency, was actively sabotaging both the man and the institution, and by extension, the entire nation, while enjoying the presumption of regard—all of this going mostly unchallenged by the media.

I felt a growing sense of foreboding at the realization that my two daughters were growing into a future increasingly in the hands of awful people. The better life we had come, stayed, and worked for was retreating into the past, like the forest rushing past a train. Their future was my barometer—what I used to judge my boss, for example. Every time I sat alone with her, searched her face, and saw no sign of a soul, I would ask myself: *Would you want your beloved girls to have her as their boss?*

The answer was always a resounding "No!" My children deserved better.

The same principle had applied to the national leadership since January 2017. We deserved better. The world deserved better, but what could we do? What could I do?

As I watched the hearing that day, I tried to fathom the crippling dissonance I had been battling since Trump became president. I thought of him sometimes as a scarecrow with a rudimentary likeness to a human being but missing all the essential elements. His vileness bothered me, but his ever-present red necktie was becoming its own source of annoyance and discomfort, and I did not understand why. It came together that day as I looked at images of him and of his surrogates and faithful supporters mimicking his ways and dress code.

Trump, I realized, had loosely two kinds of supporters: the "poorly educated" MAGA-hat-wearing crowd who attended his rallies and did not bother to invest the energy in concealing that they were unapologetic bigots, and those in professional spaces or who turned up on national television to advance his message and defend him. They were the so-called evangelicals—senators, congresspeople, lawyers, mega-rich businesspeople, neighbors, and Ivy League graduates, people of "standing" who should be shown regard and from whom society has generally been taught to expect rational and decent behavior. They were rabidly dishonest, illogical, and manipulative—spewing propaganda with no concern about its impact on individuals or the society at large. They used the same playbook, and they all wore their red neckties, transmitting the same message in the most benign way: an acceptable but seemingly useless piece of clothing hanging down their chests and ending in arrows pointing toward their penises.

I realized then that the red necktie was not a harmless or useless piece of masculine attire intending to convey nothing more than sartorial elegance and related considerations at all. It was a blatant symbol of ill intent, and not because it was an old call sign for male prostitutes. Rather, it was intentionally worn to communicate aggression, coercion, and a desire to dominate—all key attributes of misogyny and White supremacy. Thus, their "power" ties, under the guise of being well dressed, communicated their affinity to old, archaic, and oppressive structures and what they are after: the power and privilege they believe they are entitled to, opportunity and access to enrich themselves, and the ability to keep others at bay. They have no qualms about hurting those who were already suffering, particularly those who do not align with their views of what it means to be human. There was a certain homogeneity in their personas—vacuousness, narcissism,and unabashed depravity. The red neckties served as a unifying symbol, just like the MAGA hats, posing as a formal male accessory.

Ultimately, while some men wear them out of a misguided sense that they are being fashion forward, red neckties are ever-present reminders that there are people whose goal in life is to control, dominate, and exploit others. This is among the worst human impulses, and it has led to some of the greatest tragedies of our civilization: slavery and colonialism, the annihilation of native peoples throughout the Americas, apartheid in South Africa, Nazi rule and the Holocaust, genocide in Rwanda, and ironically now, the subjugation of the Palestinian people by the Israeli government. It has also been the chief characterization of the relationship between Whites and Blacks in the United States, with one group determined to control the other in every sphere of interaction and leaving the other no choice but to fight back—or to exist in a permanent defensive posture.

I finally understood my increasingly negative psychological response to men wearing them and to women who behave as if they were. Like Donald Trump, from whom the attire is inseparable, they are profound symbols of everything that is wrong in American society.

Consequence be damned! I resolved to fight ill intent and injustice however I could, including in my workplace, where I was experiencing so much hostility in a self-styled anti-oppressive space.

Early in the spring, I had added my name to a roster of volunteers to present at the weekly staff meeting at my workplace. I picked November 29 to give myself as much time as possible to prepare a good presentation and execute it before the end of the year. It turned out to be exactly two months after the Senate Judiciary Committee voted 11 to 10 to send Kavanaugh's nomination to the full Senate with a favorable recommendation.

As the date drew closer, I decided to use the opportunity to open a discussion about the nature of oppression from the perspective of someone with multiple marginalized identities, interrogate some of the underlying premises of White supremacy as they played out within the organization, in the US, and globally, and reiterate social justice as an imperative for the better world they claimed to want. To me, it was entirely in keeping with the organization's purported purview.

My Australian colleague laughed when I told him the topic of my upcoming presentation. We were not yet lunch buddies, but I thought it was in the realm of possibility if we stuck around long enough. In the meantime, we bonded over cricket, and he was professional, polite, and kind—all I needed from anyone to function in the workplace. No coddling, condescending inclusion, or allyship required.

"'The Global Social Justice Agenda and the Need for a New World Order!' That's it," I said, laughing with him.

"Oh, come on, Grace!" he retorted. "You have to come up with something more practical than that."

That he found the topic of my presentation more than a little quixotic was unsurprising and amusing to me too. By then, I had seen enough to understand that the culture at many nonprofits like mine was largely performative. I saw a great deal of posturing, an ingrained addiction to PowerPoint, and a devotion to using keywords to ensure their blog posts rose to the top in Google searches. I saw little actual knowledge or desire to better understand the condition that we call poverty: what it is, how it manifests, what causes it, what sustains it, why solutions are so intractable, and why nothing short of radical restructuring of the global system and destruction of the narratives that support it would be sufficient to change things. I saw far less conviction or even pretense at ethical considerations, which are baseline considerations regarding issues like poverty and marginalization from my perspective.

Therefore, while I laughed with my colleague, I was entirely serious about the topic. I thought my coworkers needed to understand better, at the very least, that poverty does not happen without structural societal failures that cause and support it, and solutions cannot be found in isolation of historical and contemporary social injustices; the framework for analysis must be ethical principles, including a commitment to social justice—not public relations. I saw the presentation as my first and perhaps last opportunity to put the issues squarely before my employers and coworkers and demonstrate what it means to live within an oppressive paradigm and, just as importantly, what it means to live outside of it.

I also wanted them to understand what social justice is and what it means to me—that it was not a liberal or progressive political concept or any such superficial construct but a principle grounded in my lived experience, in the essence of my faith as a follower of Christ and what my education has taught me. Most importantly, I wanted them to hold up a mirror to their "anti-poverty" work and understand why their refusal to even use the words "fairness" or "justice" concerning the conditions and necessary outcomes for marginalized communities was hugely problematic for me, who lived, saw, and understood deep-seated material lack—an insoluble condition without widespread systemic reforms.

The need to eliminate cultures of oppression was everywhere in our social environment, and the Kavanagh hearing demonstrated how easy it is for even cornerstone institutions to be diminished, if not corrupted, by the determined dishonesty of a coterie to whom right and wrong are one and the same if they are benefiting.

Twenty-one days after Kavanagh was installed on the court, a gunman stormed the Tree of Life Synagogue in Squirrel Hill near Pittsburgh, Pennsylvania, killing eleven elderly worshippers during Shabbat worship. That afternoon, Mayer and I walked along one of our favorite routes, through Kemp Mill Shopping Center and onto the Sligo Creek Trail toward Dennis Avenue local park. I was overwrought; Mayer was pensive.

Together we had already logged hundreds of hours walking in and around our mostly Orthodox Jewish community, and often much farther away—time we enjoyed as exercise and a commune with nature to combat the hazards of growing old. It was also time spent deconstructing national politics, other current events, and the vagaries of our lives, whatever they happened to be in the moment.

Before retiring from his career as a public relations executive, Mayer had been a journalist at the *Wall Street Journal*. Like me, he had a lifelong love affair with the profession and remained interested in the world of news and ideas. On the surface, he—an Ashkenazi Jew—and I were Kemp Mill's "odd couple," but beyond whatever people saw when they looked at us, we shared deep personal and professional interests and similar ideas about humanity and our places in the world.

A car came bearing down on us as we crossed Sligo Creek Parkway slightly east of University Boulevard. I scampered to the left and watched Mayer as he followed at his usual part-dignified and part-indifferent pace—as if daring the driver to hit him and never seeming to think they could do it. With my still healthy fear of the volume and speed of traffic, I always thought he was courting disaster. Once we were safely on the other side, I urged him not to be so nonchalant about crossing the street. He blew me off, and for the first time, I voiced my fear that the driver could have been a White supremacist and that the two of us—a Jewish man and a Black woman—might be their idea of trophy-hunting.

The Tree of Life shooting was one more reminder of how the US under Donald Trump had become so filled with hate and racial and ethnic tensions that even in suburban Maryland, one of the most progressive states, the fear of a racially motivated attack was far from unfounded. I was increasingly wary whenever Mayer and I ventured deep into the woods, where our voices could be lost among the thick stands of oak and magnolia. More than I feared a stray pit bull, I feared encountering an insecure, maladjusted White man, angry because I exist or because Mayer exists.

As much as I hate guns, I had been thinking about getting one—something small that I could put in my pocket with my keys and phone and pull out and handle quickly and efficiently if I needed to. Yes, it was a contradiction of my values and fear of violence, but if children were not safe in schools, Christians were not safe in churches, and Jewish people were not safe in synagogues, then I knew that grace might not be enough on some days.

"What's causing this, Mayer? Where is all this hatred coming from?"

I had my ideas. I had seen and experienced enough. I was being fretful, and I needed his comforting wisdom.

"It's greed," he responded glumly. "Greed and irrational fear. Some people just want too much, and we do not know enough about each other."

A part of me wanted to believe the answer was more complicated—that it required the wisdom of the sages speaking or writing voluminously in flowery prose but in terms searing and straightforward enough to explain the rise of Trump and the relentless effort to suppress non-White people. But I knew that in Mayer's simple answer lay flawless wisdom. Society was not sufficiently integrated; it lacked real bonds of sisterhood, brotherhood, and community where people see each other as fellow humans first as opposed to whatever label they choose to respond to, and people were growing further apart.

Add to this to the perception of human worth purely in material terms—money, title, possessions, and other externally validating indicators—and the unending quest for wealth and power for its own sake, as well as the ego of those in charge who believe that the more they have, the more worthy and important they are, and the fragility of the social fabric becomes clearer. Greed is not only about money but about worth, power, space, attention, and regard.

This ethos is everywhere, including the workplace, and maybe more so in the workplace. I question the future of our civilization if there is no real commitment from people in power to build a better and more just world.

Mayer's brief analysis stuck with me as I contemplated my presentation. When the day came, ten months after the Black History Month dust-up, I began with a Bob Marley classic:

One love, one heart
Let's get together and feel all right
Hear the children cryin' (one love).

I was soon explaining to my colleagues that in the context of the organization's work, I wanted to see more focus on understanding the causes of poverty and the social deformation of many communities of color in the United States and the Global South, where they claimed to want to eradicate it. For how does one eradicate a condition without awareness of its causes? And I suggested that any genuine attempt to understand and solve global poverty requires bold and honest questioning of old narratives that Western societies perpetuate about non-White people, our humanity, and our place in history. The same approach is required regarding how words like philanthropy, charity, and development are conceptualized and used by first-world governments and NGOs working to end poverty.

Specifically, I invited them to examine the actions of France, the home base of one of our highly regarded European partners, whose condescension toward Haiti was always noticeable and exasperating to me, yet I was expected to treat them with reverence. The poster child for social and political underdevelopment in the Americas, Haiti is a primary target of the NGO community. Our French partners did not seem to know that in addition to 300 years of slavery, Haiti had to contend with 125 years of extortion by the French government, beginning with an 1825 demand for compensation for loss of property after the Caribbean nation declared its independence from colonial rule. Compliance meant that Haiti could not afford the public services its newly freed people needed, which has much to do with why the country is so poor, why its public institutions are so warped, and why its citizens so often seek stability outside their borders.

In the context of this historical injustice, I asked, how should one characterize whatever France now gives to Haiti? Is it charity or aid based on the goodwill of the French people, or is it giving back to Haiti what was theirs to begin with? What would constitute fairness, justice, and equity in the relationship between France and Haiti, given the well-developed state of the former and the impoverishment of the latter?

And what of Belgium's responsibility to the Democratic Republic of the Congo? Coincidentally, I had been in Brussels that summer with my sister, who had lived there for two years, to keep her company while she tied up loose ends. I wandered around the Grand-Place, contemplating its golden facade and how much of it was maintained through the exploitation of the Congo and whether it mattered to contemporary society that Leopold II enslaved and abused a whole nation, killing or mutilating an estimated fifteen million people in the process. So, does Belgium owe reparations to the people of the Congo? Taken together, is it a mere coincidence that Haiti and the Democratic Republic of the Congo, two of the most historically exploited countries in the world, are also the two poorest?

Finally, I pointed out the parallel between African Americans who suffered through slavery and Jim Crow and contemporary patterns of political, economic, and social discrimination. The education system, which, in any society, should be an avenue for transformation and better quality of life, was itself the primary vehicle transmitting White supremacist ideology, and this at the most elite levels of the system. The inequities were baked in, requiring deeper transformative change than what currently obtained. For example, it took Harvard University well over 200 years to recognize the humanity of Black people and admit its first African American student—as an experiment. Georgetown University, meanwhile, executed one of the most egregious crimes against humanity when, in 1838, it participated in the sale and trafficking of almost 300 enslaved Black people to get ahead of emancipation and pay off its debt.

I saw the rapt attention. I heard the dead silence in the room. I reveled in the opportunity to be who I was despite their efforts to diminish me. I had stayed quiet in the ten months following Black History Month and knew I was at my best in the setting I was now in—prepared and speaking passionately about a subject in which I was comfortably knowledgeable. I finished in tears, weighed down by a confluence of emotions:

"Even if the Georgetown case was not criminal by the standards of the day, it represents extreme moral and ethical failures when measured against the standards of Christianity to which Georgetown subscribes as a Catholic-owned institution, and the intent of education as outlined by the ancient scholars and the ethical pillars upon which even contemporary institutions are built. Centuries later, that case and other similar ones require full distillation, analysis, and proper restitution to the victims or their descendants.

"Over centuries, nation-states and private institutions have not sufficiently acknowledged their roles in the poverty and trauma of some communities and have instead created false narratives to cover up their wrongdoings. It is increasingly difficult to imagine a peaceful and progressive future without powerful leaders of the world engaging honestly and effectively in redesigning society to reflect a more just and authentic path forward. This means they must accept responsibility, make restitution, and hasten the pace of the just and respectful society that people deserve and are clamoring for.

"This is what social justice means to me. It is a moral imperative first, and to that end, it must mean a fundamental reversal of old patterns of behavior and the promotion of new paradigms that are anti-oppressive, life-affirming, and liberating for all."

I felt triumphant at having finished the presentation and making myself fully understood. I had done so without fear of consequence, which I find to be the greatest inhibition to truth, justice, and progress in the American workplace. There was not even vague apprehension of what would come next—just a resolve that whatever it was, I would be just fine because what was the worst thing that could happen?

I did not want to be a martyr. I was merely perplexed by the purposeful ignorance and exhausted by the duplicity people wore like Trump did his red neckties. I felt I owed it to myself for all the years I spent going to school; to the lived experience that drove me; to my ancestors who suffered centuries of brutality in captivity; and to my daughters, who, in the name of progress and justice, should not have to fight the same battles I faced.

Was that disrespectful? Revolutionary? If so, what does the workplace want from an educated person? I do not always understand.

My first trip to the African continent loomed ahead by only a few days. I was on a mission to train a group of medical professionals and advocates from across the continent on how to connect with and use media to promote child health and proper nutrition and to show them how to prepare for and present themselves in international forums like the World Bank, the United Nations, and the World Health Organization, in particular.

As fate would have it, I was going to Kenya, a part of Africa to which I had always felt connected even though my ancestors came mainly from Nigeria, Ghana, Liberia, and Sierra Leone. It was enough for me to know I was about to visit the continent and to be away, for even a short time, from the racial hostility in the US.

"You took the whole damn place to church!" my Ethiopian colleague exulted when the presentation ended. "You took us to church!"

Several others expressed similar sentiments, but my biggest takeaway was the expression of the chief administrative officer, caught on-screen behind me and slightly to my left as I neared the end of my presentation. He had been working remotely and joined the meetings via a video-conferencing program. Regardless of how good the presentation was and how loud the applause, I knew what I saw was a look not of satisfaction but of profound disturbance.

I felt a fantastic sense of peace. At some point, I thought, one must live without fear; otherwise, the entire journey of life will be meaningless.

I already knew I was being fingered as the cause of the team's dysfunctions—never mind that the entire organization had been rooted in dysfunction long before I joined them. It did not matter what I did. If I tried to fly below the radar and was generally quiet and measured in my comments, someone would complain that I was not speaking enough. If I tried to be more involved, someone would complain that I was talking too much. If I left my desk for five minutes for a bathroom break, one of the women would report me missing, and the whole team would be looking for Grace—the runaway slave.

It took a while to understand that the problem was because I existed in my skin as a Black woman in spaces where the dominant majority did not think I belonged as an equal. They would have been fine with me in a subordinate or nonthreatening position, as they were with the African partners, but I was there as a professional with better relevant qualifications and lived experience than they possessed and uninterested in either performative allyship or forced camaraderie. I also challenged organizational practices such as unpaid internships and how that was counter to their mission to end poverty and excluded people from the communities they needed and claimed to serve. It should have been helpful to them, but they perceived it as negative criticism. Nothing I did short of leaving or walking in front of a truck would help. I am certain they would have sent me off with expensive flowers and glowing tributes and proceeded to happy hour to celebrate with wine and hors d'oeuvres. It never crossed my mind. I simply liberated myself from the fear of being fired.

I was intentional about using the presentation to do something different from the daily mind-crushing banality and to expound on a worldview grounded in a set of ethical principles I thought was essential to international development but which remained absent from the organization's work. I wanted to examine the meaning of justice in a space that refused to use the word or see it as vital to its ethos.

I was old enough to understand that meaningful change in the context of social struggles requires deliberate disruption of cultures and mores that accommodate oppression, and I was committed enough to risk losing a steady paycheck. I have always believed that without the willingness to take the risk myself, I should not expect it or ask it of others. This belief is central to who I am, and the older I get, the more deliberate I am in ensuring that small, cumulative acts of injustice are addressed with the same urgency as the big ones that garner global media attention and become trending hashtags on social media. If they are not, they grow and flourish.

This crucial lesson draws from far back in my life—from Patrick Bryan and all the historical figures, individuals, or groups whose efforts have had far-reaching impacts in the struggle for human liberation, including the abolition of slavery. A name like George Fox comes readily to mind, reminding me of the beauty of history, the value of the written word, and how I can draw a parallel between some of our mutual influencers—our belief systems—and how early in our lives we began to question the structures of our societies and reject what did not make sense.

Fox lived in England in the mid-seventeenth century, took the Bible seriously, and recognized and questioned unjust societal patterns. He eventually broke from the Church of England and founded the Quaker movement, which became the first organized anti-slavery group in Great Britain. Some Quakers continued to enslave, but by the late-seventeenth century the organization had denounced the practice and voted to abolish it completely almost a century before the United States.

Quakerism would influence Martin Luther King Jr.'s nonviolence theology during the civil rights movement indirectly through Rufus Jones, a noted Quaker philosopher, and directly through Howard Thurman, a Black Morehouse College graduate pursuing further studies at Haverford College in Philadelphia. Thurman's book *Jesus and the Disinherited*, which interprets the teachings of Christ through the experiences of the marginalized and discusses nonviolent responses, influenced much of King's work. Though not much in the limelight now, I count these men among the forces who recognized early and correctly that God is present in every human being—not just in men, White people, rich people, or Christians—and helped change the world for good.

William Wilberforce, a central figure in the abolitionist movement in Britain, challenged the slave trade at age twenty-six and fought for the next two decades to end it. Meanwhile, Granville Sharp's hugely consequential advocacy against slavery began when he found a battered Black teenager on a London Street and took him to William, his physician brother, for treatment. Together, they nursed him back to health, only for him to be recognized and snatched back by his enslaver, a planter from Jamaica who had beaten him within inches of his life. Granville subsequently became a founder of the Society for the Abolition of the Slave Trade.

I met the English abolitionists in history classes in Jamaica, and their American counterparts much later: Benjamin Rush, John Greenleaf Whittier, William Lloyd Garrison, and others who vigorously opposed slavery, even if some unwittingly projected their White savior complex in the process. I put that down to the impossibility of entirely transcending beliefs and behaviors that are hardwired in one's socializing environment or divorcing from language thought to be appropriate throughout one's life. There were also those in later years who supported the civil rights movement, helping with organizations, joining public protests, and protecting Black people from racism when necessary.

Generally, though, White support in the United States has not been sufficient to combat normalized anti-Black oppression. Had it been, we would be much further along in the quest for a more just and ethical America. While I do not believe most White Americans are racist, there is no doubt that the majority have been socialized within an anti-Black culture and are often unable to separate their biases from reality. I also believe that a significant minority is dangerously racist, and they form the core of Trump supporters and the Republican Party, whether they wear MAGA hats or red neckties or neither.

These contemplations were merely efforts to grasp how the Quakers and Wilberforce, Sharp, Rush, and others like them recognized, understood, and accepted the idea of one common humanity unimpacted by the superficiality of race nearly 400 years ago, yet here and now, people like me and countless others remain targets of racism from colleagues and neighbors. So, as reasonable as I knew the presentation was, I knew it would trigger a backlash. I was not sure what form it would take, but whatever it was, I was fully prepared for it.

Preoccupied by the prospects of what awaited me in the office, I was caught off guard by a confrontation on a Montgomery County Ride On bus on my way to the Wheaton metro station one morning soon after. A White woman with seemingly no intention of getting off the bus suddenly decided she wanted to disembark. By then, I had boarded and was safely out of her way, but she demanded that I get back off so she could get off—because the rule was that boarding passengers should yield to those getting off, even though she had decided at the last minute.

The last thing I wanted was to acquiesce to an unreasonable request, but I also did not want to be drawn into a battle over something relatively trivial. The urge to resist rested in both the reality and metaphor at play—me, a Black woman, being overtly bullied by a White woman on a public bus for no reason. There was so much of this behavior at work and in the broader environment already, manifesting in more harmful ways, that I did not want to engage with it.

The minutes ticked by. No one uttered a sound, but several passengers shook their heads in bewilderment. The driver, a Black man, did not seem to know what to do. I thought about the police officers with real work to do who would have to be called for something that would have been petty at best, except for the racial dynamic. I did not want to be in the middle of that. I got off the bus thinking how proud my daughters would be that I stood down rather than being sucked into a drama not of my choosing.

They were disappointed, particularly my mild-mannered firstborn. They thought it was one time when I should have fought like a Maroon instead of allowing myself to be bullied by a misguided woman. I put my decision down to the wisdom of growing older, declining a fight that would have cost me and everyone else more than it was worth. I chose Grace—or resignation; after all, this was not someone I would likely see again. This was quite unlike my workplace, where one interaction might define all future interactions.

It is not pejorative to say workplaces are spaces where all forms of bigotry—sexism, racism, nativism, elitism—collide and combine under the imperative to create profit and keep the capitalist system humming. In most societies, they also operate on hierarchical structures that determine what benefits are available to whom and when. They are therefore generally contested spaces where people and groups are almost "naturally" pitted against each other based on age, race, ethnicity, religion, and whether one attended Howard or Harvard. Survival often requires wearing the mask, which my rural Jamaican upbringing did not prepare me for.

I recognize that the fixation on these selected variables exacerbates conflict more than it offers the possibility of a liberating future. Intersectionality and experience have taught me that the one factor common to cultures and systems of oppression and which requires deep interrogation is power—what it is, who has it, how it is derived, and how it is used. Built as it is on layers of power relationships, the workplace invites exactly this kind of deconstruction, toward equity, justice, and genuine liberation.

CHAPTER NINE
GRACE

I longed to ignore the news and live in blissful ignorance of what was happening around me, but I could not be that person. Every new comment from Trump designed to belittle and incite attacks against vulnerable populations wore on me. With gasoline spewing from his fields of hate, the racist flames that smoldered under Obama's presidency became raging infernos that we could not ignore. I feared for my safety, knowing that while I could try to keep my mouth shut so no one heard my island accent or my views on race, there was nothing I could do about walking through America and the world as a Black woman.

I continued to fervently hope that Trump would go away—that something in the great American system, supposedly built on rules and laws, would prove its mettle in the face of its greatest internal threat since the Civil War. As the much-hyped Mueller investigations into Russian interference in the election dragged on, I feared that it too would be manipulated to serve the interests of power; no truth was forthcoming, no affirmation of the existence and importance of moral correctness as a prerequisite for high office or the law as equitable, enforceable, and binding. There would be no accountability and justice applied regardless of the race and status of an offender.

I felt a growing sense that the system was a sham in many ways and that Trump knew it as much as he embodied it. He never failed to remind us with his red necktie, nor did his most faithful lieutenants, like Rudy Giuliani and Jared Kushner. Rachel Maddow's breathtaking nightly takeoff on MSNBC kept me hopeful in the early stages, but eventually I began to feel like, even there, I was being taken for a ride. The rise increasingly was not worth the inevitable thud each night. She remained a lifeline nonetheless.

A friendly colleague at the nonprofit, seemingly imbued with the wisdom of her Aztec ancestors, had been skeptical from the start. She was much younger—my children's age—but where I had been optimistic, she was certain that nothing sufficient to hold the president accountable would come of any investigation into his conduct. He would serve out his term. We each felt so strongly that we had a bet: I owed her dinner if the report came to naught and Trump served out his term, and she owed me if there were any real consequences for Trump. We know who won.

I credited her surety to a greater understanding of the system, having been born into it while maintaining a parallel set of outsider's eyes as the child of immigrant parents. It was harder for me to accept that in a country heralding itself as one of law and order, a con man could publicly solicit an adversarial foreign power to help him win an election, flout the laws and norms, and violate nearly every principle of common decency but nonetheless be able to serve out an entire four-year term as commander in chief of the armed forces, with access to national security apparatuses, and all this while being accorded the same respect to which a legitimate president was entitled. All of this in the same country where his predecessor had to show the world his birth certificate to prove that he was who he said he was and was born where he said he was.

The times I spent outside the US became my saving grace. The trips were mostly short, but I benefited from being beyond the reach of Trump's toxicity and the parts of American society that were more than happy for the official license to oppress. I realized how much one's enervation under those conditions is best understood when one is rid of it, even temporarily—how much lighter my spirit became without the need to endure or challenge the arrogance of racism.

The experience of being in physically and culturally new places also reinforced the pleasant reality of a bigger world beyond the United States. Every day outside provided the fresh oxygen necessary to return and endure for a little while longer. I looked forward to those reprieves, as well as the opportunity to understand the conditions and belief systems that determine how other societies are programmed and what glue holds them together, particularly those substantively different from either Jamaica or the United States.

As Father Charles explains in *Race, Trauma, and the Doctrine of Discovery*, the United States is toxic for Blacks and other non-White people because White supremacist ideology was embedded in its DNA and remains intractable. This means that organizations like the two major political parties, the media, the church, and the education system are carriers, participants, and drivers, even if they claim not to be. Spaces where it is less present will be more pleasant for Black people.

This felt true of my experience in Japan, beginning with immigration officers at Narita Airport. No one looked at me with suspicion or hostility—as if they thought I was coming in to steal, kill, or at least had some cocaine in my makeup bag. There was no tension. I felt no threat to my integrity as a human being and none to my physical or psychological safety, even as I uncharacteristically walked the streets late at night with friends or alone, shopping, eating out, and visiting ancient temples. I visited the Imperial Palace and the Akasaka Palace, where a trio of security guards sensibly made me drink from my water bottle before leaving me alone to wander the grounds to my heart's content. When I asked for help on the subway, I found myself surrounded by six or seven men, each earnestly trying to make sure that I got the most straightforward directions, in the best English, that would take me closest to where I wanted to go.

I recognized that as an American on a work trip, I was cocooned somewhat. This status assigned me a value other than as a disempowered migrant seeking long-term opportunities. People typically react differently when they know others are not trying to take anything away from them. My enthusiasm was also checked a few times by my Korean colleague, who felt much less optimistic about the country and the culture than I did. She had strong reservations about a country that had once annexed hers, held it as a colony for almost four decades, and severely abused her people at times, notably during World War II when millions of Koreans were forced to support Japan, including hundreds of women who were forced into sexual slavery.

Still, some things felt different, and with good reasons.

The Japanese committed to peace after the war. It is a widely held belief in international circles that the country has tried to follow that path and has prospered as a result. Their approach, I felt, was noncombative—not predicated on me as a lesser "other" or as a natural enemy in the way racial differences often present in the US. This assumption is why it is so instinctive for White people to call the police on Black people, whether they are birdwatching in a city park or fishing in a neighborhood lake.

It also explains racialized policing and the cycle of fear and distrust it breeds in minority communities, as well as the hostility to Black people in the workplace and why, two decades into the twenty-first century, employers are trying to create cultures of "belonging" and still experiencing pushback from those opposed to change. When DEI is deconstructed and stripped of its peripheral issues, it is exposed as a clumsy attempt to address ongoing racism. It is a sideshow—feel-goodism that does little to address the problem. So of course, it quickly became popular in corporate America.

My trip was just long enough to form an impression of what it means to be Black in Japan, and it was far more pleasant than being Black in the United States. The fact that people are not allowed to own assault rifles and routinely act out their resentment by killing people in bulk is one enormous factor.

That the place where I stayed felt like a garden in full bloom also helped tremendously. Nature is healing. The historic New Otani Hotel sits in the middle of a 400-year-old samurai garden with Eden-like enclaves of koi ponds, camellias, roses, and an endless variety of plants and flowers. I lost myself in the outdoors after delivering the opening plenary at the conference I attended on advancing positive change in the world, particularly for the people of the Global South. As always, I made my crucial point: I understand that the world cannot be perfect, but I also know it can be more just. Getting there requires genuine commitment—and action.

It was well received, and in that space, I felt like the different parts of myself were in full sync. I was enjoying the lure of faraway places and advocating for the disadvantaged in a place that deeply satisfied my abiding love and respect for the natural world.

Even Germany, where I visited in 2017 and 2018, seemed surprisingly comfortable. I never felt any great affinity to it previously, but once I had my American passport, I honored a promise to visit a friend who had moved there shortly after I left Jamaica. Traveling there as a tourist also meant experiencing a culture with some similar characteristics of the US but without the tension of interacting with it beyond a superficial level. I was not looking for a job or health care or housing, and the trip had a certain end. I could simply enjoy walking in and out of neighborhoods and boutiques in Wiesbaden, a city in the state of Hesse, or the drive to a hilltop with a stunning view of Rüdesheim, a winemaking town in the Rhine Valley, or a riverboat cruise past ancient castles and little villages that took me back to *Grimms' Fairy Tales*. I reveled in a favorite pastime, wandering the neighborhood and photographing old churches.

Twice I walked to Evangelical Market Church (Marktkirche), a skinny-looking redbrick structure with dozens of soaring spires. The market held in its shadows on Wednesdays and Saturdays was a surprising and inviting attraction, festive and colorful like the harvests of my childhood in Old House, when villagers took the best of their produce as gifts to God and laid them across the altar at church. I lost myself among the bevy of vendors, sampling fresh strawberries, homemade ice cream, cheeses, meats, and breads from Germany, Poland, and Hungary. It was glorious!

Whatever the theology, I loved the idea of a church as a marketplace for wonderful organic foods and small producers to earn an income so much that I forgot all about being a Black woman in an entirely White space, far away from Old House. I felt like a person—one with similar needs, interests, and vulnerabilities to the people around me. No one looked at me differently, gave me a side-eye, or acknowledged in any way that I looked different from them. I felt, however naively, that the implicit acknowledgment was of one common humanity. The experience reinforced my belief that race can and does fade into the background with deliberate effort and once we recognize even small parts of ourselves in the values and ways of others. Somehow, it seemed to require much more effort in the United States.

I blamed myself the two times I experienced race-based anxiety. While nothing happened, it could have, and it would have been the result of less-than-smart choices, in one case at least. In the first instance, my youngest sister, Sadie, and I arrived in Wiesbaden close to 3 a.m., after a trip to Brussels and Amsterdam. We had spent a wonderful few days trudging around the cities and unexpectedly meeting up with Marjan de Bruin, my old journalism professor from UWI. I had not seen her in years and had no idea where she was, but she came to mind as I crossed the border from Belgium into the Netherlands and spotted the first windmills. I remembered she was the first Dutch person I had met, and nearly thirty years prior she had been my inspiration to someday visit her country. I posted a message on Facebook saying as much. She replied immediately. She was still living in Jamaica but was in Amsterdam for the International AIDS Conference and within a bike ride of my hotel. We caught up over dinner one evening, and over breakfast on our way out. It was just what my soul needed—a reminder of all the good people in my life and a break from the excessively stress-inducing environment that I was existing in.

I even got to indulge my secret dream of experiencing as many of the world's cities as possible by water and took a cruise around Amsterdam. It got unexpectedly more interesting when from my seat on the right, I caught sight of a building with a large sign: THE DUTCH WEST INDIA COMPANY. I had encountered them in tenth-grade history class as the most prolific "slave traders," responsible for trafficking hundreds of people from Africa to the Caribbean and South America during the 1640s. I suddenly wished I was on the ground so I could explore what was inside the structure and why it was still there.

My sister and I ran out of juice and aborted our plans to try to reach Switzerland, instead catching a train back to Wiesbaden. It malfunctioned and sat on the track for several hours, resulting in our late arrival at our home station. Instead of calling a cab, we decided to walk approximately twenty minutes to our friend's apartment. We met no one, and not even a car passed, but there in the dead of night, I did wonder, *What if we run into skinheads or anyone hostile to Black people?*

Another time, we took the bus to Fasanerie, a wildlife and botanical park outside the city. In a world without anti-Black racism, it would have been just a nice afternoon outing in nature for a couple of curious Jamerican tourists. We felt no threat at all while trudging through the woods, watching the goats, deer, bears, otters, and foxes, and stopping to swap stories and laughs when we encountered a newly arrived Jamaican man from Westmoreland Parish and his German husband; the odds seemed long, but not for a people who pride themselves on showing up everywhere from the North Pole to the South and all points between. One day, one of us will plant our flag on Mars. I am certain.

As the sun dimmed and we turned homeward, we became two little specks of color in a sea of White faces. We waited at the bus stop, more than a little apprehensive in a tight crowd that did not seem hostile but was not friendly either. Again, I wondered, *What if one crazy person acts on their bias and comes at us? Would others join them, or would they help us?* I was relieved when the bus came and we were on our way back home.

I challenged my own assessments whenever I found myself making a comparison—wondering, for example, how much of the society's attitudes and my comfort level generally had to do with the fact that then German chancellor Angela Merkel, who grew up heavily influenced by the teachings of Christ and social justice ideations, much like I did, was not stoking racism against Black people or anyone else or dehumanizing migrants who showed up at her borders in search of refuge from war and famine. To some degree, societies take on the character of their leaders, with their influence and impact lasting for generations sometimes. In an unfortunate example, Germany itself was a case in point under Adolf Hitler.

The country has still not eradicated White supremacy, but Germany has made it difficult to propagate the ideology in a way that the US has not. Where hate speech is protected in the US, it is banned in Germany, as is the presence of artifacts, like giant statues and monuments, dedicated to White supremacy. They remain present in US public life despite ongoing battles in some places to remove them. Beyond the legislation, Merkel was believable as someone committed to decent human values, while Trump was unfamiliar with the books of Corinthians. When I left the United States, it felt idiotic and chaotic like Trump, far from the Shining City on a Hill. When I arrived in Germany, it felt calm and sedate like Merkel. I hope it lasts and gets better.

Long before Merkel or Trump, some Black people with the wherewithal to do so left the United States for Europe because they experienced it as less hostile, notwithstanding the damning colonial history. France, traditionally, has been a popular destination. James Baldwin, Richard Wright, Josephine Baker, and Sidney Bechet relocated there. Francophone Caribbean scholars like Aimé Césaire, Maryse Condé, Frantz Fanon, and Senegalese Leopold Senghor were respected anti-racism advocates whose work and presence in Paris fostered a welcoming space for Black professionals and artists from the US.

I had a small taste of the capital city when I arrived there in January 2017 for a one-week work trip. I began mostly from a point of indifference, with little to no expectations. I had not bought into the romantic narrative that is key to Paris's brand, but I had sufficient awareness of the space I was in and its relative significance in Black liberation struggles.

Most of my days were spent in the hotel with the women from

my office in DC and their European counterparts, some of whom manifested the same kinds of behavior I experienced at home. The trainees from Asia, Africa, and the South Pacific, the African staff, and an erudite Canadian woman provided respite.

She was a younger White woman without supremacist views or attitudes. I was curious and engaged with her intensely to uncover what made the difference, including the night of a scheduled dinner at a restaurant behind the Notre-Dame cathedral. I learned that her parents had sent her to a private school where Marxism and liberation theology were taught alongside North American history. She reinforced what I know to be true: that the antidote to White supremacy requires an entirely different cultural orientation among all the agents of socialization and extensive contact with other cultures not grounded in Eurocentricity.

What I saw of Paris outside of work came via a young Guadeloupean woman named Laure, whom I met in 2007 when I signed up with a small, Maryland-based organization to host an international exchange student in my home for three weeks. Intrigued by the idea of housing someone from the French Caribbean, a part of the region with which we did not often get to interact, I welcomed the opportunity as a convenient way to further my interest in different cultural backgrounds, even those with which I had much in common.

Laure was my children's age, a beautiful spirit at the beginning of high school, and she fit seamlessly into our family. According to the program requirements, she should have taken public transportation to her classes every morning. Instead, with my memories of rural Jamaica and how different it was from the US, I drove her to Takoma Park every morning for two weeks. She did not mind, and nor did her mother, with whom I spoke on the phone. She was immensely grateful for a temporary mother hen protecting her child, even if it meant slightly retarding the speed at which Laure learned English.

Thanks to Facebook, we kept in touch, and ten years later, we reconnected in Paris, where she had graduated from university and was working as a teacher. She picked me up in the evenings and took me through the maze of a subway system to the Eiffel Tower, then for a ninety-minute cruise down the Seine, past the Notre-Dame cathedral, the Louvre, and the tunnel where Diana, Princess of Wales, was chased to her death by paparazzi.

My affinity for traveling by water had developed considerably since my very first time in New York. I missed the opportunity in Tokyo but enjoyed it tremendously elsewhere, including in Paris.

Unlike Germany or Japan, I did not have time to fall in love with anything specific about France. The hotel was in a construction zone, and elsewhere I was disappointed by the grime in parts of the city center and surprised by the number of panhandlers and homeless people I observed. I could not look past them to appreciate how sophisticated Paris was or how many high-end restaurants and jewelry stores there were, and I did not have time to venture outside the city. France, albeit from limited exposure, struck me as a rich country, like the United States, with many structural dysfunctions to address before it could become a genuinely liberating space.

I left Paris via the Eurostar and fell asleep before it left the station, waking intermittently to catch fleeting glimpses of the English countryside. I awoke fully as the train pulled into London's St. Pancras International Station. Now I was in a city I had heard about almost since I was born but had never visited. England, not just London, was one of those places I had always wanted to see because, like it or not, much of my early heritage was connected to the place. As time passed, I surrendered my desires to my children's needs and let them travel instead, hoping that one day I would make it. I finally did, for a few days.

My uncle Maurice, a home improvement contractor, had lived in Streatham, South London, during my growing-up years. He was responsible for upgrading Mammy's little bungalow in Old House and building her a new pit latrine closer to the house. Throughout her life, he wrote her faithfully, once, or twice a month. The letters arrived in blue-and-white airmail envelopes, which I collected from the post office, and they nearly always came with some British pounds. Most of the money would be hers, but like my aunt Priss, he also sent money for my father, for Sa Bea, and for Mammy's sister, my great-aunt Doris.

I had seen so many envelopes with his address written in a beautiful, exuberant flourish with what seemed like the same royal-blue fountain pen ink that I had known it by heart from about age six. When I was eleven, he promised to take me to London for a visit. He never followed through. Mammy died a year later, and he did not visit as much anymore. I promised myself that if I ever set foot in London, I would head immediately to his home in Streatham, even before Buckingham Palace.

My cousin Berris, who owned the little house in Old House, lived in Aldershot, Hampshire, a little over an hour from London. Auntie Minzie, Mama's sister, lived a little closer, in Ilford, Essex. My maternal grandfather, whom I never met, lived in London too, but I knew nothing else about him except that he had a new family; I had aunts and uncles from him that that I did not know, along with others, and numerous cousins in and around London.

Then there were the books connecting me to this place. *The Lonely Londoners* by Samuel Selvon, *The Emigrants* by George Lamming, and the diet of British literature that was a standard part of our education in postcolonial Jamaica. For all these reasons, London felt more familiar, despite my never having visited.

I did not end up going to Streatham. I saw my decision not to go as part of my evolution and realization that some of what was important in childhood did not matter as much anymore. I had only a few days, and it was early February. While it was not unbearably cold, I am still an islander. Cold weather exploration was not appealing to me.

Plus, Uncle Maurice had been dead for almost thirty years, passing unexpectedly in his early fifties from a deep vein thrombosis. I would not have been able to go inside the house or the backyard. I let it go and rode the tour buses through London a few times in different directions.

I walked to Harrods in Knightsbridge and breezed through the first and second floors, laconically accepting a few perfume samples before beating a hasty retreat through the nearest exit.

I could not imagine any circumstances under which the mountain of pricey clothes, jewelry, and knickknacks could be relevant to my life or to anyone from Old House or elsewhere. In my construct, Harrods was for the birds! I had seen it, though, and understood why Uncle Maurice used to complain to Mammy about his wife buying curtains there.

I stopped by Kensington Palace—for Diana Spencer, perhaps the most visible abused woman in the world and a courageous rebel against the patriarchy. She died on August 31, 1997, the same night my children joined me in the United States. I remember waking from a nap on the sofa, where I had fallen asleep with my younger daughter on my lap, to see Diana's face emblazoned across the television screen with her date of birth and death. I was crushed.

Next was a quick stop at Buckingham Palace, home to Elizabeth II, then ninety-one, whom I had met in Kingston more than two decades previously. I saw a humongous old structure, the seat and symbol of the twenty-first century's most glaring anachronism. The incongruity was heightened by the thing I remember most: a compact blue car leaving the entrance of the building and approaching the gate. I had no expectation. It simply seemed out of place given the scale of the building. It seemed like a collision of different worlds—of fantasy and reality. I turned and walked back across the park to the train station.

There was no time to see Stratford-upon-Avon, the medieval market town where William Shakespeare was born, or the Lake District, the inspiration behind the work of William Wordsworth, the very first poet I read and whom my father occasionally recited from his memories of school; or Lincolnshire in the East Midlands, the setting of *The Mill on the Floss*—still the biggest novel I've ever read; or Thornton, Yorkshire, birthplace of the Brontë sisters; or Steventon in North Hampshire where Jane Austen was born. Regardless of how these books entered my lexicon, I had engaged in the realms I explored through them. I would have liked to walk a little in their actual worlds, even centuries beyond their time.

In the end, my most memorable experience in the UK happened at a little eatery called Double Six Café near the Euston subway station. I was returning to my hotel near Heathrow Airport on my last evening in London and decided to eat dinner before catching the bus back. The food was bland for a Caribbean palate. The service, however, was impeccable. The server, a thirtyish-year-old woman of Asian descent, treated me like I was either a person of note, her old friend from high school, or just her best or only customer for the day.

I finished my dinner and asked for the check. When I offered my Bank of America Visa card, she said she only accepted cash. I reached in my purse for the only cash I had—a US twenty-dollar bill. The bill was twelve pounds.

"Nope!" she said. "Pounds or euros only."

It was the first time in my life that anyone had refused to accept US money from me! I was in a spot. I never had pounds to begin with, and I had used up all my euros in anticipation of going home the next day without foreign money that would end up sitting in a drawer.

"I have to find an ATM," I said, pushing my laptop down in my tote bag and handing it to her. "My travel documents are in there, and I have an early-morning flight tomorrow. I will be right back."

"No," she said, shaking her head. "Take it with you."

"You are letting me walk out of here without paying? How do you know I will come back?" I asked her.

"I can't put my finger on it," she said, still shaking her head. "But there is just something about you."

Somehow, a woman I had met no more than forty-five minutes prior knew she could trust me. She did not question my integrity nor assume that I planned to con her out of the cost of a meal. It was particularly touching because I had been struggling for more than three months to get the basic respect I needed to do my job at work—to get past the hostility of my colleagues. She saw Grace and decency and extended her trust. I reciprocated.

Blinking back tears, I followed her directions to the nearest ATM and returned with her money. It would be a slightly less dignified exit through Heathrow when the random additional screening almost caused me to miss my flight, but at least I had that one warm, fuzzy memory of London.

I had long ago ceased to be apprehensive in spaces not originally intended for people like me, so I was excited about going to the G7 in 2017, but not intimidated. I had been to the White House twice and met President Clinton the second time, and I interviewed Alexis Herman, his labor secretary in Jamaica, before that. I had spent an evening at Vale Royal with Johnnie Cochran, the defense attorney who got O. J. Simpson off his murder charge, and had walked across the university campus chatting with one of my favorite politicians, then Barbadian prime minister Lloyd Erskine Sandiford.[13]

I sat with my hero Michael Manley in the living room of his townhouse in Allerdyce, St. Andrew, while a census taker interviewed him, and multiple times with Sir Howard Cooke, the fourth governor-general of Jamaica, and his wife, Lady Ivy Cooke, at King's House.[14] They were rural Jamaicans like me and initially had great difficulty adjusting to city life. Lady Cooke confided how much she missed her chickens and wished she could bring them to Kingston, and how much she wanted to sew her clothes instead of taking the government clothing allowance, which she thought was too much. For a while I was the only journalist they would trust.

I arrived in Taormina, a medieval hilltop town near Mount Etna on the east coast of Sicily, for the summit. I was interested in the G7 as a news event and eager to explore how I could potentially draw

---

13   Vale Royal is the official residence of the Jamaican prime minister.
14   King's House is the official home of the governor-general, the British monarch's representative in Jamaica.

attention to child nutrition and tuberculosis in the Global South as the assignment called for.

With the top global leadership converging, hundreds of journalists followed them. This was also the first summit with Trump in attendance as the US president, and the anticipated circus around him meant an even greater-than-usual need for a remote, highly controlled environment. Taormina, more than 800 feet above the Ionian Sea, offered that. While the leaders themselves were inaccessible, the media and civil society were camped out as close as was practical in the Hilton Hotel near the foot of the summit. My task, and that of dozens of representatives from civil society organizations, was to ensure that our stakeholders' voices were heard and would influence the summit's decisions on global health.

Arriving at Catania-Fontanarossa Airport from Rome, I took a taxi to a villa in Giardini Naxos, an unexpectedly long trip into rural Sicily. The driver spoke no English. I spoke no Italian. He talked all the way nonetheless, yelling and waving wildly as he tore around hairpin bends. Until then, I never thought I would ride with anyone more dangerous than a Jamaican taxi driver high on ganja. I was more than ready for it to end when he pulled in front of the villa and gesticulated me out of the car. About an hour later, I left on foot for the Sant Alphio Garden Hotel and Spa for my first meeting.

It was only a fifteen-minute walk, but in the fading evening light, my subconscious reminded me that I was a Black woman walking alone in a rural community far from home where no one else looked like me. It mattered especially because migrants from North Africa were turning up in Europe, including Italy, on rickety boats, looking for safety and finding hostility in many places. A baby had recently died and washed ashore, and sometimes dozens of people drowned all at once. Supposedly, it was one issue on the leaders' agenda at the summit.

I was not a refugee, but I knew I could so easily be, and in some fundamental ways, there was no distinction to be made, so I did not fear being misidentified as one. I only feared hostility because someone might think I was one.

--- ❦ ---

"Back! Back!"

I had made a right turn at a fork about two blocks from my villa. A Sicilian man in his thirtie, perhaps, was walking toward me and making urgent hand gestures. I stopped, reading insistence in his actions but no hostility.

Once he got to me, I showed him the paper with the hotel's name, and he directed me—back up, right turn, and right turn again. Soon, I saw Mount Etna's peak in the distance, towering over fields of wildflowers to my left and orange groves to my right. Doves cooing soothingly from palm trees or building overhangs reminded me of Old House, a world away. I was beginning to see why Ernest Hemmingway thought Sicily was so pretty that it hurt to look at it.

At the hotel, I joined the discussion on how to get the attention of leaders from the world's seven largest economies: the United States, Italy, France, Canada, Germany, Japan, and the United Kingdom. Using media was the goal, but the media were there to cover the ready-made drama, and in 2017, it was named Donald Trump. I returned to the villa that first night and wrote an op-ed, "Why the G7 Should Fund Nutrition," for Inter-Press Service, a news service concentrated on the Global South. It was certainly not the best place to get Angela Merkel's attention. But the upshot was that it would be on the World Wide Web, and who could predict where it might land?

The NGOs busied themselves with a lot of manufactured chatter. The more deluded they were, the more certain they were that whatever gimmick they came up with would make a difference. To me it was mostly performative. Staffers were in the hotels and on the beaches in Sicily, already planning for Tokyo in 2018 with little to show for their presence the previous year. There was a strong sense that the trips—jetting around the world—was the point. I imagined if Tokyo followed the same template, there would be little to show from there either. The organizers might have been well meaning, but their behavior seemed insufficiently serious or authentic to be believable or satisfying to someone who knows what it means to need food, water, sanitary conveniences, and proper shelter. I calculated how many poor people could have been fed and housed with what it cost to have everyone there, including me. Direct aid to people who need it seems to make more sense than taking circular routes through so many NGOs, especially those just advocating and not offering measurable direct service or care.

Over and over, women from the Global South with whom I engaged expressed their frustration with not having enough to do or being unable to make their voices heard in meaningful ways. As is too often the case with some nonprofits, women of color became props or inserts in the narratives and drama for those from the North. The Italian performer talked on and on—race and celebrity gave her that right; but the woman from Malawi, the only one to attribute her country's poverty to unfair domestic tax practices and global trade practices, had less sway.

I realized more than ever that for the wretched of the earth, liberation lies in our own hands and not with foreign-based NGOs claiming to be acting on their behalf. Not with the G7. Hardly with billionaires bearing gifts with conditions that serve their interests above all. In the shadow of those entities feigning interest in the plight of those they call the "global poor," I heard echoes of Manley from half a century ago, telling the people of Jamaica, Latin America, the Caribbean, and Africa the same thing. People called it communism and sabotaged him. Yet from what I have seen, capitalism has not moved the needle much. The disparities have only grown.

In that state of contemplation, I left one of my meetings to return to Villa Alcantara. I took the shortcut through the San Alphio hotel's property, where bougainvillea of every color sprouted from the earth below or spilled from window boxes overhead. From the corner of my eye, I glimpsed a splash of color through the trees and shrubs and approached the tiniest chapel I had ever seen. Visible through the glass door were four tiny pews arranged in two rows, each capable of seating three people—four at a squeeze. The windows to the back arched above the tiny pulpit bearing a cross with the image of Jesus, his head crowned in thorns and drooping left. I tugged at the door, feeling an urgency to enter the peace of the delightful little sanctuary and pray at the feet of Jesus.

He would understand how I needed help quelling my existential unrest on behalf of Jamaica, Haiti, Somalia, South Sudan, Yemen, Nigeria, and even the United States. I wanted to pray that the global power structure would apply the Jesus principle to public policy and refrain from playing rancid games in the face of so much suffering—children dying from hunger, diseases, guns, and bombs. And I wanted to pray, really pray, for myself.

The little door was unyielding. Even the sanctuary had to be locked. I prayed as I left, my back now toward Etna. A few days later, I took the train to Rome and wandered around Vatican City, ultimately failing to reach the Sistine Chapel, my intended destination, after abandoning the long line. Although I am not Catholic, I find common ground in the church's social justice teachings and works. I went to St. Peter's Basilica, where there were several chapels, all with open doors.

Two weeks after my big November 2018 social justice presentation at work, I landed in Nairobi, Kenya, for a week of advocacy training for medical professionals from several African countries, including Nigeria and Sudan. The goal was to bring them together to work on common issues affecting their patients, connect them with journalists and local policymakers, and train them in how to use media to help effect change, specifically around child health and nutrition.

The thirteen-hour flight from Dulles to Doha, with my knees pressed against the seats on Qatar Airways, allowed more than enough time to think about my ancestors packed like sardines on cargo ships from Africa to the Caribbean, half-starved and living in filth for months. The six-hour leg from Doha to Nairobi was more comfortable, thankfully.

I was excited, having long felt the absence of real connection to Africa. I would still be a good way off from Nigeria, which accounts for 53 percent of my DNA; and Ghana, Liberia, and Sierra Leone, which account for 13 percent; but it still meant the world to me that I would be on African soil, doing something useful for a cohort of professionals and experiencing a slice of life on the continent.

I stumbled out of the airport near midnight and bent low to touch both palms to the ground on my way to meet my driver; he was holding up a large sign with my name on it. Minutes later, we were driving off into a perfect tropical night. I remember asking him a few questions, then waking up outside the Four Points Sheraton Hotel in Hurlingham, where several men were reaching for my bags. The whole trip had taken just over twenty-one hours, and I had no juice left for the thirty-minute drive from the airport.

"Karibu!" they were saying. "Karibu!"[15]

I crashed as soon as they deposited my bags in my room, excited for the morning and the days ahead.

Those days were rich and rewarding, inside and outside the training room. I enjoyed the training, as always, and chatting with the trainees and the hotel staff outside the structured sessions. The area seemed so much like parts of Mandeville that I felt entirely at home popping inside grocery stores and buying things I did not need. I tried traditional Kenyan dishes and made return trips to the Maasai Market in search of native art and jewelry.

Prior to the trip, I had been given latitude to hire a consultant to help with media training. I hired Carol Mayne-Rose, my old boss from the newspaper in Jamaica. She had migrated to the United States several years ahead of me, earned her master's in journalism, and had been an editor at the *Palm Beach Post* in Florida for more than fifteen years. I hired her because I knew she was competent, we were equally goal oriented, and we would execute without drama.

---

15 The Swahili word for welcome.

"Gosh, Grace, this is the work you have always wanted to do," she noted feelingly, complimenting me at the end of a workshop. "You were always so passionate about making a difference." When I completed the cultural competence workshop where I spoke about accent biases and how to counter them, she said, "That was superb. You are the perfect person to do this kind of training."

Our major field trip was to a little clinic called Alice in the middle of Kibera, said to be the largest slum in Africa and one of the largest in the world. The scope of poverty was staggering, with an estimated 250,000 people living there in conditions too inhospitable for even a hardy woman from Old House. There were vast acreages of tiny shacks made from corrugated zinc and dirt or concrete floors, some housing as many as eight people. I looked away from the little culverts, some carrying fresh feces in dirty water and understood that while much of Nairobi was like any large, cosmopolitan city, the setting I was navigating was what inspires the "poverty porn" pictures used mercilessly by Western NGOs to raise funds, ostensibly to improve conditions. Alice was a little oasis run by a Kenyan sister-and-brother team trying to provide reproductive, prenatal, and maternity care in honor of their mother.

I took it all in, wondering about all the global philanthropists working to alleviate poverty in Africa and how in God's name the world ignores such horrific conditions that have existed for more than a century. If the United Nations and its numerous agencies are working to alleviate poverty, why does Kibera exist? And what about the World Bank? What about the world's billionaires with the capacity, individually or collectively, to solve the myriad problems leading to Kibera? Do they think this is Black people's lot in life?

I chatted with the clinic staff and the housekeeper in the kitchen and noted their determined efforts to keep the place clean and meet international standards in the quality of care offered, including the storage of medication and other supplies at temperatures specified by the United Nations. Against the odds, they were succeeding.

Filled with both despair and hope, I stepped outside, quietly observing a hundred or more goats in a small pen to the left. They reminded me of Old House and the goats my brother and I tended as children; our goats had provided food and were sold occasionally to buy our books or pay for something else we needed. These goats, however, were too close to the clinic. They were dirty like I never knew goats could be, perhaps because ours were kept on grassland.

I looked up to the heavens, trying to better understand why the world works the way it does. The conditions I was born in did not come close to what lay before me. Our tiny house was clean, with a concrete floor. We had a pit latrine with a seat cover. Trees and birdsong surrounded us. Kibera looked like hell.

I would be late for my evening workshop. I had made a valiant effort to keep the program moving and to balance the American perspective of time with that of my African colleagues, which was worlds apart, but I was desperate for a long, hot, soapy shower—to wash away the things I saw before they could take hold of my consciousness and haunt my dreams. I was the first out when the bus pulled up in front of the hotel. I ran to my room.

A trip to the Nairobi National Park three days later provided a vastly more pleasant experience. It was the perfect elixir for the melancholy that had overcome me. Under a primrose sky, I drove with my friends through the park, marveling at the vast expanse interrupted by huge herds of rhinoceroses silhouetted against the sky. Closer to us, dozens of gazelles stared curiously, unmoving but seemingly poised to take off if the need arose, and next to them, towers of giraffes stood perfectly still as if posing for the pictures they knew we were trying to take in the thin dawn light.

The scene could not have gotten any more surreal as I stood inside the rover while it rolled behind a peeved-looking lioness about five feet below. She stayed nearby for about a mile before disappearing into the underbrush. That day was an exhilarating, hyperintense escape from the troubles of the world. The experience got even better when I came within touching distance of the elephants at Sheldrick Wildlife Trust and fed a giraffe named Stacy from my hand at the Giraffe Centre. I was a goatherd again, enjoying time with some more exotic companions. I could have stayed forever, but time was up.

I took an Uber from Hurlingham to Jomo Kenyatta International Airport to catch my midnight flight out of Kenya on December 15, reflecting on my experience during the half-hour ride. This trip offered a small taste of Kenya, a stimulating and tranquilizing bite of a heritage I would never have enough time or resources to enjoy. I left wishing I could have spent time in Africa in my youth, enough to see more of Kenya, and Nigeria, where most of my ancestors came from. Am I Yoruba, Igbo, or Fulani? And there are still Botswana, Cameroon, Ethiopia, Tanzania, Ghana, Malawi, Sierra Leone, South Africa, and other places to see.

On my trips abroad, I exited each country feeling like I had done what I needed to, satisfied a curiosity, and experienced a little of a different culture. Japan presented some ideals to strive for; I love how they make use of modern technology while preserving their history and ancient charm. Kenya helped me understand, in part, the magnificence of the African continent, its enormous potential to develop differently from the West, and how much lip service is paid to ending global poverty.

The airline representative at the airport reminded me of the courtliness of the Kenyan men I met in ordinary encounters—bus drivers, waiters, bellhops, vendors, and airport workers. This was the same level of courtesy I experienced in Japan, with giant doses of African warmth. I asked him to please ensure I had legroom on my flight from Doha to Dulles to keep my right knee from freezing. With a half-moon smile, he assured me he would. On board, I realized he had given me the best possible option—an aisle seat in a row with nothing in front. I stretched my legs all the way out. I thank him still.

Back home in Maryland, I experienced a deep satisfaction at completing my work, along with profound physical and emotional fatigue. It had been a most intense ten days.

Mayer was happy to have me back and to hear how my mini trip stacked up against *Love, Africa*, the 2018 memoir by Jeffrey Gettleman, a Pulitzer Prize-winning *New York Times* journalist, which he had bought for me hot off the press. He smiled when I told him I had taken the California Republic compact he had brought me from his trip home that summer and how useful it was for quick fact-checks between workshops. We had been kindred spirits for more than a decade. I loved how highly he thought of me and the pleasure he took in my accomplishments, big or small.

Despite some cultural differences, approaches to time being the major one, the training had gone off without a hitch. I had well-laid-out plans, but I rolled backward or forward whenever there was a significant change because a key speaker showed up too late, spoke too long, or did not show up at all. My media roundtable started almost two hours late. The trainees said it was one of the most important sessions for them.

My colleague, a Hispanic woman, and Carol, trusted my leadership and commitment to getting the job done. As if to cement how much we were on the same page, all three of us had arrived in Nairobi with the same book clutched under our arms: Michelle Obama's *Becoming*.

To the consternation of the leadership I reported to, we completed the work without so much as a disagreement worth mentioning. Had I responded aloud to their wonderings of how and why, I would have simply said, "There was no one there fighting for power! We were able to focus on the work!"

I was happy with the outcome. My fatigue was due partly to jet lag and partly to the forceful emotions engaged before the trip, during, and upon my return to the United States.

Kenya had been a perfect escape from the duplicity of the workplace and the ever-oppressive presence of White supremacy. There was no constant need to expend one's creative energy trying to decipher authenticity from deceptive camouflage. With an ever-expanding understanding of how power distorts truth, and why there is so much more humanity among the powerless than the powerful, came increasing sadness. I wished for a world where power means more than greed and empty ambition. I needed to decompress. Three days later, I flew to Kingston.

There was the familiar warmth of the Jamaican sun and old friends and family, along with a blissful normalcy worlds away from Kenya's intensity or America's weariness. From smoky blue mountains to grassy lowlands, sleepy inland villages to bustling marketplaces, shimmering waterfalls, and aquamarine seas, Jamaica was home and incomparably sublime.

Birthright, familiarity, place, and belonging supersede mostly everything, and at no other time is this more deeply felt in Jamaica than at Christmas. It does not matter to me if it is a White man's holiday, as some say. It is a jewel in my crown of memories of home and family. It will forever bring me joy, even blunted by the fact that the accident that took Papa from us happened on Christmas Day 2010.

This was my first trip back since traveling to Sicily and falling under the spell of Mediterranean magic. The comparisons were inevitable. Jamaica's natural beauty did not come up short, though I worried about the number of white patches in the eastern hillsides facing the airport, where too many trees had been cut down. Undisrupted poverty persisted in the communities along the airport route into Kingston. Time stood still for those living there. I stopped at UWI for the usual sentimental trip around Ring Road, to gaze at the mist over the Blue Mountains and honor the closest thing to a liberating education I ever experienced.

Treasure Beach, a rustic fishing village in St. Elizabeth Parish, southwest of Kingston, was my choice for a lazy afternoon. Relaxing on the beach with friends and watching children playing in the sand, villagers chasing waves, and fishermen coming ashore in dugout canoes made from the trunks of big cotton trees felt just like the old days—like I had not missed years away from home.

The drive back took me through Old House, meandering along the narrow, winding valley roads of my childhood. The little house was no longer there, the spot covered in shrubbery. I felt nothing, merely an acknowledgment that this was where my life began.

On Christmas Day, I arrived at Hibiscus Place, our little bungalow. It was shuttered, all the doors locked. I could not get inside. The feeling was as unexpected as a gallon of ice-cold water thrown in my face.

At no time during the trip from Maryland did it occur to me that I could not just walk up the steps at any time and let myself in or knock on the door and have someone let me inside. I have never had a key. I never needed one. A door was always open. Someone was always there. It was the first time I could recall seeing that dear little house shuttered and utterly silent with no one inside. Why wouldn't someone be at home on Christmas Day?

I wandered into the backyard. It was overflowing with ackees, pineapples, coconuts, naseberries, soursop, and breadfruits. Not even a single goat or pig was there to eat the produce. The food and fruits Papa planted had never stayed unused for long, certainly not long enough to rot on the ground. I marveled that there could be so much food now unharvested when once my mama would have given anything to find something for us to eat.

They were right there, my parents, lying next to each other near a clump of banana trees, along with my sister, who had rounded off the perfect dozen but died in utero.

I wondered what they would say if they could see the bounty—and me, their third child, looking helplessly at it and the closed doors.

"Tings change eeh, dawlin? But a yard yuh dey. We glad fi see you," Mama would say ahead of a smiling and nodding Papa. "Dem bwoy will soon come open the door. Siddung and rest yourself meanwhile. Yuh look so tired."

EPILOGUE

I rested and returned to the United States in January 2019 with enough juice to start thinking about how to help Democrats win the 2020 election. Once again, I was ready to dedicate my efforts to stopping Trump. Joe Biden was clearly the best pick out of a crowded field and the perfect choice to stabilize the country. I eventually cochaired the Biden–Harris campaign in Montgomery County with a man named Mark Feinroth, who signed up later. We worked together to help spread awareness and do whatever we could to make sure Biden got elected. With all its contradictions, I believed in the US and its place in the world. I believed I had a responsibility to contribute my widow's mite.

One week after I returned to work, the nonprofit announced a reduction of force, cutting six staff members—five women and one man, and half of them Black or Brown. I was cut along with the Hispanic woman who went on the trip to Kenya trip with me and the administrator the two women had been harassing because he did not try to force me to apologize for showing the short film. I later learned that five of the six of us had at some point raised concerns about issues within the organization. It ended up gutting itself, with most of the remaining staff resigning. The nonprofit rebuilt over time and hired a DEI specialist.

In the years ahead, I would learn how typical my experience was for Black women in predominantly White workplaces and particularly in the NGO sector. The world would see the hostility we often face played out in the belittling treatment of Justice Ketanji Brown Jackson, the first Black woman nominated to serve on the Supreme Court, in her confirmation hearing; in the incessant mocking of Kamala Harris, whose nervous laughter is no doubt driven by discomfort under the glare of a country where a significant portion of the population does not think she belongs; and in the public lynching of Dr. Claudine Gay, appointed as the first Black president of Harvard University only to be forced out after six months in 2024, casualty of a brutal conflict in the Middle East between the State of Israeli and Hamas, a group designated by the US as a terrorist organization.

I took the opportunity to undergo therapeutic surgery and then rested for ten weeks as my doctor instructed. I began applying for any jobs for which I was qualified as the end of my recovery neared—and that was how I ended up, for the next two years, teaching public affairs at the Department of Defense Information School based at Fort Meade, Maryland.

Prior to that, I had no interest in working in a military environment, nor did I share any romanticism about it. For me, militaries are about wars, and military personnel are instruments of war. Wars mean death and destruction, often for innocent people, including women and babies. Therefore, wars are bad. My interest in journalism, history, sociology, and anthropology kicked in, however, and I knew that, come what may, I was embarking on a journey of learning about an important and often problematic societal institution. It did not disappoint.

As fortune or misfortune would have it, I was there when George Floyd was murdered in 2020.[16] The leadership attempted to facilitate open discussions like many other workplaces. They went the same way as most others I had encountered. Still, some of the Black servicemen aired their views, and it was poignant and disappointing at the same time.

In one noteworthy response, a Navy commander with almost

---

16 George Floyd was a Black man who was murdered by Derek Chauvin, a White police officer, in Minneapolis, Minnesota, on May 25, 2020. Floyd died after Chauvin handcuffed and pinned him to the ground with his knee on his neck for almost ten minutes. The killing sparked widespread global protests and became a symbol of the oppression that Black people face.

twenty years of experience revealed that his wife was due to give birth shortly, and he hoped his next posting would be in Japan so his son could grow up without the fear of being abused or killed in the United States because of his race. He explained that even in uniform, he was never out later than 9 p.m. for the same reason. His views confirmed what I felt about Japan.

I was there too on January 6, 2021. I returned to my desk after teaching a morning class to see CNN broadcasting images of a mob storming the Capitol to prevent the certification of the election results. It was a moment of profound shame for me as an American, and it cemented my disappointment in what Trump and the Republicans have done to further damage the US and its image abroad.

By then, I had completed a small but insightful case study of the school as part of my coursework for an executive leadership certificate from Yale School of Management and realized how thoroughly racism was baked into the military's DNA. While I had developed great friendships with some colleagues, I felt increasingly unsettled—enough to debrief one of them about who around me might be armed or not. Amid the anxiety, I learned that the trainees generally had little interest in wars, though they were committed to duty, disciplined, and highly trained. They were bright, friendly, and all-around lovely people who wanted peace and safety for the world. They have my abiding respect.

However, there was a sizable element devoted to preserving White spaces, and those who were dissimilar to them were seen as interlopers. This attitude was about race, but it was also about self-glorifying industry norms—the belief that everything military was superior and it should be preserved for superior people. For this reason, I was not surprised by the high representation of people with military backgrounds in the insurrection, and I knew my fears when I walked the hallways were not unfounded. I needed to get out. The decision was taken out of my hands when they did not renew the contract with the company I worked for, likely because they were hiring too many Black people. Yet they were the best employers I have had in the United States.

I view all my experiences now as part of life's tapestry, from which I have derived great joy at times, learned essential lessons, and gained invaluable experience. In the quest for social justice, especially in the workplace, I understand better the complexity of the forces working together and how effective they are at keeping some individuals on the margins of society. More than ever, I am cognizant of the binding role of culture and the forces that perpetuate values inimical to justice and peaceful coexistence in a genuinely multicultural society.

I understand, too, why change cannot occur without deliberate and sustained social movements or other kinds of events dramatic enough to deliver an overpowering shock to the system, where it is disassembled to a significant degree and cannot be rebuilt on the same template—events like COVID-19, which brought the most far-reaching changes to the workplace since the Industrial Revolution. Working remotely eliminates long commutes and saves time and money, and for many women of color, it provides an escape from toxic office culture.

Also of great importance, COVID-19 revealed more clearly the misshapen education system and the need for revolutionary changes. As in Jamaica, too much of the system in the US is built on values and practices that perpetuate inequities in ways that society has been conditioned to consider reasonable but are anything but!

As for media, it is safe to say my interest remains, but more so from a critic's perspective than a fan's. Outside of Whiteness, media companies are too ideologically biased toward authority, even when it is corrupt or when it makes no sense to give it the benefit of the doubt. This was obvious in the treatment of Donald Trump, who had little credibility but was treated by the media as if he did, from his candidacy to his presidency. Ultimately, the media's determination that the US presidential election campaigns are most valuable as entertainment rather than in providing a serious evaluation of character and competence gave the world the Donald Trump presidency in 2016—and all that came with it.

In the same way that the education system divides the United States along racial and class lines, media drives deep ideological wedges. The liberal–conservative dichotomy, for example, is in large part a media construct that oversimplifies how people arrive at the positions they hold. It disregards the fact that such stark divisions do not exist in reality; human beings are complex, and we have the capacity to reason and change our beliefs over time.

I am a woman of color, and I identify as a social justice advocate, for example, but I believe in the rule of law, and I see no conflict between the two—except where laws are unfair and, in their existence, or application are more punitive to any group of people over another. I believe in a woman's right to choose, but I despise the way some so-called liberals talk about abortion as if it should be the norm or routine to terminate a pregnancy—something that birth control or more responsible sexual behavior can often prevent. I cannot see how society benefits from treating human life as cheap or meaningless at any stage.

I am a feminist, one label I do not mind wearing, but I believe men, women, and children thrive more within the context of strong family units, and I see no incompatibility with these two ideas.

I am an immigrant who believes in the value of immigration and celebrates multiculturalism, but I do not believe in involuntarily open borders, because they are unsustainable and unsafe, and they make the US look weak and vulnerable. I believe the paths to legal immigration should be more rational and that there are endless opportunities to utilize labor from the Global South in sectors like hospitality, agriculture, health care, and direct care services in ways that could be treated as part of US international development aid, to assist in community development in Latin America and the Caribbean, and to disincentivize people from entering illegally. I believe immigration opportunities should be treated as less as a favor to the immigrant and more of a mutually beneficial exchange. This cannot include illegal immigration based on the simple logic that illegal entry is incompatible with the rule of law.

Media, my old love, has a crucial role to play in social formations as among the principal purveyor of culture. Change there is necessary too for society to move beyond White supremacy and other oppressive practices and social dysfunctions. This is fundamental to a world that can never be perfect but can certainly be more just. Mayer would agree with me. Sadly, he transitioned somewhat suddenly in May 2022.

www.ingramcontent.com/pod-product-compliance
Lightning Source LLC
LaVergne TN
LVHW041759060526
838201LV00046B/1050